Frederick Denison Maurice

The Epistles of St. John

A Series of Lectures on Christian Ethics

Frederick Denison Maurice

The Epistles of St. John
A Series of Lectures on Christian Ethics

ISBN/EAN: 9783337165284

Printed in Europe, USA, Canada, Australia, Japan

Cover: Foto ©Lupo / pixelio.de

More available books at **www.hansebooks.com**

Messrs. Macmillan and Co.'s Publications.

BY THE SAME AUTHOR.

COLLECTED AND UNIFORM EDITION.

Crown 8vo. 3s. 6d. each volume.

CHRISTMAS DAY AND OTHER SERMONS

THEOLOGICAL ESSAYS.

THE PROPHETS AND KINGS OF THE OLD TESTAMENT. A Series of Sermons preached in the Chapel of Lincoln's Inn. Fifth Edition.

THE PATRIARCHS AND LAWGIVERS OF THE OLD TESTAMENT. A Series of Sermons preached in the Chapel of Lincoln's Inn.

THE GOSPEL OF THE KINGDOM OF HEAVEN: a Course of Lectures on the Gospel of St. Luke.

THE GOSPEL OF ST. JOHN. A series of Discourses.

THE EPISTLE OF ST. JOHN. A series of lectures on Christian Ethics.

LECTURES ON THE APOCALYPSE: or, Book of Revelation of St. John the Divine.

THE FRIENDSHIP OF BOOKS, and other Lectures. Edited with a Preface by THOMAS HUGHES.

SOCIAL MORALITY. Twenty-one Lectures delivered in the University of Cambridge.

THE PRAYER-BOOK, considered especially in reference to the Romish system. Nineteen Sermons preached in the Chapel of Lincoln's Inn; and THE LORD'S PRAYER. Nine Sermons preached in the Chapel of Lincoln's Inn in the months of February, March, and April 1848.

THE DOCTRINE OF SACRIFICE DEDUCED FROM THE SCRIPTURES. A Series of Sermons.

SERMONS PREACHED IN LINCOLN'S INN CHAPEL. New Edition. In six Vols.

MACMILLAN & CO., LONDON.

Messrs. Macmillan and Co.'s Publications.

BY THE SAME AUTHOR.

THE CONSCIENCE. Lectures on Casuistry, delivered in the University of Cambridge. By FREDERICK DENISON MAURICE, Professor of Casuistry and Moral Philosophy. Third Ed. Cr. 8vo. 4s. 6d.

DIALOGUES BETWEEN A CLERGYMAN AND A LAYMAN ON FAMILY WORSHIP. Cr. 8vo 4s. 6d.

THE KINGDOM OF CHRIST: or, Hints to a Quaker respecting the Principles, Constitution, and Ordinances of the Catholic Church. In two Vols. Third Edition. Cr. 8vo. 12s.

LEARNING AND WORKING. Six lectures delivered in Willis's Rooms, London, in June and July 1854. THE RELIGION OF ROME AND ITS INFLUENCE ON MODERN CIVILIZATION. Four lectures delivered in the Philosophical Institution of Edinburgh, in December 1854. Cr. 8vo. 4s. 6d.

THE LORD'S PRAYER, THE CREED, AND THE COMMANDMENTS: a manual for parents and schoolmasters. To which is added the Order of the Scriptures. Pott 8vo. 1s.

MORAL AND METAPHYSICAL PHILOSOPHY. New Edition with preface and a Portrait. Vol. I. Ancient Philosophy and the First to the Thirteenth Centuries. Vol. II. Fourteenth Century to the French Revolution, with a Glimpse into the Nineteenth Century. 8vo. 16s.

THE RELIGIONS OF THE WORLD AND THEIR RELATIONS TO CHRISTIANITY. Considered in eight lectures founded by the Right Hon. Robert Boyle. Third Edition. Cr. 8vo. 4s. 6d.

SERMONS ON THE SABBATH-DAY, ON THE CHARACTER OF THE WARRIOR, AND ON THE INTERPRETATION OF HISTORY. Fcap. 8vo. 2s. 6d.

SERMONS PREACHED IN COUNTRY CHURCHES. Second Edition. Cr. 8vo. 6s.

THE UNITY OF THE NEW TESTAMENT. A synopsis of the first three Gospels, and of the Epistles of St. James, St. Jude. St. Peter, and St. Paul. Second Edition. In two Vols. Cr. 8vo. 12s.

LESSONS OF HOPE. Readings from the works of F. D. MAURICE, selected by J. LLEWELYN DAVIES. Cr. 8vo. 5s.

THE COMMUNION SERVICE, from the Book of Common Prayer, with select readings from the writings of the Rev. F. D. MAURICE, M.A. Edited by the Rev. JOHN WILLIAM COLENSO, D.D. Lord Bishop of Natal. 16mo. 2s. 6d.

THE LIFE OF FREDERICK DENISON MAURICE. Chiefly told in his own letters. Edited by his Son, FREDERICK MAURICE. With Portraits. In two Vols. Second Edition. 8vo. 36s. Cheap Edition. Two Vols Cr. 8vo. 16s.

TIMES.—" The book is one of profound interest."
SPECTATOR.—" A unique piece of biography; few of those of our generation whose names will live in English history or literature have exerted so profound and so permanent an influence as Mr. Maurice."

MACMILLAN AND CO., LONDON.

THE
EPISTLES OF ST. JOHN

A Series of Lectures

ON

CHRISTIAN ETHICS

BY

FREDERICK DENISON MAURICE

London
MACMILLAN AND CO.
AND NEW YORK
1893

TO

THE STUDENTS

OF THE

WORKING MEN'S COLLEGE,

45, GREAT ORMOND STREET

𝔗𝔥𝔢𝔰𝔢 𝔏𝔢𝔠𝔱𝔲𝔯𝔢𝔰,

DELIVERED TO A FEW OF THEIR NUMBER,

ON A SUBJECT WHICH CONCERNS THEM ALL,

ARE DEDICATED,

BY THEIR FRIEND AND FELLOW WORKER,

THE AUTHOR.

ADVERTISEMENT.

THESE Lectures were delivered to a small Class of Students in our Working Men's College at eight o'clock on Sunday mornings. I have not scrupled to tell this Class that I consider the question whether there is a foundation for human morality—or whether it is dependent upon the opinions and fashions of different ages and countries, to be *the* question in which, as a body and as individuals, we are most interested; the question which most affects our studies and our daily lives. And I have told them also where I find the answer to that question. But I have never used the plural pronoun; I have not assumed to speak except in my own person; and I should be very sorry if my colleagues—no one of whom has heard or read any of these Lectures—were held responsible for the sentiments contained in them. Any Manuals which they may hereafter publish for the use of the Students in their own departments will embody the results of their thought and experience. The present Volume does not profess to be a Manual of Christian Ethics, composed by me. St. John supplies the Manual which I wish my pupils to use; if they study him they will soon discover the feebleness and insufficiency of his interpreter.

TUNBRIDGE WELLS,
Sept. 14*th*, 1857.

CONTENTS.

LECTURE I.

INTRODUCTORY.
                                                                PAGE

Meaning of the words Ethics and Morals—Whether Christian Ethics and Human Ethics are the same—The Ethics of Aristotle—Their great excellence and utility—They refer all morals to life—Exclusion of theology from the Aristotelian Ethics—They are not Ethics for all men—How Aristotle compels one to ask for that which he does not give—Whether the Scriptures supply what we are in search of—The most perfect book, which is merely a book, cannot supply it—The Bible professes to set forth a Life—Its method as a history considered—St. John gives us the result of its discoveries—The first verse of his Epistle tells us of a human Life—It tells us also of a divine Life . . . . 1—18

LECTURE II.

THE GROUND OF CHRISTIAN ETHICS.

What doubts must have arisen in the minds of Christians when they were losing sight of the eye-witnesses of the acts of Christ—St. John's answer to these doubts—What he had seen and handled—What had been manifested—What he could declare to all—The Word of Life—The Eternal Life—The message concerning God—Fellowship with the Father and the Son—Ethics must start from Good and not from Evil . . . . 19—33

LECTURE III.

LIGHT AND DARKNESS: SIN AND PURIFICATION.

Use of language drawn from the senses—Its superiority to abstract language—Special fitness of the words Light and Darkness in a letter addressed to the Ephesians—The God of Light—How a Jew regarded the worship of Sun and Moon—Christ the Light of

Men—Light enjoyed, not appropriated—What the Apostles said to the worshippers of Light—Connexion of Darkness with Falsehood—Light social; Darkness separating—How we discover the nature of SIN—Cognate words—Sense of Sin awakened by the message that God is Light—Strong in proportion to the strength of that message—Demand for purification—*What* the purification must reach—The purifying Blood—The Confession of Sin—God's justice in Forgiveness and Cleansing . . . . 34—52

LECTURE IV.

THE TRUE IDEA OF MAN.

St. John and his little children—How the phrase is connected with the business of the letter—The Family—Heathen and Jewish notions of an Advocate—A deeper feeling discoverable at the root of these notions in each—The Representative of the Family—The Representative of *Man*—Force of St. John's expression, '*for the whole world*'—Heathen and Jewish idea of Propitiation—Deeper feeling latent beneath these notions—How that feeling was brought out in the Jew by his education—St. John's doctrine of a Universal Propitiation—How it redeems Prayer from a false and superstitious use and makes it the great organ of humanity . . . . . . 53—68

LECTURE V.

DOING AND KNOWING.

The story of the young Ruler in the Gospels—Eternal Life connected with keeping the Commandments—Expression, '*We do know that we know Him*,' illustrated—How we know that we know a man—Knowledge of God treated by the Apostle as more possible than the knowledge of Men, and as the ground of it—The word '*keep*' illustrated—Use of a '*keepsake*'—Application to the Ten Commandments—How a Jew could '*keep*' each of them—GOD: The Deliverer, Idols, The Name, Rest and Work, Honour of Parents, Murder, Adultery, Stealing, False Witness, Covetousness—St. Paul's language respecting the Commandments on stone—How he was led to use it—Perfectly consistent with St. John's—The initiated or perfect man according to certain refined teachers—The initiated or perfect man according to St. John . . . . 69—86

LECTURE VI.

THE OLD AND NEW COMMANDMENTS.

Walking and Resting—Use of these expressions—Are they mystical when applied to spiritual creatures, or simple and universal ?—How to ascertain their force—The Teachers who opposed the new age to the old—What St. John says of the old time—The Commandments not on stone, but a *Word*—The Law coming forth from *the* Word—The Manifestation of the Word the ground of a *new* Commandment—Wherein it differs from the old—The parable of the good Samaritan—The love of *Neighbours*, the principle asserted in Law—Christ the Universal *Brother*—Brotherhood in the Gospel takes the place of Neighbourhood—Application to modern Politics . . 87—100

LECTURE VII.

THE CHILDREN; THE YOUTHS; THE OLD MEN.

Whether the Jewish Ordinances were *additions* to the old Commandments—Whether any Gospel Ordinances were *added* to the new Commandment—The significance and use of both—The stages of growth in the Christian Family—(1.) The Lesson to the *Child*; how it is trained by a wise human parent—God's discipline the archetype of this discipline—Forgiveness a means of securing Obedience, in an individual child—Forgiveness exhibited as a part of the divine order, of the divine character—Forgiveness of Mankind in Christ's name, the Gospel principle—(2.) The Lesson to the *Fathers*—Reliance on the Nature of God—(3.) The Lesson to the *Young Men*—The Evil Spirit overcome; strength to fight—(4.) Repetition of the lessons with significant changes—The Word of God dwelling in the young men . . . . 101—116

LECTURE VIII.

THE WORLD AND THE FATHER.

The Children of a Family going out into the world—Dangers of the change—Why we should rejoice in it—The World an *Order*—How the Order becomes a *Disorder*—God's love of the World—How can we be told not to love the world seeing we are to be like Him—Effect of the World upon us—Testimony of Wordsworth—

—Man between God and the World—Man becoming the servant and child of the world loses his strength, his freedom, his power of appreciating the world, his sense of beauty, his capacity of enjoyment, all *God's* love of the world—Forms in which the love of the world in its evil sense presents itself—St. John's classification illustrated—Its practical value—Possibility of loving the outward world with a true and divine love—Quotation from Cowper . . . 117—133

LECTURE IX.

THE LAST TIME; THE CHRIST; THE ANTICHRIST; THE CHRISM.

Opinion that the Apostles made mistakes about the coming of the last days and of God's Judgment—Reasons against that opinion—Periods in History—Ancient History according to Guizot the period of national divisions—Modern History the period of Unity and Universality—Popular division of Ancient and Modern History contradicts this doctrine—The Scriptural division into the period before and after the fall of Jerusalem, favours it—That division explains the uniform language of the New Testament—The destruction of Jerusalem a revelation of the Christ and of His Universal Kingdom—That revelation of Christ the end of an age and the beginning of an age—This earth always contemplated by the Apostle, as the seat of Christ's kingdom—The Revelation of the Christ contemporaneous with the Revelation of the Antichrist, and of many Antichrists—Characteristics of the Christ—Characteristics of the Antichrist—The anointing from the Holy One—How it enabled humble people to '*know all things*'—That phrase illustrated—'*No lie of the Truth*'—That phrase illustrated—How we may use St. John's words in our time . . . . 134—151

LECTURE X.

THE PLACE OF THE DOCTRINE OF THE FATHER, THE SON, AND THE SPIRIT, IN CHRISTIAN ETHICS.

The expression, '*He that denieth the Son hath not the Father*,' illustrated—How the Apostles regarded a Christ who is not a Son, but an independent being, as an Antichrist—How they regarded a Self-Willed, Independent God, as a false God—How the idea of a Father and a Son was inseparable from the idea of God—How the Universal Baptism was into the Name of the Father, of the Son, and of the Spirit, in whom they are One—'*Abiding in the Father and the Son*,' this phrase illustrated—The Eternal Life the blessing of this abiding—Those who withdrew from the fellowship of the Church denied the existence of a *common* life for all, of a *divine* life for any—Connexion of the Anointing of the Spirit with the Unity of the Church illustrated by the 133d Psalm—This Anointing never withdrawn—Connexion of Theology with Morals—Pope's line, 'He can't be wrong whose life is in the right,' considered and vindicated . . . , ... 152—167

LECTURE XI.

HOPE; ITS GROUND, OBJECT, AND EFFECT.

The Death of souls—How is it to be explained—The root at which Life may be renewed—The discovery of this root by the Jews and Heathens to whom the Gospel was first preached—The command '*to abide in it*,' illustrated from St. John's Gospel—The words '*that ye may not be ashamed before Him at His coming*,' illustrated—The passage from natural to human emblems—The phrase, '*He that doeth righteousness is born of Him*,' illustrated—This divine birth the ground of righteous acts—Also the ground of *Hope*—Hope directed to the appearing of Christ and His the manifestation of the Father whose children we are—That appearing treated by the Apostles as no less certain than the rising of the Sun—Hope therefore not dependent on contingencies—Hope of that which is '*to be*' a continual witness of that which '*is*'—Hope the means of purification—All therefore should be encouraged to hope . . . . 168—183

LECTURE XII.

THE DEVIL AND HIS WORKS.

The Accuser or Slanderer—Was St. John following an old Hebrew tradition in speaking of such a Spirit?—Experience of thoughts that are presented to our Minds—Whence do they come?—To say that we are responsible for them is strictly true, but nothing to the purpose—Suggestion of a Crime involves no obligation to commit it —The words, '*The Devil sinneth from the beginning*,' considered— Do they involve the notion of Evil being as ancient as Good ?—They merely assert the presence of Temptation to Evil in every period of the World's History—That fact testified of in the Old Testament—But the Tempter little spoken of there—Why the New Testament alludes to him so continually—Christ, the answerer of slanders and accusations against God, against the race of Man, against each member of that race—The Good Seed produces only Good, the Evil Seed only Evil—Why this statement appears to involve a contradiction—St. John no Sentimentalist—Not a Witness for the pleasing side of Morality and of the Gospel, but for facts, be they agreeable or disagreeable . . . . 184—199

LECTURE XIII.

RELATION OF LOVE TO RIGHTEOUSNESS.

Justice and Mercy supposed to be characteristics of two different kinds of Men—Proof from experience that each implies the other—Notion that the Righteousness of the Old Testament stands in some sort of opposition to the Love of the New—Answer from the story of the First Murder—The command, '*Love one another*,' implied in the relation of Cain to Abel—Law could not be broken without an outrage upon Love—But if the Cainites become the Majority?—how St. John deals with this question—The nature of transgression cannot be decided by Statistics—The appeal to experience and conscience—The state of Death; the state of Life—How we know Love—Christ's Death in what sense a Definition of Love—How Self-Sacrifice is proved to be the Law of Human Life; not an act of Supererogation—Proofs that the Conscience of Men in the Old World and in the New confirms this idea of it—The words, '*How dwelleth the Love of God in you?*' illustrated—'*Loving in word and tongue*'—How to assure our hearts—The condemnation and acquittal of the heart—The commandment to believe and to do . . 200—214

LECTURE XIV.

SPIRITUAL POWERS IN OLD TIMES AND IN MODERN TIMES.

Interest of Working Men in the Substitution of Living Language for School Language—That Living Language very awful—Why it is impossible for us to avoid the subject of spiritual powers and influences—St. John's recognition of them as widely diffused, and as needing examination—What comes under the head of spiritual powers or influences—The notion of communications from celebrated men who have left the world, considered—The notion of communications from personal friends, considered—The mystery of Memory—The spiritual world made utterly frivolous by those who deal with its secrets in our days—How the Apostles treated the workers with spiritual enchantments in their times—The deliverance from evil spirits, what it meant—The Apostles, asserters of human rights against Men who were trafficking for their own reputation or pelf —The Apostle's test of Spirits, '*whether they were of God*,' considered —The two possible meanings for the words, ' *We are of God ; he that is of God heareth us, &c.*'—Which was St. John's meaning?—The words, '*Beloved, let us love one another ; Love is of God*,' an answer —Whether those words confine Love to the Church—Difficulty of love within a small circle greater than within a larger one—The assertion '*God is Love*,' not agreeable to our evil natures, but most offensive to them—It is not ecstatic language, but the scientific explanation of all previous revelations, itself the final revelation—The attempt to make the Incarnation and Death of Christ a limitation of this principle, instead of a proclamation of it, how crushed by St. John—God's love the only foundation of all human love—All spiritual influences which cannot be referred to this source, must be futile and evil . . . . 215—235

LECTURE XV.

THE PERFECTED LOVE.

The words, ' *The Father sent the Son to be the Saviour of the World* considered in reference to the subject of the last lecture—St. Paul's Speech to the idolaters at Athens—The blessing of those who *believed* that in God they lived, and moved, and had their being—Men's feelings respecting God illustrated by their thoughts of a judgment—St. John's boldness in the prospect of judgment—The warrant for it—Words, ' *There is no Fear in Love*,' considered—The apparent limitation of them, why it does not apply to that love of which St. John speaks—Words, ' *We love Him because He loveth us*,' considered—Do they refer to the ' motive of gratitude ? '—Love again asserted to be the obedience to a commandment—Love, in our day, supposed to be incompatible with fervent hatred—It is worth nothing unless it be fiery, and intolerant of what is unloving —How we may become worse than our forefathers—How we may become better than our forefathers . . . . 236—251

LECTURE XVI.

FAITH AND LOVE—THEIR RELATION TO EACH OTHER AND TO THE WORLD.

PAGE

Love and Faith represented as two graces imparted to men—Their respective values a subject of continual dispute—St. John's method of treating them altogether different—The words '*Every one who believeth that Jesus is the Christ is born of God*,' considered—St. John sets Faith as high as St. Paul in the Epistle to the Romans—He places Faith in the same subordination to Love as St. Paul does in the Epistle to the Corinthians—The words, '*He that loveth Him that begat loveth Him that is begotten of Him*,' explain the previous words, '*He that loveth not his brother, how can he love God?*'—Ground of all love to men in God—Test of our allegiance to God, the love of man—The war with the world—How Faith wins the victory—What faith wins it . . . . 252—265

LECTURE XVII.

THE WITNESSES.

The different worlds in which the Ephesian Christians found themselves—The actual victory of the Son of God over these worlds—Cause of this victory—Can it be ascertained by speaking of Christianity and its high moral code?—How St. John speaks of it—Words, '*Jesus Christ came by water and blood*,' considered—How the Gospels explain them—How the history of Christendom explains them—How the Spirit witnesses with the Water and the Blood—The spurious text, its irrelevancy to the subject of the passage—How these three witnesses on earth explain the blessings of Christendom, and its sins—The worth of Testimony—Testimonies of God and Man—Outward and inward Testimonies . . . . 266—283

LECTURE XVIII.

THE NATURE OF PRAYER—VENIAL AND MORTAL SINS.

St. John writes to believers in the Son of God that they *may* believe in Him—What this means—He declares Eternal Life to be given—Why then does he speak of Prayer?—Prayer part of the gift of Life—

'Praying according to God's will,' not the natural notion of prayer—
Why it is the complete idea of prayer—How it gives the only practical solution of the problem about the existence of Evil—The limitation to the efficacy of prayer—Mortal sins—The doctrine which has been grounded on the Apostle's words—These words examined by the light of their context—How the Apostle avoids all definitions of Mortal sins—Motives for defining them—The subject connected with excommunication—How St. Paul treats that subject—Consequences of the Romish doctrine—Cure of it . . . . 284—302

LECTURE XIX.

CHRISTIAN CERTAINTY.

What St. John says we may be sure of—(1) *'He that is born of God doth not commit sin'*—How we arrive at this knowledge—How the division of persons as believers and unbelievers robs us of it—How an ETHICAL SCIENCE is possible—(2) *'We know that we are of God, and that the world lieth in wickedness'*—This language considered—Illustration from Galileo's saying, 'Nevertheless it moves'—How we may imitate his boldness—What we may affirm—No truth depends on majorities—Uncertainty not certainty leads to persecution—(3) *'We know that the Son of God is come, and has given us an understanding,'* &c.—How the Ephesians arrived at this knowledge; how we may arrive at it—St. John lived to proclaim the living and true God and to witness against Idolatry . . . . 303—315

LECTURE XX.

TRUTH IN THE WOMAN AND THE MAN.

What the early Church would have expected in a letter from St. John to an Elect Lady—What is actually found there—The Lady a Mother—TRUTH, the place it holds in St. John's Ethics—Truth said by the doctors to be found only in *Propositions*—The Truth of which the Apostle speaks in a PERSON—It is Truth in which we dwell, and which dwells in us—The command not to bid God speed to the false Teacher, considered—Its application to the first age, and to ours—Wherein the Second and Third Epistles are alike—Wherein they differ

—Characteristics of the woman and the man—Truth, the foundation of both their lives—Question respecting the feminine and masculine virtues—The Life of our Lord has not exalted the former above the latter, but has brought them into one—What this Life shows to be the end and aim of Human Life—Is it Happiness? is it Perfection? is it Truth? . . . . 316—341

NOTE ON POSITIVISM 343

THE EPISTLE OF ST. JOHN.

LECTURE I.

INTRODUCTORY.

I HAVE given some lessons on Ethics, or Morals, to a class in the College, which met me on one of the evenings of the week. I have had a Bible class on the Sunday evenings. I propose at this time to give a lecture upon Morals, or Ethics, which shall be drawn from a book in the Bible.

Some of you, I dare say, will wish to ask one or two questions. I have spoken of Morals, or Ethics. First, what do I mean by the word Morals? It is a word derived from the Latin; it signifies Manners. I understand by it the manners and habits which belong to us as human beings. That is the sense I have always given it in my lectures. Do I intend something different by Ethics? No; I intend the same thing. It is a word derived from the Greek. It expresses, I think, a little more delicately and accurately than the other word, that the manners are not outside manners, not mere deportment. It answers more nearly to what we call character. I have, therefore, adopted both expressions; but either will serve our purpose.

If this be the case, then you may ask me, in the second place, why in the programme I have prefixed the adjective Christian to Ethics? Did I not propose to speak of the habits or character of a man? Do I mean that a Christian is to be something different from a man? Do I think that he can be anything better than a man? Or do I suppose there is one kind of morals for week-days and another for Sundays, and that the last is to be got from the Bible, the first somewhere else?

You cannot be more anxious to ask these last questions than I am to answer them. I have little hope that we can understand one another till I have quite cleared my meaning about them. And I feel very confident that I shall be able to make you, the members of this College, understand me even if I fail to make other people understand me. I think so because I believe you come to study morals, and every other subject, for the sake of work, for the sake of life. I think so further, because I know that my colleagues, and that all who come by accident to lecture among you, cultivate that disposition in you and try to show you that books only exist to make us acquainted with facts and with laws which God has established for us and for the world. Some of you may have listened to a beautiful lecture, which was so kindly given here last night, upon Natural History, by Mr. Huxley. You will have observed how he proceeded. You will remember that he did not give us a system out of a book; that he did not entertain us with an eloquent panegyric on his study. He took a lobster; he explained to us the different parts of its frame, the uses to which each part was applied, the type upon which the whole was constructed. So he led us by degrees to perceive what the objects of Natural History are, how it interprets one and another portion of the Universe to us, how it may cultivate our own minds. I cannot follow an eminent and accomplished man of science, but I should like at least to catch something of his spirit, above all of his modesty. And I should like you to try me by the same kind of test, severe as it is. If I cannot help you better to understand the facts and laws which most concern yourselves, my words ought to go for nothing.

Perhaps I shall be able to explain the plan which I have endeavoured and am endeavouring to pursue in this College of Working Men, if I tell you a little of my own experience when I was a student in a much older and more august society. From what you have heard of the University of Oxford, and of its being confined till very lately to members of the Church of England, you will perhaps fancy that the book on Ethics, or Morals, which is used there, is a book written by some eminent divine. By no means. It is a book written by an old Pagan philosopher. Out of that I learnt lessons on this great subject. What other books I read there on Ethics, were chiefly for the purpose of illustrating the Ethics of Aristotle. How did this answer? I cannot venture to speak for others; but I will for myself. I owe quite unspeakable gratitude to the University of Oxford, for having put this book into my hands and induced me to read it and think of it. I doubt if I could have received a greater service from any University or any teacher. For I will tell you what this book did for me. First, it assured me that the principles of Morals cannot belong to one time or another, that they must belong to all times. Here was an old Heathen Greek making me aware of things that were passing in me, detecting my laziness and my insincerity, showing how little I was doing the things which I professed to do, forcing me to confess that, with all the advantages which I had, he was better than I was. That was one great thing. Whatever takes down a young man's conceit must be profitable to him. This book might have done it much more effectually in my case than it did; that was my fault, not the writer's. Next, I could not but learn from him, for he took immense pains to tell me so, that it is not by reading a book, or learning a set of maxims by heart, one gets to know anything of morality; that it belongs to life, and must be learnt in the daily practice of life. I repeat it, he tells us this very often. English and Christian writers might have told it me also. But I am not sure that their words would have gone as much home to me as Aristotle's did. I might have thought that it was their business, part of their profession, to utter that maxim; and also, there would have been so much in these books which I did not find in Aristotle, that I might have trusted them more, and not have thought that I wanted some inward experience to expound them. For this is the third good that I got from the old Greek; he did *not* satisfy me. He told me a number of things which I believed then, and believe now, to be of continual use. He made me see the worth of habits, the worth of acts, the worth of moral purposes. But when I asked him what was to be the standard of my habits and acts and moral purposes, he did not give me any distinct answer. And the more I questioned him, the less could I extract from him what I wanted. He had made me know that it was not a mere book standard I needed, that all the theories and all the laws in the world would not give it me. For that I was infinitely obliged to him. But I positively wanted to learn where it was, since without it I felt I could not practise the things he wished me to practise, I could not be the worthy man he was trying to make me. Nay, I should have been a very unworthy man; for I had reason to think there was such a standard, and I felt strange twinges for having departed from it, which twinges he could not explain to me.

Of course many people would have said to me at once, 'If you want this standard you must turn to the Bible.' The common religious opinion of my country said so; the University in which I had been studying this Heathen book said so. But I found a difficulty in practically attending to the recommendation. I had got the conviction thoroughly worked into me, that this standard could not be contained in any letters, though they were the most wonderful letters ever written in the world. It did not signify how good they were, how much authority they had. Aristotle's was an imperfect treatise, a treatise containing plenty of errors. But if there were a perfect treatise, one in which were no errors at all, it would not be the standard that I wanted; still less would it enable me to follow a standard. The standard must be a LIFE. It must be set forth in a living Person. If it is to do me any good, his life must in some way act upon my life. Aristotle had been, as I said, a blessing to me for making me understand that this was so; he had failed from being unable to show me such a life as this. Neither the authority of my country's faith nor of my University, though I had reason to reverence them both, could warrant me in practising a self-deception in so important a matter. If the Bible was merely a book, though it might be the best of all books, though it might be a book without a flaw, I could not hope to find in it that which I was seeking.

There was another lesson I had learnt from Aristotle,—had learnt from that which he did tell me and from that which he did not tell me. He believed that there was one Creator of the Universe. He might pay a sort of reverence to the gods whom his country worshipped, but they evidently did not affect his speculations in the least about Nature or about Morals. All his inquiries as to the course of the world and as to man's life were pursued independently of them. He arrived at the conclusion, that it was most likely there was one Ruler over the whole Universe, by reasonings that were quite independent of any he had received by tradition.

Well, I said to myself, this acknowledgment of a one Ruler in him is very good, I am very glad he was able to make it. But has it anything to do with *me? I* dwell in this world. Is there any sort of relation between *me* and the Maker of it? I found from the history of the world that men everywhere had been dreaming that they had something to do with some powers or rulers whom they could not see. I found that these dreams had not been confined to a few people here or there, who might perhaps have leisure for dreaming; that they had affected the condition of all people from the highest to the lowest; that what they thought of their gods, and the worship they had paid to their gods, had influenced their civil life, their opinions about Nature, their notions of what they themselves were to do and to be. It had influenced their conduct to each other, it had influenced their inward characters. Aristotle no doubt had discovered that the honesty of their investigations and the honesty of their practice was very seriously interfered with by the terror with which the gods inspired them, and by the notions they had of the feelings and passions of the gods and of the demands they made upon men. He had little hope that his countrymen would fairly study the facts of nature or the facts of human life, while these confusions about the gods, and their connexion with them, were continually intruding themselves into their minds. So he simply gave all these thoughts the go by. His physical studies and his moral studies were pursued without reference to them.

One could not help admiring Aristotle for taking a course which seemed to him the most honest under his circumstances. It showed him to be a brave man, that he did not profess to understand what he did not understand, and that he tried to make the best of what he did. To those who act thus more will be given in due time. One said so whose words I believe; who never said anything which I do not expect will come to pass. But then I was bound to inquire for my own sake whether this course was a reasonable or a possible one. Certainly the effect of it was to cut off an immense body of facts which had told upon the condition of all generations of men, all tribes of the earth. Certainly the effect of it was to confine the study of the Morality which is for all human beings within a small circle of human beings. But was this all? Could I for myself dispense with thoughts of this kind? No; those twinges of which I spoke, were they not just like what other men had felt in other ages and in other regions of the world? Were they not witnesses to me that I had a common nature with them, that I was not free from their doubts and fears and griefs? Did they not show that I needed what they needed? Could I make up a scheme of morality for myself which should take no notice of these facts in myself? And what did these facts imply? Did not they seem to say, 'There *is* some connexion between you and a Being 'who is higher and better than yourself? He *is* calling 'you to account for these acts of yours and these thoughts 'of yours. If you had nothing to do with Him, you might 'be easier than you are; but you would be more of a mere 'animal, you would be less of a man.'

A person who finds this out is likely to be in great perplexity. For he cannot be satisfied with only talking of a one Creator of the universe. What he is thinking of is of a Being who has something to do with *him*, who is *his* Ruler, who is the standard of *his* life. And yet he cannot help perceiving that men's opinions about this Being have often led them to strange crimes and cruelties. He cannot wonder that Aristotle, and many men since his time, should think it safer to lay down the plan of their existence without any direct reference to Him. What is to be done? For to stand still in such a state of mind as this is impossible. The world does not stand still. Our own years and days do not stand still. We are swept along, whether along in the right course or in the wrong one.

Then perhaps it may occur to a man to ask, 'Was I
'doing justice to the faith of my country, when I supposed
'that it was merely setting up a book, even a divine book,
'as the standard of man's acts, and life, and morality? Is
'not that Book commonly spoken of as a Revelation of
'God? Is it not spoken of as the Revelation of One who
'was the Son of God and the Image of God, and who
'became Man? Supposing it were this, might it not tell
'just what Aristotle shows me that I need to be told?
'Might it not set forth to me a *Life?* Might it not set
'forth the Life that is the standard of my life, the standard
'of the life of all human beings? Might it not explain the
'dreams there have been in all men about the relation
'between them and some Being that is above them?
'Might it not clear those dreams of that which has been
'so mischievous in them? Might it not place Ethics, or
'Morals, on a true and universal ground?'

Those of you who have attended my Bible class on Sunday evenings, will know that I have taken some pains to show you that the Bible may be read as a continuous history, and that it is the history of the unveiling of God to the creature whom He has made in His image. I have tried to show you this by taking separate books in the New Testament, and examining them chapter by chapter, verse by verse. I have tried to show it you by beginning at the beginning of the Old Testament. and tracing the course of its narratives. I have tried to show it you by comparing the Old Testament with the New. I have not used any arguments to prove that the book was divine or was worthy of our attention. If it was divine and worthy of our attention, I thought it would make good its claims for itself, though I could not make them good. All I wanted was that we should find out what it is saying to us. I believe if we question it, it will answer more honestly than any book in the world. There may be mistakes in our translation of it which ought to be set right, as all mistakes ought to be set right where they can be, especially when they have to do with the most important matters. But in our way of proceeding with the Old Testament, this was not a very serious matter; for we wanted to find out the upshot of the history, the principle which was involved in it; and that did not depend much upon the interpretation or the construing of particular texts. Whenever I could give you any light that I thought might make a passage clearer, especially in those books which we were examining more carefully, I was bound to do so. But what I chiefly desired was, that I might put myself as little as possible between you and the revelation which I was sure the book contained, and that we should question ourselves and each other to see whether it did reveal anything to us, whether it did scatter any darkness that was in us before. That was what I aimed at in this course of lessons. I believe the aim was right and the method was right, whether I have succeeded or not.

In the Lectures which were said to be on Ethics, or Morals, I pursued an entirely different method. I had no text-book; I rather carefully avoided text-books; I was afraid you should think I was delivering a system which was contained in them, not making you acquainted with facts which were in you. I was equally afraid that you should think I was working a system out of my own head. I tried to avoid both dangers by speaking to you of what you all knew. When any of us is born into this world, he is surrounded by objects which he is by degrees to get acquainted with through his senses. But he has also human relations—a mother at all events, a father; perhaps brothers and sisters. He sees their faces, he hears their voices, as he sees the curtains of the bed and hears the noise in the streets. But his relation to them must be something different from this. We all are sure that it is. All the seeing and hearing in the world do not fulfil that relation. We speak of affections. Evidently a man's relation to his fellow-men fails utterly, is not fulfilled, unless he has these affections. They are as necessary to it as seeing and hearing are to his intercourse with any thing that is not human. To these relationships and to these affections, then, we addressed ourselves first of all. The consideration of them gave rise to a number of observations and a number of questions. If we merely confined ourselves to the life of a *child*, we were met with a variety of serious inquiries as to how its affections were to be directed, as to the distortions to which they were liable, as to the influence of the senses upon them, and their influence upon the senses. We seemed to learn a good deal by examining the words which we use to describe these facts, as well as by comparing our experiences of the facts themselves. What the members of my class said to me, and the difficulties which they raised, were very useful to me and helped me to see many things more clearly. If I did not remove their difficulties, I hope I may have shown some of them a way of removing them for themselves, by doing the duty which they are called to do.

Duty? What did that mean? That word introduced

us to another series of questions which belonged to the second division of these lessons. At some time there arises in the mind of each of us the sense that he is an individual person, not merely related to certain other people. I pointed out this feeling to you as especially characteristic of a *boy*, as being indicated by certain exhibitions of self-will and independence, and determination to put forth power, such as we had only seen the germs of in the *child*. I tried to show you that if these feelings are left to themselves, he becomes a savage; but that this is not the state that is intended for any one of us. I urged that all the efforts of schoolmasters, where they had been wise, had tended to awaken a sense of responsibility, to make the boy feel that he is subject to laws which must be executed in punishments if they are not obeyed. This dread of punishment may deter from crimes; but it can never lead any one to do a single right action. Till we understand that there is something *due* from us, till the sense of *duty* is awakened, we have no freedom, we are not even in the way to become men. To understand what this sense of duty is, I was driven to speak to you of that mysterious *Conscience*, which all men in some sort confess, which those who deny it in their theories bear witness of in their acts and in their habitual language. Some of you will remember what pains have been devoted to this inquiry during the last term, and how we were driven at last by facts, and in defiance of the speculations of eminent men, men worthy of all reverence, to think that the conscience is not a power of its own, but is a witness to us of some One speaking to us, commanding us, judging us.

Very deep questions indeed started up unawares while we were engaged with this topic, and suggested the third division of our subject, which concerns especially the full-grown *man* after he is loosed from the direct restraints of parents or teachers, questions concerning our Will and our Reason: how the one is only free when it is delivered from self-will; how the other is only in its proper state when it is seeking for truth and does not think that it can make truth; how both together are the very signs of what man is as distinguished from the animals; how both together are proofs that we are members of a race and family, and not a mere collection of individuals; how both together demand a perfect Will and a perfect Reason, that they may not miss the object and fail to fulfil the work for which they exist.

I do not go over this ground which some of us have travelled before, from a notion that no one will profit by these Sunday morning Lectures who has not attended my former courses. I refer to it that both the old and new students may see for what purpose I do use, and for what purpose I do not use the Holy Scriptures. I use them because I think they will show us what is the ground of those affections, of that conscience, of that reason and will, which we have to do with because we are human beings, and which we must have to do with supposing there were no Scriptures at all. I do not use them because I look upon them as substitutes for these affections, or conscience, or reason, or will. I use them because I look upon them as God's revelation to us of ourselves, who are made in His image, and of Himself, who has made us in His image. I do not use them as if they would mean anything to us, or be of any worth to us, supposing we were not made in

His image, supposing it were not possible for us to be acquainted with Him. I use them because I conceive they set forth Christ as the Son of God and the Lord of every man. I do not use them because I think they set forth some standard which is good for a set of men called Christians, who are different from other men, and who have not the same God with other men. I use the Scriptures to show us what I believe is the law and the life for all of us, that law and life of which men in the old world had only a partial glimpse. I should not use them if I thought them less universal and more partial than the books of heathens or of later moralists.

Now, then, I have answered the questions with which I began. I am most anxious that you should not think of Christian Ethics, that is to say, of the Christian character, as different from human Ethics, that is to say, from the proper human character. I am anxious that you should not think of Sunday Ethics as different from week-day Ethics. But I am also anxious that you should think of the Ethics which are set forth to us in the Christian Scriptures as being the Ethics for men, of our Sunday lessons as interpreting the experience of the week. That is my reason for wishing to meet you here on these mornings. We form a Working Men's College; that is to say, a college of men not distinguished from other men by any advantages; who want only to be men and to do the work of men. Sunday, the day of rest, is, I believe, given us especially for this end. Work has its ground in rest and its termination in rest. Man is made to work and to rest. In his hours of rest he is preparing for work; in his hours of work he is preparing for rest. One great preparation is to learn what the blessing of rest is, in whom he may rest, that we may learn also what the blessing of work is, and under whose guidance he may work. If the Sunday gives us that wisdom, I believe it does more for us than if it gives us merely animal rest; though I am far from undervaluing that either. At any rate, it is my business to do what I can that those who desire it may obtain the former gift. It is my duty to consider how I may help them most to attain it. And after much consideration, I can find no way in which I can aid them better than by trying to work out with them the meaning of this Epistle of St. John.

As I have told you, generally, why I think the Bible may be our best teacher in Ethics, I will tell you now why I select this book of the Bible as serving that purpose more perfectly than any other. I have been endeavouring, as I said just now, in my evening Lectures, to show you in what sense I regard the Scriptures as a *history*. I should not give them that name if I did not discover in them a gradual unveiling of the divine purpose and divine life to man, a gradual education of men to understand, through their own wants, and weaknesses, and sins, what this purpose and this life is, and how they may be the better for it. Through all the patriarchal period of the Jewish history, through all the legal, through all the prophetical, I trace, and I wish you to trace, this revelation and this education. But if the revelation and the education are good for anything, they must be leading to some result.

I find this result expressed in these words:—'*That which was from the beginning, which we have heard, which we have seen with our eyes, which we have looked upon, and our hands have handled, of the Word of life (for the life was manifested, and we have seen it, and bear witness, and shew unto you that eternal life, which was with the Father, and was manifested to us;) that which we have seen and heard declare we unto you, that ye also may have fellowship with us: and truly our fellowship is with the Father, and with his Son Jesus Christ.*'

Do not suppose that I expect you to take in the meaning of these sentences all at once. If I did, I should not have thought it necessary to examine carefully into this letter. I hope, next Sunday, to go with you into the meaning of the principal words in these sentences, and to consider them in their connexion. But I think you can hardly hear them read to you without feeling that they have something to do with those questions which I said that a Heathen had taught me I must engage in, and those in which I have endeavoured to interest you by recalling to you different portions of your own experience. The very language which perhaps puzzles some persons on first taking up the book, about the Life and the manifestation of the Life, fits in with our previous thoughts and difficulties. Something like this is what we were asking for. The writer clearly means to tell us of a Person whom he has seen and handled, in whom he believes a divine and perfect life was shown forth, with which life, he says, he himself and those to whom he is writing, may have fellowship. I do not care who holds out to me this kind of promise. It so exactly answers to what I am looking for, that I must perforce give heed, I must beg the speaker to tell me what he means; I must look further into the account he gives of this matter, to see whether it is consistent with itself, whether it only seems to meet the demands of my spirit, or does actually meet them. Let the writer be who he will, I have a right to examine his words, not for his sake, but for my own. And if he brings a message to me from God Himself, I believe God will make it evident to me that he does.

I am glad, however, to hear anything I can hear about the speaker and about those to whom he spoke. If he were, as we in England believe him to have been, a fisherman who once mended his nets by the Lake of Galilee, and who was now dwelling, a grey-haired man, in the commercial city of Ephesus, it may be strange that he has anything to tell us who live in this far country of the west—anything to tell refined men and scholars, as well as working men, whose customs and whose language are altogether different from his, who belong to a world which is eighteen hundred years older than it was in his day. But if we shall find that what he spoke to the fathers and young men and children in Ephesus, who had been worshippers of the goddess Diana, or worshippers in the Jewish synagogue, and who had come to think that there was a Person who bound Jews and Gentiles into one; if, I say, we should find that what he told them has some deep interest for us—does make known to us secrets which we need to be acquainted with—we, at least, shall not care less for him because he was a fisherman or a Jewish fisherman. We shall hope that he will not, at all events, speak of accidents that belong to rich and comfortable people, when we want to know of principles which are for all equally. We shall hope that, as he was a Jew, he may be able to explain to us what the law and history of his own people had to do with mankind, and how he himself, being born a Jew, had been led to seek fellowship with men of other tribes. We shall hope that he may tell us how we are bound to our forefathers, and how we shall be bound to those who may dwell upon the earth when we have left it. We shall hope that he may have proved us and our children to be of the same family with the Ephesians to whom he wrote,—not to have a different Father from them or from him.

LECTURE II.

THE GROUND OF CHRISTIAN ETHICS.

1 John I. 1—6.

That which was from the beginning, which we have heard, which we have seen with our eyes, which we have looked upon, and our hands have handled, of the Word of Life; (for the life was manifested, and we have seen it, and bear witness, and shew unto you that eternal life, which was with the Father, and was manifested unto us;) that which we have seen and heard declare we unto you, that ye also may have fellowship with us: and truly our fellowship is with the Father, and with His Son Jesus Christ. And these things write we unto you, that your joy may be full. This then is the message which we have heard of Him, and declare unto you, that God is light, and in Him is no darkness at all. If we say that we have fellowship with Him, and walk in darkness, we lie, and do not the truth.

WE call this book an Epistle, and I do not know that we have any right to say that it is not one. But it does not open like a letter. It is not addressed to any body of men, or to any one man. The author does not speak of himself. He does not introduce any greetings, such as you would expect of one who is at a distance from his friends. In all these respects it differs from the other Epistles in the New Testament, specially differs from those which St. Paul sent to the Gentile Churches which he had founded. The words '*These things we write to you*,' and others of the same kind which occur afterwards, do not permit us to suppose that it was a discourse delivered with the lips. Otherwise we might have fancied an aged man standing up in an assembly of men among whom he had dwelt a long time, to remind them what lessons he had taught them, and for what end he had lived. And that I doubt not was his design. He may have been too feeble to speak what was in his heart, or he may have been away from Ephesus for a while, in his exile at Patmos. Anyhow, it was ordered that his words should be committed to enduring letters, and that we should profit by them as much as those who lived in his day.

The absence of a special superscription has led people to call this Epistle a catholic or universal one. It well deserves the name. Its words, I think we shall find, are as good for London as Ephesus; for the nineteenth century as the first. And we shall understand better how fitly the opening words apply to us, if we consider for a moment what a peculiar fitness they had for the men who had sat by the old Apostle; who remembered that he had talked with our Lord on earth, and had been with him at the last supper; who had listened to him while he recalled the words which had fallen from his Master's lips, the acts which had been done by his Master's hand. Do you not think this thought must have often come into their minds?—
' Shall we not be terrible losers when he is taken from us?
' —losers, not merely as all are who part with a dear friend
' and guide, but in this sense—that henceforth we shall
' only have the lessons of Christ at second-hand; we shall
' only have scattered and broken memorials of His works
' and His life. And will it not be worse for our children
' than it is for us? Will not the tradition become fainter
' and fainter in each new generation? Will it not become
' more mixed with reports that are not true? To be sure,'
they may have gone on, ' we have books which contain

'accounts of His words and deeds, which are trustworthy.
'These we prize now; these we may transmit to the men
'who come after us and teach them to prize. But will not
'that be very different from hearing a living voice? Will
'reading a book be ever a substitute for that? And may
'there not be false reports which are handed down along
'with the true ones? Have not lying accounts of our
'Lord's deeds and words been put together already, which
'His Apostles have told us not to care for? Who will
'give these warnings to our descendants? Who will help
'them to discern between the honest record and the coun-
'terfeit one?'

I cannot doubt that such things were said at this time, because, in some form of language or other, people have been saying them ever since. They *have* fancied that each age was less likely to be right than the last, because it was further from the age of the Apostles. They *have* supposed that our knowledge of Christ can only be second-hand, or third-hand, or fourth-hand knowledge. They *have* disputed whether we are dependent on oral traditions or whether a written book is sufficient without them. They *have* asked who is to determine between the false reports and the true reports. They *have* debated these questions backwards and forwards, and are debating them still.

Now, St. John's words, it seems to me, meet these confusions, and answer them as no others can. He begins with speaking of that which he saw and heard and handled. Those who read his letter could have no doubt that he was referring to the time when he saw the face of Jesus Christ, when he heard His discourses, when he grasped His hand, when he leaned upon His breast. There might be some still upon earth who had been in Jerusalem at that time, who had even been disciples of Christ. There would not be any of them upon the earth long. And there was none of them who would have thought he had as much right to use these expressions as the son of Zebedee had. Here, then, he claims for himself the full dignity of an Apostle. Whatever advantage there was in this kind of intercourse with Jesus, he could say, 'It was mine.'

Yet there is something peculiar in his mode of speaking. Why does he not say, '*He* whom we saw and heard and handled?' St. John certainly meant this. Would it not have been more simple and natural to adopt that form of language? Before we decide, let us hear what he does say: '*That which we have seen with our eyes, and our ears have heard, and our hands have handled, of the Word of Life.*' The preposition *of*, which our translators have adopted, does not exactly answer to the one which St. John uses. I do not know whether I wish that they had rendered it '*about,*' though that certainly would have been more literal. That would be nearly as unintelligible as '*of,*' if we do not exercise our minds upon the passage; if we do, either may be intelligible. Think of the friend whom you have known best and loved best. Let each ask himself, 'What is it that I have known and loved in him?' Suppose he is gone away. You will recollect his look, the tones of his voice, the pressure of his hand. But you would not call these *himself*. You would not say these *were* your friend. You would say these were of him or about him. You would say that what you could not see or hear or handle was much more that which attached you to itself, that which you rested in. You would say—would not you?—

'There was a life in him, which took hold of me. It was
'in that I found the difference between him and other
'people. It was with that I could converse. It was that
'which conversed with me. The goodness, the wisdom,
'the power which I recognised, were in that. The hearing,
'the seeing, the handling would have been nothing without
'that. They brought me in contact with the outside of
'the man,—an outside that was dear to me because of that
'which it expressed,—but *he* was within.'

Now, St. John says exactly this about that Lord and Master who called him from mending his nets, only he says something more than this. He says that that face of His which he saw, that voice of His which he heard, those hands of His which he handled were 'about the WORD *of Life*.' A life was there within that body, just as there is a life within the body of each man whom we converse with. A life revealed itself or was manifested through those outward organs of His, just as a life is manifested through the outward organs of every person who speaks to us, who looks at us, who approaches us. But St. John says that this life which was in Him was not merely *a* life, but *the* Life; the life from which all the life that is in us and in the other creatures is derived. That there must be such a Life, such a central fountain of life as this, we all, I believe, feel more or less strongly. It is what men have been asking for in every country and every age. I showed you last Sunday how one who is seeking a ground for his own moral life is led to perceive the necessity of it. And I observed then how the thought of this life in man associated itself with the thought of God; how men had dreamed that the true standard and ultimate source of their life must be in Him. To that conviction, also, St. John does justice; the phrase '*Word* of Life' intimates that the life which was in this Person was, in very deed, the expression or utterance of that which is in God. Just as the word I speak contains the thought that is in me and that I put into it; so this life with which St. John had held converse, was, he says, the Word of Life; the expression of the whole Mind and Nature of Him from whom all things have proceeded. We say sometimes of a speech which strikes us as very sincere and very powerful, 'The speaker threw his whole soul into it.' We mean that that speech showed or expressed to us very much of what we think was in the man who delivered it. But we know that no man can tell us *all* that is in him, by a speech. We must compare one thing that he says with another, we must be acquainted with his acts as well as with his sayings; both together help us to understand his mind and purpose. And there is so much in us that is variable and contradictory, that one act or one word may not represent the same mind and purpose with another. You may say to-day, ' I fancied that person was one of ' the gentlest of human beings; now I have seen him ' in a passion, I find another kind of man in him; I ' cannot tell what to think of him.' But supposing there were a being with nothing variable or contradictory in his nature, whose purpose was always the same, who was himself always the same; the sayings which he spoke and the acts which he did would be always in accordance; each one would tell the truth about him, each one would tell us of himself. And his acts, and his sayings together, would represent one life. Supposing, then, that you could

ever say of the life of a man, 'This life perfectly ex-
'presses the mind and purpose of God, this life per-
'fectly shows the life that is in Him'—then you would
say, 'This is the Word of God. In him God speaks
'out Himself. In him God manifests Himself.' You
would not mean merely that something which he spoke
proceeded from God, and declared what He intended or
willed. You would mean that he, the whole person, was
and is the Word of God.

You will think perhaps that I am in a hurry to put this
meaning upon St. John, when perhaps his expressions can
be explained in another way. There is nothing that I
wish less than that any one should take my interpretation
for granted. There is nothing that I wish more than that
they should compare St. John's different writings together,
and see whether this is not the kind of thing that he is
telling us in all of them. I say the *kind of thing;* for
I am sure that what he is telling us is much better, and
deeper, and larger than I have been able to express in
my language. Perhaps one of the first discoveries to
which such an examination would lead you, is the feebleness, the poverty, the circumlocution of my phrases, as
contrasted with the strength, and the richness, and the
directness of his. This, however, you may ascertain
for yourselves. The meaning of these expressions '*Word
of God,*' '*Word of Life,*' has not been left by the Apostle
for other interpreters to bring out. His whole Gospel
is an elucidation of it. There is not one narrative in
that Gospel which does not help to present it in some
new aspect. In doing so, I think—indeed, I have endeavoured elsewhere to prove—that he has made the force

of the expression '*Word of God*' in the Old Testament, and so the whole history and purport of the Old Testament, beautifully clear and consistent. And I am also convinced that this language of his is only obscure to us just as the great principles of science are obscure—not from *their* want of simplicity, but from *our* want of simplicity; and that like those principles, we shall at last be led to it by finding that we cannot explain the facts which most need to be explained, without it. Many circumstances in the history of our time, are, it seems to me, tending to this result; none more directly than the conviction, at which we have all arrived, that the deepest knowledge is intended for all classes equally. The full idea of a Word of God, a Word of Life, a Word who is the Light of men, will come out, I think, as we try to act upon that conviction, and not till then. We shall not see our way through the puzzles of education, till we have taken firm hold of this truth. When we do, we shall find it a very levelling one; we shall find that we are all learners from first to last, and that we have all a perfect Teacher. You will not wonder, therefore, that I should dwell upon this subject in a College of Working Men.

I am advancing but slowly with the passage which I have chosen. But I gave you notice that I should have to dwell upon the separate words of it; and St. John himself stops us when we are over-eager to proceed. Here you will see that he introduces a parenthesis, one, however, which is very necessary for the complete unfolding of his design. '*For the Life,*' he says, '*was manifested, and we have seen and bear witness, and declare to you that eternal life which was with the Father, and has been manifested to us*'

Of that thought he is full. He must make the Ephesians understand that this is the beginning and end of all he has been saying to them since he began to dwell among them. *A* life has been manifested; *the* life has been manifested. That which he saw of Christ, while he was with Him upon earth, was to enable him to testify of this life. He had no other business than to tell them that it had been fully revealed. But that he may perform that task properly, he must tell them what kind of life it is. It was the eternal life. Not a life of years, and months, and days, and instants; but a fixed permanent life—the life of a Being in whom is no variableness, nor the shadow of a turning. I am only seeking for expressions that may give you some help in entering for yourselves into the force of this word; I do not want to change it for any other. We all oppose Eternity to Time. Each of us in his heart recognises that distinction as a true and necessary one. The more serious we become—the more we begin to think about what we are—the more real and deep the distinction becomes to us. And yet we are apt to lose ourselves in utter vagueness when we try to contemplate Eternity. It seems to us something not distinct from time, but a very very long time. Unawares, we begin to measure it by our clocks, even while we say it cannot be measured by them. And so by degrees we dismiss the consideration of it as much as we can, because if we put it far from us, it seems to fade into nothing, and if we bring it near to us, it seems too dreadful to endure. May I give you this hint about it? The Bible way of presenting it to us—St. John's way—is the safest and the most rational. He joins *eternal* to *Life;* he joins *Life* to *God.* If the Life is that which was manifested in Christ, in His words and acts, it is a life of gentleness, justice, truth. You cannot measure these by the clocks; you do not wish, or try to measure them. You never did so when you were thinking about the gentleness, or justice, or truth of a friend. And if that is the life of God, surely it is not a terrible thing—though it may be an awful thing—to recollect that He is, and was and is to come, and that He is not far from any one of us.

But is that what St. John means by *eternal Life* here. Look at the next clause, and you will not doubt it. He speaks of the '*Life which was with the Father and has been manifested to us.*' You will not doubt that when he speaks of the Father, he means the Eternal God. I would not have you satisfied with saying that. The name *Father* is not a name that is ever used carelessly. It is *the* New Testament name. It is that name which we pray to have hallowed. We should ask ourselves, why it is the New Testament name; why every little child may use it now? And I do not think we can get any other answer than this, that He who came into the world, and showed forth that life in it whereof St. John speaks, said, 'I come from a 'Father. My Life is the image of His Life. Therefore 'it is an eternal life. It did not begin at a certain time; it 'will not end at a certain time. And as you are partakers 'of my nature, you are intended to partake of this eternal 'life; you are the children of Him who has declared me 'to be His only-begotten Son.'

I have thus brought together two names which are never long separated by St. John, the name '*Word of God*,' and the name '*Son of God*.' Neither gives forth a complete sense without the other. We might suppose that the

'*Word of God*' was only a sentence or decree of God—that it did not point to a person at all. If only the name '*Son of God*' was used, we might mix associations of time with Him who is declared to have an Eternal Life. The two expressions, when they are compared together, discover the full intention of the Apostle. He who shows forth the true life to man is as much one with God as the word is with the thought that it makes known. But that we may understand how personal and perfect the relation is, we must resort to the highest and tenderest of human relations. The union and sympathy between a son and a father, is most imperfect among men. There must be some perfect original of it. It could not be what it is to us if there were not. We are told that the original is where the original of all our life is—in God. The union of the Father with the Son is involved in the very idea of God as it is declared to us in the New Testament. We shall see also that it is involved in the idea of the way in which men are to partake in the life of God.

This is the subject of the third verse, '*What we have seen and heard declare we unto you, that ye also may have fellowship with us; and truly our fellowship is with the Father and with His Son Jesus Christ.*' There is nothing, you see, which he claims for himself as an Apostle, that he does not claim for those to whom he writes. The very highest privilege which can belong to him, he affirms to be theirs. His reward is, that he has the delight of announcing to them that it is theirs, and how they may enter into the enjoyment of it. Fellowship or communion with God, he is to tell them, is possible for man. The inferior being may partake the nature of the superior. The creature who has fancied himself limited to threescore years and ten may enter upon the eternal life of the Creator. The declaration sounds wonderful, the promise incredible. But the Christian revelation means nothing unless this assertion is true—unless this promise can be fulfilled. It professes to be the revelation of a Father through a Son, who has taken the nature of men upon Him—who has entered into our conditions of birth and suffering and death. If it is so, all who have that nature must stand in a direct filial relation to this Father in this Son; there must be some means by which they may acquire His mind, His character, or, to use once again St. John's more comprehensive word, His life.

'*These things*,' says St. John in the next verse, '*write we unto you that your joy may be full* or *fulfilled.*' I supposed that there might be a question among the Ephesian Christians, how they would fare after the Apostle had left the world—how their children would fare after they had left it. Would they be dependent upon a tradition, upon the things which the Apostles had recorded concerning their Master; a tradition that might become more muddy every year? Would they be dependent upon a mere written book? The Apostle answers emphatically 'No,' to both these demands. He saw and handled Christ; but it was that he might bear witness of a life that was in Him, an eternal life—one which had been in Him before the worlds were— one which would be in Him if all worlds were to come to an end. He had seen and handled that which was about this Word of Life, that he might tell them, because they were men—though they were not Apostles at all, though they had never seen and handled Christ at all—that His life was manifested to them, and that they might participate in it. He now adds, '*And these things we* WRITE *that your joy may be full.*' They are written down, not that you may be satisfied with a set of letters, but that these letters may testify to you and to all generations which shall come after—when Apostles shall have been for centuries in their graves—of a life which cannot cease; of a life which must be the same always because it is in God; of a life which it is God's will to communicate to His creatures, and which it is their highest joy to receive.

One verse more, and I have finished this Lecture. I cannot separate it from those which have gone before, and you will see immediately how it belongs to the subject of my whole course. '*This then is the message which we have heard of Him, and declare unto you, that God is light, and in Him is no darkness at all.*' This was the revelation which had been made to men in Him whom St. John had seen and handled—had been made not only with His lips, but in His acts—in the powers which He had exerted for man's benefit—in the death which He had died. If He was the Word of God, if the whole life and purpose of God were manifested in Him, then it was possible to say boldly, 'There is not one dark spot in this Being, not one evil malicious thought against any creature whom He has formed. All is clear unbroken light.' And this word 'Light' is at once the simplest, and the fullest, and the deepest which can be used in human discourse. It is addressed to every man who has eyes, and who has ever looked on the sun, or to whom the sun has discovered the ground at his feet. The more you think of it, the more it satisfies you. It does not only tell you of a

Goodness and Truth without flaw, though it does tell you of these; it tells you of a Goodness and Truth that are always seeking to spread themselves abroad, to send forth rays that shall penetrate everywhere, and scatter the darkness which opposes them.

Here, then, is the answer to those terrible conceptions which I said in my last Lecture men had formed of the Divine nature and character; those conceptions which made Aristotle think that it was better and safer to leave what was divine out of his scheme of morals. I did not wonder that he had done so. I could find no fault with him. And yet I could not understand how that which affected men so much, and acted upon their character so much, could be treated as if it had nothing to do with the formation of their characters. In Christian ethics it is the foundation-stone. This proposition, '*God is light, and in Him is no darkness at all*,' is the proposition from which all others start. How it has been demonstrated to men I have tried to show you. That demonstration in a Son leads on to the next proposition, that this divine light is not merely hidden inaccessible light; that it has shone out in a Person Who makes us understand what He is by doing human acts and bearing human sorrows. And so we arrive at the third proposition, that the highest end of man's existence is to have fellowship with this Life and Light. And then a fourth, which we shall have to speak of more hereafter—that fellowship or communion with each other is implied in this fellowship or communion with God and with His Son.

These I regard as the fundamental maxims of Christian ethics. In any true study of them which is grounded upon the teaching of the Apostles, these maxims will precede any considerations respecting the condition of man as an erring and sinful creature. We shall know nothing about that condition unless we understand first what our true and proper state is. We must measure the crooked line by the straight, not the straight by the crooked. But in the next Lecture I hope to show you that these great principles of Christian morals, which St. John has declared to us, are not applicable to some imaginary, perfect world, but to ours—not to some pure and saintly beings, but to you and me.

LECTURE III.

LIGHT AND DARKNESS: SIN AND PURIFICATION.

1 JOHN I. 6—10.

If we say that we have fellowship with Him, and walk in darkness, we lie, and do not the truth: but if we walk in the light, as He is in the light, we have fellowship one with another, and the blood of Jesus Christ His Son cleanseth us from all sin. If we say that we have no sin, we deceive ourselves, and the truth is not in us. If we confess our sins, He is faithful and just to forgive us our sins, and to cleanse us from all unrighteousness. If we say that we have not sinned, we make Him a liar, and His word is not in us.

YOU will remember the words which immediately precede these. '*This then is the message which we have heard of Him, and declare unto you, that God is light, and in Him is no darkness at all.*' I have spoken of that message already, but I must speak of it again, as all the rest of this chapter depends upon it. I can quite imagine a person saying,—' Light! Darkness!—What exactly does he ' mean by these expressions? They are figurative. What ' is the literal force of them?'

Now I am very glad to hear questions of this kind, and I will answer them as well as I can; but I must tell you why I do not expect that I shall ever be able to answer them as those who propose them may desire that I should. I have explained to you already that the student of morals does not want letters first and chiefly. He wants a *Life*. He wants letters only as they assist him to the know ledge of a Life. Well, then, if I am bidden to find a *literal* meaning for these phrases, 'Light' and 'Darkness,' I must consider what I am about. They certainly are very living expressions. They belong to the life of us all. Every man who cannot read or write has to do with them, and knows something of what they signify, if he cannot convey his knowledge accurately to another. Nay, sometimes he *can* do that; an ignorant man may tell me something about the effect of darkness or light upon him, which may make me feel what they are more truly, more exactly, than any long descriptions of them which I meet with in a dictionary or encyclopædia composed by learned men. He may say, 'My companion and I walked on pleasantly ' and cheerily enough as long as the sun was shining upon ' us. We saw the sky over our heads, and the trees, and ' the corn-fields, and each other's faces. But night came ' on. All things were huddled together; we mistook old ' stumps of trees for houses, we were continually stumbling ' against each other; it was dreary work enough.' If he only said this to me, I should understand him better—he would give me a fuller and more accurate impression of what light is and what darkness is—than if he had been able to supply me with the best definitions of them that were ever invented. Do you not see, then, that to get what are sometimes called literal equivalents for these words, which are just what a dictionary or encyclopædia affords, might be to lose clearness instead of to gain it? Let us not be deluded with phrases. If what is called figurative language brings us into closer contact with reality than what is called literal language, it must be better for our purpose; and we should resolve to let no one rob us of it under pretence of giving us something more substantial in exchange. If he can prove that it is more substantial, we will take it; if not, we will keep what we have.

Moreover, these expressions were wonderfully suitable for those to whom St. John wrote. The Ephesians had paid an especial worship to Artemis or Diana. They connected her with the moon, the night-ruler. They had paid a worship, in common with the other Greeks, to Apollo; him they connected with the sun, that rules the day. They *connected* them, I say, with these beautiful objects; but they were never satisfied with doing so. The god of light was the god whom they went to consult how they should manage states, conduct wars, make peace. They felt that a higher light than the light which the eyes could see must proceed from him. That could never enable them to choose the right path and avoid the wrong one. That could never keep them in fellowship with each other. But that which could, they were sure must *be* a light. They could not describe it in any language so well. It must be a better, purer, diviner light, than that which they perceived with their eyes. It must be a more human light; the other affected men in common with animals and plants; this must have to do with that in which they were different from animals and plants. So these old Greeks thought. And the more one reads of them, the more one perceives how much all that was great in them and in their deeds was produced by these thoughts. Yet they were perpetually confusing the light which came from the sun and moon—the light which they saw only through their eyes—with that light which they could not see with their eyes at all—which came directly to *them*. They were continually exalting the lower light above the higher light, and supposing the higher to come from the lower. This was their idolatry. They worshipped the visible things from which they thought that the light proceeded. All the time they felt that men were better than these things; therefore, if they worshipped these things, they must also worship men. And men could make wonderful things. They could imitate the works of nature. They could express the thoughts of their own minds in pictures and statues. Why should not these be worshipped too?

St. John had been taught almost from his birth, that he was not to worship things in heaven, or on earth, or under the earth, or the works of his own hands. He had been taught that the Lord his God was one Lord, that He was the Unseen Deliverer, Guide, Teacher, King of Israel. He had clung to this teaching. He had believed that all the institutions of his land were appointed to keep him and his people from forgetting it. He had believed that this was their distinction from the nations that were round about them; that they were a wise, and understanding, and united people, while they trusted in this Deliverer and King, whom they could not see; and that they became a stupid and ignorant and divided people as soon as they began to bow down to things which they could see. *Now* he had believed that this God had revealed Himself to them, not in the sun or in the moon, but in a humble and crucified Man. With this conviction becoming every hour deeper and deeper in his mind, he had settled in the city where Apollo and Diana were worshipped. He saw the mischiefs and dangers of that worship more clearly and fully than he did when people told him about it on the Lake of

Galilee. But he did not think that these Ephesians had been wrong because they had dreamt of a God of Light. That was a true dream. Christ had come to fulfil it. The God of Abraham, and Isaac, and Jacob, whom Jesus had revealed, was this God of Light. The sun was His, the moon was His; He had created them for the blessing of all creatures. But that Light which belongs especially to man,—that Light by which he is to guide his steps,—that light which keeps men in fellowship with each other,— that was His own true Light, His own proper nature; that was what He had manifested to men in His Son. For this was the message which they had heard of Him and declared to the Ephesians, that '*God was light, and in Him was no darkness at all.*'

If, then, I had told you that 'light' meant goodness, wisdom, justice, truth—and that 'darkness' meant the opposite of all these—I should have said exactly what St. John will tell us in very distinct words hereafter, and what he has intimated to us already. But I am so afraid of your thinking of these great realities as if they were mere words, that I have taken what may seem to you a roundabout course for the purpose of showing you how both Heathens and Jews were taught in their different ways to feel that Light, which is the great blessing of all in this creation of ours, is the symbol and witness of these, and that He, who is Himself Wisdom and Goodness and Justice and Truth, may be declared in one word to be LIGHT. And I have endeavoured to show you also how there was a perpetual tendency in men to confine this Light by their own notions and imaginations; that is, in better and more intelligible language, by their own darkness; and how this confusion would have multiplied more and more, if He whom St. John saw and handled had not manifested forth this Light in its purity, free from any darkness at all.

But, as I hinted to you last week, there is another reason closely connected with this, why St. John could not abandon the word 'light' for any that was more formal and less living. A man may easily fancy that goodness, wisdom, truth, are possessions of his own. Whether he thinks he has got them for himself, or that some god has given them to him, he may still believe that he holds them just as he holds a freehold house or a purse of money. But you can never suppose that you hold light in this way. That I can never boast that I possess. When I go out and walk in the light, my eye receives it, my whole body is the better for it. I shut myself in a room with the blinds and shutters dark, or I close my eyes; the blessing is gone. Now the message which St. John brought to the Ephesians was not concerning a blessing of the first kind, but of this last kind. He did not tell them that God had given them certain possessions here, or had promised them certain possessions hereafter, which they could call theirs. He declared, ' God has established a real intercourse between Himself ' and you. I have no better news for you than this: the ' fulness of joy lies in this.' And he had a right to say so. For it was precisely this which men in all ages, and in all countries, had shown that they were craving for; not this, for the sake of other things, but other things for the sake of this. The religion of every people under heaven had meant a longing for intercourse or fellowship with some superior being; it expressed or indicated a conviction, that that superior being must be actually holding now, or be willing to hold some intercourse with them. The belief was strong, that all the arts of life, everything that made existence upon earth tolerable, as well as everything that had purified or elevated it, was owing to some visitation of mysterious celestial beings, or to some communication from them. The knowledge of the husbandman, as much as the inspiration of the poet, was traced to this source. Then came a terrible conviction that this intercourse had in some way been interrupted; that men had somehow failed in fulfilling their part of the relation. They could not tell exactly how; but it seemed likely that they had withheld from the gods that which they wanted, or had disobliged them as men disobliged their fellow-creatures. These were very natural thoughts; men were certain that there must be a truth at the bottom of them. For intercourse with the gods could not be an imaginary thing; it must be as real at least as intercourse with their fellows; it must have some direct resemblance to that, and connexion with it. Therefore they asked wise men to tell them what the gods wanted which they had not given; what had offended them; how the quarrel might be made up, and the intercourse renewed. Therefore they paid all respect to the soothsayers who pronounced that this or that was the god they had displeased—that this or that was the wrong they had committed—and to the priests who offered sacrifices to bring the gods into harmony with them.

You see that all these acts and services presume the existence of a being or beings above men, and of an intercourse between that being or those beings and men. It was possible for a teacher to come among them with the message, 'There is no such being; there can be no such 'intercourse.' I do not say that such a message would not have found listeners. I do not say that some who had been oppressed with the thought of the enmity which was between them and some power whom they did not see and could not approach, might not have felt that message a relief. But then I am not sure that any one could have received it fully; whether every one would not have had misgivings about it which would have made his life often as terrible as if he were afraid that the gods were always plotting against him. And I am quite sure, that if a man, or a nation, had been able to receive that message completely, it would have led to the death of all hope—ultimately, of all interest in the world—of all struggle to improve it—of all human cultivation. But supposing this message was not brought to men; then the only alternative was, that another should be brought to them. And that was St. John's message: 'You are not mistaken. 'The one living and true God does seek fellowship with 'you—has created you for fellowship with Him. He has 'opened the way for a complete fellowship between us and 'Him in His Son. That Son has made us understand, by 'His own words and acts, that God is not the suspicious, 'grudging, covetous being you have taken Him to be; 'that He has in Him no suspicion, no grudging, no covet-'ousness; that all these have come to you because you 'were not holding fellowship with Him, because you were 'not walking in His light.'

That is the subject of the next verse. '*If we say that we have fellowship with Him, and walk in darkness, we lie and do not the truth.*' I hope what I have said will make you feel what an honest simple expression that *walking in darkness* is, and how impossible it is for us to find some better and more intelligible one. We have only to remember our experiences on a dark night, and then to compare these with the experience we have had in our own minds when we have been playing with some malicious or foul thought, to know exactly what St. John means. Walking in darkness is, alas! the phrase about which we have the least need of an interpreter. Every one interprets it himself. It addresses itself with terrible force to the rich and the poor, the wise and the unwise. Whatever else we have not learnt, we have learnt something of that. That darkness is in us, that it is possible to choose darkness rather than light—this every person can tell for himself. It is just the secret which he *can* tell to himself, and which he can impart very imperfectly to his neighbour. For this darkness comes to each man from his being shut up in himself, from his not seeking to get beyond himself. That is a thick darkness, a darkness which begins to be felt the moment a little light breaks in. When a man is hiding himself from all but himself, then the light never reaches him; it is to him as though there were none. And yet a man may go on walking in this darkness. Day after day he may become more used to it. Then how startled and shocked is he at even a glimpse of light! How he wishes to quench it, and cannot!

It is possible for a man to be in this dark selfish state, and yet to say that he has fellowship with God. He may repeat prayers, he may offer sacrifices, he may pass for a religious man. But his life, the Apostle says, is a lie. It is not only that he speaks a lie; he acts a lie. He *does* not the truth. This, indeed, he would have us to understand *is* falsehood—the very root of falsehood. If we are made in the image of God, it is a false and unnatural state for a man, not to be looking up to God but only to be looking down upon himself. It is the same sort of falsehood and contradiction as for the earth to be excluding the sun; only there is this more in it—the man *feels* that he cannot shut out God, if he tries to do so ever so much; he is haunted with the thought of Him; the thought of Him mixes with his bad deeds and bad purposes. Then he tries to worship God on purpose that he may persuade Him not to molest him. His prayers and his sacrifices are entreaties to God to go away from him, to leave him to do what he likes, to be as dark as he likes. Surely St. John's words are the only proper description of this state of mind. We cannot make them stronger; we must not try to make them weaker. It is a lying state. The man who is in it is a liar. And yet every one of us has been in it, and may be in it, and may sink into it utterly.

And then comes the next sentence. '*But if we walk in the Light, as He is in the Light, we have fellowship one with another.*' The darkness of which St. John speaks is an utterly unsocial condition. A man thinks about himself, dwells in himself; the rest of the universe lies in shadow. It is not that he has not continual transactions with other people; it is not that they do not supply him with things that he wants; it is not that he could dispense with them. But all they do is only contemplated in reference to himself; they work, and suffer, and think for him. It is not that the things which he looks at are indifferent to him; he depends upon them; whether he has less or more of them is his chief concern. But he does not wonder at them or enjoy them; they, too, are only his ministers. Emphatically, then, he has no fellowship with men, no fellowship with Nature. All the world is only a looking-glass which reflects himself. What, then, is the opposite state to this? St. John says, '*If we walk in the Light, as He is in the Light, we have fellowship one with another.*' The Light is all around us, while we are most dark. I cannot extinguish the creation because I do not think about it or care about it. Man is living a wonderful life; there is a wonderful life going on in earth, sea, and air; though I am only troubled about what I shall eat, and drink, and put on. But this recollection is not enough to bring me out of my dark pit. My selfishness is too strong for all, however bright, in earth, and sea, and air to overcome. It is not too strong for God to overcome. If I remember that He is in the Light; if I look upon the light which is in these things as coming from Him; if I believe that the light of men—the light in me—is from Him; if I believe that He *is* Light, and that in Him is no darkness at all; then I must believe that I am resisting His will when I am walking in that darkness—when I am acting and thinking as if I had no concern with any being but myself. All those strange intimations which come to me that I am not what I am meant to be, must be flashes of light from the source of light. They are painful flashes. I have often wished and tried to get rid of them. They have discovered me to myself in a way in which I did not wish to be discovered. They are just what men have tried by their false religions—by their insincere professions of fellowship with God—to drive away. But if, instead of

doing that, we will hail them; if we will turn to Him from whom they flow; if we will receive them as His messengers, we may enter into His true order. We may walk day by day as if we were in His presence, as if He were looking at us and guiding us, and guiding all our brethren, and all this universe. And then we have fellowship one with another. The proper social life is restored to us, even if we are far away from our brethren. Yes; Alexander Selkirk in a desert island—John Bunyan in a prison—thousands of sick men and women in lonely rooms, may, in this way, have had a fellowship with the human race, such as we, who walk about the streets and talk with a number of people every day, know little of. By walking in light, as God is in the light—by continually recollecting that He was with them, and that He was with those whom they could not see—they may have acquired a habit of fellowship with those in the world now, and with those who had been in it generations before, which might make us covet their island, their prison, or their sick bed, if those could impart to us the same privilege. But they could not, there was no charm in them; St. John tells us the secret: 'If we walk in the light, as He is in
'the light—wherever we are, in lonely rooms or crowded
'streets, we may have fellowship with each other: we
'may see each other, not as reflections of ourselves, but as
'images of Him.'

But what are these words which follow? *'And the blood of Jesus Christ His Son cleanseth us from all sin.'* They will strike a person who is making out a system of divinity or ethics, as very much out of place. For he will say, 'The Apostle has given us no definition of *sin*. He 'has not even spoken of it in the verses we have read. 'And though he has spoken of having fellowship with the 'Father, and with His Son Jesus Christ, he has not un-'folded any theory concerning the object or the effects of 'the death of Jesus Christ. How much, then, must be 'assumed and explained before this language can have any 'force or meaning for us?'

I have spoken to you about definitions already. I am convinced that if there is one word of which a definition will tell us nothing, unless we have learnt the signification of it first in some other method, that word is 'Sin.' And I am equally convinced that it is by that method, and not by a theological theory, that we must learn how the blood of Jesus Christ cleanseth away sin. What this method is, St. John, it seems to me, teaches us better than any one ever did. He appeals to our experience. You desire to be true yourself; you desire to have fellowship with other men. The moment that first desire is awakened in me, then arises along with it a sense of falsehood: 'I have 'done false acts. I have been false. I have an inclina-'tion to do false acts, and to be false now. I have some-'thing in me which violently resists my craving to be 'true.' The moment that second desire is awakened in me, there arises along with it a sense of selfishness: 'I have 'done acts which imply that I have no relation to my 'fellow-creatures. I have been out of fellowship with them. 'I have an inclination to do such acts now, to be out of 'fellowship with them now. I have something in me which 'violently resists that craving for union with them.' About this fact there is no doubt. Each of us can bear testimony of it. We want no doctor to define it or reduce it to a formula. And about the seriousness, the terribleness of this fact there is no doubt. It must be at the bottom of the insincerity of the world. It must be at the bottom of the discord and hatred of the world. But how shall I describe this fact? What name shall I give to that which is contradicting whatever is right in individual men, whatever is for the peace of society? I am at a loss; I cannot find a name. But I discover something more about the strange fact. '*God is Light, and in Him is no darkness;*' I am intended to walk in this light. This inclination not to be true, not to have fellowship with my fellow-men, is an inclination not to walk in this light, not be in that state in which He has intended men to be. Now I am, perhaps, better able to express this inclination of mine, and what has been the fruit of it. One name, however, does not satisfy me. I try several. I call it *transgression;* that is, the passing over a boundary which was marked out for me. I call it *iniquity;* that is, an uneven zigzag course, a departure from the straight even course. I call it *sin;* that is, the missing of an aim; the going aside from the goal which I was intended to reach. All these words imply that there is one who has marked the boundary for me, who has drawn the line for me, who has fixed the goal or aim for me. All imply a disobedience to a Will which I am meant to obey. But the last is the clearest and the most significant, because it implies that the aim or goal which I miss is Himself; that I am meant to set Him before me, and that I set some other end before me; that I am meant to be like Him, and that I prefer to be like something altogether different from Him.

If this be so, the word 'Sin' expresses the fact of our disposition to be false, and of our disposition to be at war with our fellow-creatures. Yet we do not feel the power of it, or give to it its full sense, till we believe that GOD is true, and that GOD has created us all to be at one. With that acknowledgment comes the *acknowledgment* of Sin. Now, the message which St. John brought to the Ephesians was. 'God has revealed Himself to us in Jesus Christ as the 'perfect Truth. God has revealed Himself in Jesus Christ 'as the God who has created men to be one. Therefore it is 'a revelation to us of our sin; for it shows us how we have 'fought and do fight against this mind and purpose of God; 'how, in doing so, we fight against our own proper state, 'our own proper blessedness.'

I do not mean that this sense of sin did not exist before that full revelation of God in Christ. I have shown you already how strong the sense was in men everywhere of having in some way offended an unseen and powerful Ruler; how many efforts men made everywhere to remove the cause of offence, and to establish peace with the gods. And I will add now that everywhere this sense of wrong-doing was connected with a sense of defilement. Besides injuring the *gods*, they had in some way made *themselves* unclean. Purifications or lustrations were necessary for the removal of their own uncleanness, as sacrifices were necessary to appease their rulers. Such testimonies existed among heathens that they had evil in them; that they knew it. The Israelites were unlike these heathens, for they believed that the Lord had declared Himself, at the beginning of their Law, to be their Deliverer out of the house of bondage, and to be their God. They were taught that He was a righteous God, and that He wished them to be righteous. But, for that very reason, the commandments made them tremble; for they showed them what inclinations there were in them to be unrighteous, to break loose from the government of this Deliverer. Their sacrifices, they were taught, were His means of drawing them back to Himself when they had gone astray; their purifications were His way of showing that He was their Purifier. In both parts of the old world, then, there was this feeling of wrong and this feeling that they needed to be set free from the wrong. But how much deeper did each become in those who learnt that God was Light, and in Him was no darkness—that He was seeking to make them dwell in the light—that He had sent His Son to bring them into His Light! What a sense of sin must have been in them! How they must have felt, 'It is our own fault, our own '*choice* that we have been walking in darkness. We have ' been striving against a God who has been at every moment ' plotting for our good!'

If, then, the men in the times of old cried out for a purification—for something to cleanse them—those who heard this revelation must have felt the need of it immeasurably more. But what kind of purification could they have? Outward purification could not avail them in the least. It was in *themselves* they felt the sin. Into the core of each man's heart the poison had entered. What could eject it? What could make each man right? What could make society pure? Such is the question which a man is obliged to ask himself when he seeks to walk in the light as God is in the light, and to have fellowship with his brother. And to such a man, says St. John, the answer comes, '*The blood of Jesus Christ His Son cleanseth us from all sins.*' There is a new life-blood put into this nature of ours. God Himself has infused it. The Son of God has taken our flesh and blood. He is the Head of our race. He is the bond of peace between it and the God of Light and Truth. He is the bond of peace between us and all the members of our race. When we seek to rise out of ourselves—to be delivered from our falsehood—to have fellowship with God, and fellowship with our brother; then His blood—the blood which He took for us, the blood which He poured out for us—is an assurance that we have that fellowship. It removes the sense of sin against God which is in us; it removes the sense of sin against men. It gives that atonement and that purification which nothing else in earth and heaven can give.

St. John speaks here of this blood as cleansing or purifying the man. He speaks afterwards of the way in which the death of Christ is a sacrifice offered to God. We must not anticipate any of his lessons, but follow them as carefully as we can. What I have given you this morning is quite enough for one time. As I hope to show you hereafter, it is connected with all that heathen writers have told us about man's blessedness, about habits and virtues, and the choice of good and evil—with all that I have said to you in former lectures about the affections and the conscience and the will. But our Apostle never speaks of the principles of morals apart from the practice of them. He will go out of his way and repeat himself twenty times, rather than let his reader fancy that he has been listening to a disquisition when what he wants is help to live. There is an instance of this at the end of this chapter. St. John had told the Ephesian Christians that the blood of Jesus Christ cleanseth from all sin. He is afraid they should think, as many of them were in fact inclined to do, that by some charm or other, they, as Christians, had been put out of the reach of sin, and were not beset by it like other men. He hastens at once to rid them of such delusion: '*If we say that we have no sin, we deceive ourselves, and the truth is not in us.*' Instead of this fancy that you are without sin being a proof how clearly the light is shining into you, it is a proof that you are shutting out the light, for that would reveal to you your own inclination to fly from it and to choose the darkness. The truth makes us aware of our falsehoods; to deny that they are near us and ready to betray us every moment, is to put ourselves out of fellowship with the truth; with the God who is truth. Is that hard doctrine? No; for '*if we confess our sins, He is faithful and just to forgive us our sins, and to cleanse us from all unrighteousness.*' His faithfulness and justice are the enemies of our sins; therefore to them we may turn from our sins. They are the refuges from the darkness that is in us. A faithful and righteous Being is *therefore* a forgiving Being. We are unforgiving because we are unfaithful and unrighteous. But His forgiveness is not tolerance of an evil; such tolerance is cruelty. He forgives us that He may cleanse us. The forgiveness is itself a part of the cleansing. He manifests His righteousness to us that we may trust Him. By trusting Him we are delivered from the suspicion which is the very essence of sin.

It is plain simple teaching this; that a man throws off the burden of his sins by confessing them; and that he may confess to God because he knows that God cares for him, that He is true, and hates falsehood, and can understand him, and can set him free. It is simple, but oh infinitely deep we shall find it to be if we try! This confession, 'Against Thee I have sinned,' this daring to lay our sin bare; this asking to be made true in the inward parts,—what power, what victory, what peace lies in that! And thus we begin to understand the Apostle's last words which at first may sound very like a commonplace vehemently expressed: '*If we say that we have not sinned, we make Him a liar, and His word is not in us.*' If we will not confess the evil in us, we impute that evil to Him. We make Him answerable for that against which He is testifying in our consciences. We thrust away that Word which is shedding abroad His light in us; we bury ourselves in our own darkness. This is the effect of trying to make out a good case for ourselves, when it is our interest, our privilege, our blessedness, to justify God and to condemn ourselves; to say, ' Thou hast been true, and we have ' been liars. Deliver us from our lies! Help us to walk in ' Thy truth!'

7·12·42

LECTURE IV.

THE TRUE IDEA OF MAN.

1 JOHN II. 1—3.

My little children, these things write I unto you, that ye sin not. And if any man sin, we have an Advocate with the Father, Jesus Christ the Righteous: and He is the propitiation for our sins: and not for ours only, but also for the sins of the whole world. And hereby we do know that we know Him, if we keep His commandments.

THIS new chapter in the Epistle is in fact a new chapter in Christian ethics. It is closely connected with the one we were considering before Easter; still it is a step forward in our study, that is to say, a step forward in human experience, and in God's revelations.

You will remember where we stopped. The Apostle had spoken to us of sin. He had told us that '*If we confess our sins, God is faithful and just to forgive us our sins;*' that '*if we say we have no sin, we deceive ourselves, and the truth is not in us.*' Now he begins, '*My little children, these things write I unto you, that ye sin not.*'

You will be struck with the fatherly tone in which St. John speaks. It belonged to himself—the old man, who had watched over the flock in Ephesus, to whom all the members of it looked up as one to whom they owed more than any child owes to its parent. It belonged to his character as an Apostle. All the Apostles felt themselves to be fathers. Christ had told them that they were not to call any *one* man their father on earth: that would interfere with their faith, that they had one Father in heaven. They gave heed to this precept. St. John did not call himself the father of the Church generally, though he was the last Apostle left. He did not even call himself the father of the different churches in Asia Minor, though they all knew him and reverenced him. He taught them, as you will find in the Apocalypse, that each had a pastor or angel of their own, and that that pastor derived his authority not from him but from Christ. But though no one might usurp this universal fatherhood—though it would have destroyed the very constitution of the Church to do so—each circle or society was to be an image of the great family, each was to have its own father. The Apostles loved and cherished that name, and all that it implied, and all that illustrated it. They much preferred it to any title which merely indicated an office. It was more spiritual; it was more personal; it asserted better the divine order; it did more to preserve the dignity and sacredness of all domestic relations. It is a sad day for churches, yes, and for nations, when men begin to regard themselves chiefly as officials sent forth by some central government to do its jobs, and not as men who are bound by sacred affinities and actual relations to those whom they preside over.

But St. John had a special reason for using this tender phrase, '*My little children*,' in this place. All sin, we have seen, is connected by the Apostle with the loss of fellowship. A man shuts himself up in himself. He denies that he has anything to do with God; he denies that he has anything to do with his brother. That is what he calls walking in darkness. The inclination to walk in darkness, to choose darkness rather than light, is *sin*. We become aware of this inclination—then arises in our minds a terrible sense of shame for having yielded to it, and for having it so near to us. But as soon as we believe that God is light, and that in Him is no darkness at all—as soon as we understand that He has manifested His light to us that we may see it and may show it forth—with this sense of shame there comes also the pledge of deliverance. We are not bound by that sin to which we have surrendered ourselves in time past, or which is haunting us now. We are not created to be its servants. We may turn to the Light; we may claim our portion in it; we may ask that it may penetrate us. And then, the Apostle says, we '*have fellowship one with another, and the blood of Jesus Christ*,' of Him in whom is life eternal, of Him who has taken the flesh and blood of man, and has poured out His blood for all—that cleanses us from sin. We renounce our selfish life; we claim His life, which belongs to our brother just as much as to ourselves.

If, then, the Apostle wished the Ephesians not to sin;—not to yield to selfishness which was in them, and which was separating them from each other and from God—what could he do better than remind them that they all belonged to one family; that this was their great privilege; that the Son of God had come amongst them to redeem them out of their pride and divisions, and to make them the little children of His Father. These Ephesians might say to the Apostle, ' Why, you told us just now not to say ' that we were without sin; you told us to confess our sins; ' you told us it was a lie not to confess them. Is not that ' as good as saying that we cannot help committing sin?

'No!' he answers, 'my little children, it is not so at all.
'You are under no obligation to sin, because you have each
'of you this selfish tendency, this selfish nature. God has
'made you one flock, one family. Keep that truth in
'remembrance, and you will be able to deny yourselves,
'and forswear that separate nature of yours; to act as if
'you were bound to each other; to feel other men's sins
'and selfishness as your own; to feel that you carry their
'wrong in you; to feel that your Deliverer and Brother is
'also theirs. I tell you these things; I urge you to con-
'fess your sins, on purpose that you may not sin; on
'purpose that you may enter into fellowship with Him in
'whom is no sin, who is altogether righteous.'

'*And,*' he goes on, '*if any man sin, we have an Advocate with the Father, Jesus Christ the Righteous.*' Supposing these words stood alone—supposing there had been no previous words to explain what St. John thought of sin, and no previous message respecting Jesus Christ the Righteous—we might easily fancy that he meant something of this kind,—' It is no doubt an unfortunate thing to sin;
'it should be avoided, if possible. But if any man does
'fall into it, there is one who has such might and influence
'with God that he can persuade Him to overlook the
'offence, and not to punish, hereafter at least, the man
'who has committed it.' This, I say, would have been a very plausible interpretation; a heathen of Ephesus would certainly have concluded at once that it must be the right one. He would have said,—'No doubt we all desire to
'find advocates who can induce our gods to pardon us or to
'accept some compensation for the punishment they would
'inflict. You think you have found the Advocate who

'has influence enough with your God to secure impunity
'for your misdoings.' Many a Jew of Ephesus, perhaps,
would have been equally sure that the Apostle must have
had this thought, or a thought very like this, in his mind.
Such a Jew would have said, 'Yes! if you could persuade
'me that Jesus was the Christ, I, too, might be glad of His
'advocacy to help me in avoiding the punishments which
'my transgressions of the law have incurred. But as I see
'no proof that He is the Christ, I would rather trust to
'the High Priest of Jerusalem, and to the sacrifices which
'he offers according to the law.' But though both heathens
and Jews might have used this language, I am certain that
no heathen and no Jew would have found what in his
inmost heart he was longing for if he found an advocate
who would obtain for him *this* sort of forgiveness. No; the
best heathens perceived—every Jew who had been taught
by the law and the prophets knew—that it is not a blessing
but a misery to escape the punishment of sin. The best
heathens perceived—every Jew who was taught by the law
and prophets knew—that what a man wants is to be set
free from his sin, and that no advocate could serve him in
the least unless he could be the instrument of winning for
him that emancipation.

But if this is true about heathens and Jews, whose education and whose corrupt practices disposed them to accept this notion of an advocate—if they had the sense of needing help of a kind quite different from any which such an one could afford—think how impossible it was for St. John, after the message which he had just announced to the Ephesians, to tolerate for one moment so immoral a doctrine. He had spoken of Jesus Christ as manifesting the life of God, as declaring to men by His words and acts that God was Light with no darkness at all, as enabling men to have fellowship with that Light. Could he all at once contradict these lessons and say, 'Jesus Christ the 'Righteous does not show forth the mind and purpose of 'God, but He is one who intercedes with God to alter His 'mind, to adopt a new and different purpose?' Could he say, 'It is not the great blessing of all that God should 'detect all the darkness that is in us, and scatter it, and 'bring us into His clear Light? What we want is, to 'avoid His Light, to find an advocate who will say, Let 'these poor creatures alone, they cannot bear thy Light. 'Let them hide themselves in their own darkness; they 'are so used to it. Do not be hard upon them if they 'have a preference for it.' No; St. John had no such horrible dream as this. He did not so slander the Master upon whose breast he had lain, of whose eternal life he was to testify. He did not so blaspheme the God of Light. He did not so hate the men whom God has made in His image.

What he does say is in perfect consistency with his previous lessons, only it is a deepening and an expansion of them. 'My little children,' he says, 'you are not bound 'to sin. What I have said to you is to remind you that 'you are brought into a family in Jesus Christ your 'elder brother, and that His Father is your Father, and 'that you may have fellowship with them and with each 'other, and so may rise above your selfish instincts and 'tempers. And if any of you do sin, if you do fall into 'low, loose, selfish acts, or low, base, selfish states of mind— 'then let me tell you how you may be raised out of them--

'how you may recover your right position again. The
'effect of those bad acts, of that bad state of mind, will be
'to make you think that there is a hopeless barrier between
'you and God; that you have made Him your enemy.
'The effect of it will be to make you think that you have
'lost the privileges of a member of this family; that you
'have nothing more to do with your brethren; that you are
'shut up in your own evil nature. These thoughts will
'seem to you true and certain. They must seem so; for
'you cannot help knowing that you are at war with the
'God who is all goodness and truth, that you are at war
'with your brethren. It would be mere mockery and self-
'deception to tell you the contrary. But understand, you
'cannot set aside God's order merely because you do not
'acknowledge it. You cannot change God's countenance,
'because your eyes are jaundiced. He has made you
'members of a family in His Son. "*He is Light, and in
'Him is no darkness at all.*" And He looks upon us as
'we really are—one body in Jesus Christ the Righteous,
'though we choose to act as if we were a set of separate
'creatures. And He wishes us to act upon a true
'belief, and not upon a lying fancy. Remember, then,
'that Jesus Christ the Righteous is ever with God, the
'sharer of His counsels. Remember that He represents
'us as one family, one race before God. Remember that He
'is the same, though we change; and then you will feel
'that there is always a way open for you to return to Him
'from whom you have wandered, always a passage out of
'your darkness into His light; one which is for all; one
'which no evil act, no evil state of mind can close up;
'for it is the way out of these evil acts, out of that evil

'state; it is the way which God Himself has prepared
'for us.'

This, I think you will see, is a different notion of an advocate from the other, and one that is considerably more helpful to struggling and sinful men. The word 'advocate,' which our translators have used, is in itself a very good one. The word signifies etymologically, 'one who may be called to us; a helper and counsellor.' Here it describes Him whom St. John speaks of as God and with God; one in whom we may read and understand His mind; one in whom God can look upon men, and in whom men may look up to God. The belief that there is such a one is, I think, the most elevating, most comforting that it is possible for human creature to cherish. We are apt to look out upon the world and count heads, and then say to ourselves, 'What a hopeless mass of misery and crime is here! 'Perhaps Paris is better than Constantinople; perhaps 'London is better than Paris. But if so, how wretched are 'the prospects of mankind! For what is this London, if 'one considers it in the aggregate, if one thinks of it in 'any of its portions?' So we reason, and then we too often go on—Pharisees as we are—to wrap ourselves in our own righteousness and wisdom, and to thank God that, at all events, we are not as the great majority are. A man is stopped in the midst of that self-congratulation. The question is asked him straightly and roughly, by one who means to have an answer, 'Is not that very 'thought of thine a proof that thou *art* as the great 'majority are? What else is destroying them but the very 'selfishness, the very want of understanding that they are 'members of a kind, which you are now indulging? And

'do not you see that they are members of a kind in spite of
'all this selfishness in them and in you? Don't you see
'that they have affections one for another, however sunken
'and fallen they may be? Do not you see that they are
'related to each other as husbands and wives, brothers and
'sisters, even when they are quarrelling most and tearing
'one another in pieces most? Do not you see that there is
'an order in the world, and that God is upholding it, in
'spite—yes, in spite of you and your narrowness and pride,
'and your wish to be a solitary creature?' Then one
begins to say to oneself, 'An order? Where is it? What
'is it? Who can tell me anything about it? How is
'God upholding it? Will it triumph at last over all this
'disorder? And what have I to do with it? If I have
'been living as if I did not belong to it, how may I begin
'to live as if I did belong to it?' Then it is that these
words, 'We have an Advocate or Representative with the
Father,' acquire such a meaning and power. We need not
be separate from our kind. *He* is not separate from it. *He*
cares for it, watches over it; holds all the different elements
of it together. We need not learn what man is in Constantinople, or Paris, or London. He is the Man. It is in
Him that we know what we are, and why we were created.
In Him each man may draw nigh to the Father of all and
say, '*Father, I have sinned against Heaven, and before
Thee.*' In Him we may confess other men's sins and crimes
as well as our own, and may learn that their crimes and sins
have not destroyed them yet, because Christ is on their
side; because Christ is the advocate and supporter of that
in them which He has himself created; because it is not
His will or His Father's will that that shall perish.

LECTURE IV.

Perhaps you will say, 'It is all very well to use these 'fine words about London, and Paris, and Constantinople, 'but St. John was acquainted with none of these cities; 'one of them at least was little more than a collection of 'mud cabins in his day. And the people he was thinking 'of was a very small circle indeed, which was surrounding 'him in the city of Ephesus, or at most a set of men 'called Christians who were scattered up and down the 'Roman Empire, separated from the rest of the world, 'denouncing its customs and its worship.' Wait a moment till we have read the next verse, and then let us consider whether these were all that St. John was thinking of; whether it was possible for him to think only of them when he spoke of the Advocate with the Father, '*And he is the Propitiation for our sins: and not for ours only, but for the whole world.*' Our translators have introduced the word '*sins*' into the second clause, supposing it ought to be repeated from the first. Perhaps they are right; I am not sure; and I believe, when we have examined the principal word in the passage, we shall find that it makes no great difference whether we say that He was a Propitiation for the whole world, or for the sins of the whole world.

That principal word is '*Propitiation.*' What does it signify? I must refer you back to what I have been saying about the word '*Advocate.*' Those heathens and Jews who looked for an Advocate who should induce some Divine Ruler not to punish them, also looked for something which that Advocate should offer to the Divine Ruler, in order that He might be moved to compassion. They expected that He should give the God some adequate or sufficient motive not to execute the vengeance which it seemed to them that He was executing, or was likely to execute, upon them. No more natural notion could come into the minds of people who had done wrong, and who knew they had done it. If some fellow-creature had displeased them, this was the course they were inclined to adopt; the more inclined the harder and crueler their feelings towards him were. '*Pay me that thou owest*,' as our Lord says in His parable, is the language which one fellow-servant is apt to use to another. He does not care to make his fellow-servant better; he cares only to get an amends for some injury which he thinks he has suffered at his hands. And he supposes that the Lord of all acts upon the same principle; that He, too, wants compensation for some injury He has suffered; that He, too, is spiteful and vengeful; that He, too, cares that His servants should pay Him what they owe, not that they should become right and gracious men. How, indeed, could a Being desire them to be that which He is not himself?

But I must repeat what I said in the other case. Though this was the natural notion of both Jews and heathens, one which they could justify to themselves by arguments, one that they became strengthened in by a series of religious acts which were grounded upon it—no Jew and no heathen was satisfied with it. The conscience in each of them acknowledged a wrong which no such compensation could clear away. The conscience in them confessed that they had grieved some Being who could be content with nothing else but that they should be right and true men. The best heathens said that the Being they worshipped must be right and true Himself, and that it was dangerous and wicked to attribute any acts to Him that would be base and evil in them. The Jew, taught by the law and the prophets, believed that the God and Judge of all the earth was a righteous being, and could only do right; and that the whole scheme and purpose of His government was to make men right. Whatever sacrifices and offerings He appointed, such a Jew was sure, were appointed for this end. They were, as I said in a former lecture, God's way of bringing back those who had wandered from fellowship with Him and with each other into that fellowship. They brought an animal which God had prescribed to the door of the tabernacle of the congregation. They confessed their sins over it; the priest presented it; it was declared to be the sign and pledge of an atonement and reconciliation between God and the worshipper.

These Jewish offerings, then, were no compensations to an offended Prince. They were indications and expressions of the will of a gracious Ruler. They were acts of submission on the part of the Israelite to that Ruler. They were witnesses of a union between Him and them which could not be broken. And there was in that tabernacle in which those sacrifices were offered, a mercy-seat, where God declared that He would meet the worshippers. It was the most conspicuous object in the building; the cherubims covered it with their wings. The High Priest who offered the sacrifices died; this sign of God's presence with the people lasted on from generation to generation. It said to all Jews, young and old, 'Though you have erred and ' strayed, though you are stiffnecked and rebellious, God ' is still claiming you as His people; God is inviting you ' to claim Him as your God.'

St. John had been used to gaze on this mercy-seat when

he was a boy in the Temple at Jerusalem, when he went yearly to the feasts. He had seen it as a man. He had seen it when he walked with Jesus in the Temple; he had seen it after Jesus had died and had gone away from the world. He was far away from Jerusalem. The Temple was perhaps still in existence; but if it was, it was desecrated; it was surrounded with armies; it was soon to be burnt with fire. What had become of the sacrifices, and the priests, and the mercy seat? St. John says, Jesus Christ the Righteous, our Advocate, is the Mercy Seat. In Him God meets us; in Him we may meet God. In Him God is satisfied with us; in Him we can be satisfied with God. Why did he say so? Because he believed that the only sacrifice with which God can be pleased is the voluntary sacrifice of a self; is the sacrifice of one who delights to do His will, and to suffer it. Because he believed that Christ had offered this sacrifice. Because he believed that God had signified His delight in it, by raising Jesus from the dead. Because he believed that that act declared Him to be the Son of God—the Mediator and High Priest who had always united God to man, from whom all other mediators and priests derived their worth and meaning; without whom they were nothing. Because he believed that, being this, Jesus Christ the Righteous fulfilled the idea of the Mercy Seat, in whom God and His creatures can have fellowship, in whom the children who have wandered from their home may find it again.

But was this all? No; the Jewish sacrifice, high priest, and mercy seat were gone. Was this, then, a *Jewish* high priest, sacrifice, mercy seat? If He was that (and He was that) He must be more. The Lord had taken the nature of man; He had died the death of man. Was He not then, a high priest, a sacrifice, a mercy seat for man? Could St. John dare to say He is a mercy seat for our sins only? Must he not say, 'He also accomplishes what the 'Gentiles have been dreaming of in their miserable propi- 'tiations? He is the mercy seat for the whole world. 'The world is atoned or reconciled in Him. All have a 'right to draw nigh to God as their Father in Him. All 'have a right to cast away the fetters by which they were 'bound, seeing that He has triumphed over sin and death 'and the grave, seeing that He is at the right hand of God.' Therefore we have a right to say, 'Our race, our manhood 'is glorified in Him. Whether we live in London, or 'Paris, or Constantinople, we are no longer separated. 'There is a common Lord of us all. There is a common 'life for us all. Confessing that common Lord, renouncing 'by the strength of this common life our selfish divided 'life, we become men indeed; we obtain the rights, the 'stature, the freedom, the dignity of men.'

This, then, is the second part of our Christian ethics. The groundwork is laid in the revelation of God to man, as the Light in whom is no darkness. That revelation was made to creatures who had sinned and walked in darkness. It told them that they were meant to rise out of their sins and to walk in the light. To-day we have heard of the elevation of men into union with God. Jesus Christ the Righteous is the Person through whom the revelation of God is made. Jesus Christ the Righteous is the Person in whom mankind recovers its true position and glory. Therefore our ethics are in the strictest sense Christian; but they are also in the strictest sense human. They adapt themselves to the wants of individual men. They concern societies of men. They prove that there is a fellowship for the whole race of men.

Next Sunday we are to enter, if God permit, upon another subject:—the worth of commandments—the nature of obedience. That subject is wholly unintelligible, so long as we fancy that an advocate or a propitiation is necessary that we may escape from our obligations or from the penalties of neglecting them. But there is another practical topic of which I must say one word before I conclude.

The longing of men for fellowship with God—the sense in men of a separation from God—had both found their expression in prayers or litanies; some of these had been general, offered up by the priest for a whole congregation or society; some had been special, the utterance of an individual's cry for help under his own misery, the acknowledgment of his own evil. These prayers were, I may say, the very signs of humanity, the proof that man does not and cannot reckon himself among the beasts that perish. They point to the past: they look on to the future; they are connected with all the needs of the present. And yet these prayers might become most inhuman. They might be struggles in one man to get something which his neighbour had; they might be cries to a divine power to aid a strong man in crushing a weak one; they might be coverings for deceit and violence, and encouragements to persevere in them. Prayers and sacrifices have served these vile ends. As long as men think meanly of God—as long as they forget their relation to each other—they must serve such ends.

Christian ethics rescue prayers from these vile applications, and vindicate the strong conviction of human beings that without prayers they cannot live. When we believe that there is an Advocate or Representative of mankind, who ever lives to make intercession, that we may not sink but rise, that we may be delivered from our own darkness, that we may know the God who is Light—our prayers become cries against a common enemy—the pursuit of a common blessing. When we believe that Jesus Christ the Righteous is the Propitiation or Mercy Seat for us and for the whole world, that He has made the sacrifice of Himself which is well pleasing to God, our confession of our individual sins increases our confidence in the purposes of God for the universe; our most earnest petition being that He will make us true and loving sacrifices to accomplish His good will to us and to mankind.

LECTURE V.

DOING AND KNOWING.

1 JOHN II. 3—7.

And hereby we do know that we know Him, if we keep His commandments He that saith, I know Him, and keepeth not His commandments, is a liar, and the truth is not in him. But whoso keepeth His word, in him verily is the love of God perfected: hereby know we that we are in Him. He that saith he abideth in Him ought himself also so to walk, even as He walked. Brethren, I write no new commandment unto you, but an old commandment which ye had from the beginning. The old commandment is the word which ye have heard from the beginning.

I AM speaking to those who attend the Sunday evening class on the relation of the Law to the Gospel. *Speaking* is not the word I ought to use, if it conveys to any one the notion that I am giving lectures on this subject, or laying down certain maxims upon it. Our plan is, to read alternately the Pentateuch (what are called the five books of the Law) and the Evangelists (what we call the four Gospels). By considering them together we try to ascertain what are the characteristics of each, how they are related to each other.

For instance, it happened a Sunday or two ago that we read the fifth chapter of Deuteronomy, which contains the repetition of the Ten Commandments. Either just before or just after, I forget which, we read of our Lord's conversation with the young ruler, who came asking Him, '*What good thing shall I do that I may inherit eternal life?*' To his surprise, the young man who had fancied he was to do some great thing, which other people could not do, that he might attain some great prize which other people could not attain—who fancied that he certainly could and should do this great thing, if he only was told what it was—heard that the way to enter into life was to keep those commandments which had been addressed to all Israelites as well as himself, and which he said he had kept from his youth up. Such a doctrine, coming from such lips, forced us to ask— how heeding the commandments which bore upon such ordinary works, which prohibited such ordinary crimes, could have anything to do with the eternal life which God is said to bestow, and to bestow freely? The question offered itself to us, in one shape or another, in all our readings; we could not avoid it if we tried; and as we wanted light upon it, of course we did not try. But I refer to this one example, because the very words which occupied us when we were considering the passage about the young ruler, in the Gospel according to St. Matthew, are those which present themselves to us in this Epistle of St. John. We have been hearing of life—of an eternal life—that was manifested in Jesus Christ. Of this life the Apostle says he and his disciples at Ephesus may partake; they may have fellowship with it. That is the highest blessing, the greatest reward he can hold out to them; if they had that, their joy would be full. And now he comes to speak of commandments. '*And hereby we do know that we know Him, if we keep His commandments.*'

It is a curious phrase, '*we do know that we know Him.*' But it is a familiar one to us in other applications. I say to a friend, ' Are you sure that you *know* that man? I am ' aware that you meet him often. You see him, perhaps,

'every day; you work with him; you talk with him. But
'do you know that you know him? Have you got any real
'insight into his character? Have you any confidence that
'you are not thinking of him better or worse than he
'deserves?' These are questions which we often ask, and
to which we get various answers. Sometimes the answer
is quite confident. 'I am certain that he is, or that he is
'not, an honest, or a kind, or a wise man.' And yet it may
not inspire us with confidence. We may say, or we may
think, 'You are deceived in that man. You have been
'flattered or in some way taken in by him. In due time
'the mask will fall off, and you will find out your mistake.'
Or we may say, 'You are not just to that man. You have
'distorted his acts. You have misinterpreted his purposes.
'There is a far truer mind in him than you give him credit
'for.' But now and then one has a strong conviction that
a friend does understand the man we are asking him about,
does appreciate him. I cannot tell you how we arrive at
the belief; I think it is generally because he helps us to
understand and to appreciate that person. He throws
light upon our own experiences of him; he corrects some
wrong impressions we had formed. And when it is so, his
report, especially if it is a favourable one, never satisfies us.
We are determined to verify it. We must try to know
him whom he praises for ourselves. We must be able to
say, 'We know that we know him.'

I have supposed the case of two men who are equals, and
who associate on equal terms. But let us suppose the
case of a youth and an old man; and to be more exact, let
us suppose the one to be the son of the other. How does
a child come to *know* his father? It has been my misfortune,

I dare to say it has been yours, to meet with many sons who did not know their fathers, who did not the least understand what they were aiming at, either in the general work of their lives, or in the particular discipline of their families. I have also heard sons say, and sometimes I fear they spoke truly, that their fathers did not know them. They did not always mean that their fathers crossed them, or contradicted them, or laid heavy burdens upon them. That may be the complaint of many; but very indulgent fathers, who take little notice of the offences of their children, who easily pass them by, may exhibit what strikes them as want of comprehension. They do not perceive what their sons need, or what is leading them wrong. Their commands are seldom severe, but they appear as if they were arbitrary. They are not enforced with any consistency; a punishment sometimes follows the breach of them, sometimes not; the offender has a good chance of begging himself off; when he does suffer, he is apt to think that it was by accident, and not by law.

On the other hand, I have met, and I doubt not you have met, persons who could say honestly, 'The rules 'which our father laid down for us often cut very dis- 'agreeably against our inclinations; but we had always 'a feeling that he was just, and that he cared for us as 'much when he punished us as when he commended us. 'And then, by degrees, we found that he was wise as 'well as just in his management of us. At last we are 'beginning to see what the principles of his conduct are; 'what he is in himself. We know that we know him.'

Now St. John assumes that the knowledge of God is as possible, is as real for human beings, as any knowledge they can have of each other. Nay, he goes farther than this. There are impediments to our knowledge of each other, which he says do not exist with reference to that higher knowledge. There is an uncertainty, a capriciousness, a mixture of darkness with light, in every human being, which make us hesitate a little, even when we think he has given us the clearest evidence of what he is. We dismiss the suspicion; we say we are sure that he is substantially right—right in intention—though he has done some things which puzzle us, and which appear wrong. But still there is something that bewilders us, in him as well as in our own perceptions. And sometimes we are utterly at fault: we say such and such a person has entirely disappointed us. I think that on the whole this happens most rarely with those that have been under the government of a person, as their commanding officer, their schoolmaster—above all, their father. When you hear a person say, 'I can speak to the temper and character of that man, 'for I have been a long time under him,' you rely more upon his word than if his acquaintance had been of another kind; because you reflect that the superior had continual opportunities for exhibiting tyranny, vacillation, incapacity for guidance; and that if he did exhibit those qualities, the inferior was sure to take notice of them, and to smart under them. The testimony that he did not—the assurance of his subaltern that the service was a free and honourable service, one in which there was no favouritism, one which acted upon his own life, and made him wiser and better—is the highest testimony and assurance that we can demand or receive.

And it is just this test which St. John says we may

have in its highest perfection in our relations with Him whom we cannot see. We may know that we know Him if we keep His commandments. I sometimes suspect that we give too loose a sense to that word 'keep.' No doubt it means to 'obey;' it does not mean *more* than that; for obedience is very comprehensive, a little too comprehensive for slow and narrow creatures such as we are. The word 'keep,' if we consider it, may help us to know what obedience is, and what it is not. A friend gives me a token to keep for him; he wishes that it should remind me of him, that it should recal days which we have spent together. Perhaps it may be only a flower or a weed that was gathered in a certain place where we were walking or botanizing; perhaps it is something precious in itself. If instead of giving me anything, he enjoins me to do a certain act, or not to do a certain act, I may be said as truly to keep that injunction as to keep the flower. To fulfil it is to remember him; it is a token of my fellowship to him, of my relation with him. The injunction may be one which is in itself indifferent. We are told by the prophet Jeremiah that Jonadab, the son of Rechab, had desired his sons to drink no wine. His descendants kept the tradition; it was a homage to their ancestor's memory. The prophet set before them flagons of wine. He did not count it a criminal act to taste the liquor; but when they refused, he commended and admired them, for they were keeping their father's commandment; it was a holy pledge and token of their reverence for one whom they could not see; it kept them as a family together. But the knowledge you obtain of the person who gives the commandment depends upon the nature of the commandment. Jonadab's descendants might get a certain knowledge of their ancestor from this precept about wine. They might fairly conclude that he was a self-restraining man, who had preserved himself, and wished to preserve them, from temptations. Those commandments of which St. John speaks, are not of this limited or arbitrary kind; they are not mere signs or tokens. Still if they are *kept*, if they are watched over and thought about, and cherished as the commandments of a friend; if they are done as His commandments, they will give us an acquaintance with Him which we can obtain in no other way.

Let us consider this point a little more. Let us take the Ten Commandments; for St. John was an Israelite, a hearty Israelite, and of course would think first about the commands which were given to his nation, whatever else he connected with them. Some of you may have gone over this ground with me before; but I am less afraid of repeating myself than of passing lightly over a topic which is connected with the most practical part of Christian ethics.

The commandments open with the words, '*I am the Lord thy God which brought thee out of the land of Egypt, out of the house of bondage. Thou shalt have none other gods but me.*' How could a Jew keep this commandment? He must break it—he must acknowledge another lord than the one who was speaking to him—if he did not think within himself, '*My* God is a Deliverer, a deliverer of slaves from ' the hand of a tyrant. That is the name by which He ' wishes me to remember Him; that must denote what His ' character is.'

Next he is told, '*Thou shalt not make to thyself any graven image, nor the likeness of any thing that is in heaven*

above, or in the earth beneath, or in the waters under the earth. For I the Lord thy God am a jealous God, visiting the sins of the fathers upon the children unto the third and fourth generation of them that hate me, and showing mercy unto thousands in them that love me and keep my commandments.' How could this commandment be kept? The words *the* Lord *thy* God which were used in the former, here acquire a more distinct signification. 'I am not to
' worship things that I make, for He is *the* Lord. He has
' created me in His image. I cannot create Him in my
' image, or in the image of any of these things I see. No!
' I must not fancy Him like the most glorious of them. He
' is the Lord *my* God. He has more to do with me than with
' them. He is nearer to me than to them. He cares for
' me more than for them. He says He is jealous over me.
' He keeps hold of my heart; He will not let me give it
away to some meaner thing. And as it is with me, it
' will be with my children and my children's children; He
' will be the Lord their God, as He is the Lord my God.
' He will love us from generation to generation; and each
' generation will be worse than the last, if it sets up some
' visible thing in place of Him; and each generation will
' be better than the last, so far as it remembers that He,
' the Deliverer, our God, is the Lord.'

Next comes, '*Thou shalt not take the Name of the Lord thy God in vain: for the Lord will not hold him guiltless that taketh His Name in vain.*' How could a Jew keep this commandment? He would have learnt from the first two commandments, that he was in the presence of a Deliverer, an unseen Being who was watching over him, whom he **must not** imagine to be like even the best of the things which his eyes saw and his hands handled. The *Name* of this Being was that which denoted Him to be a real Person, that by which one could tell another of Him. To fear the Name was to fear the presence, the Person; to recollect, 'A 'true God, a living God is taking account of my acts, and 'of my words.' To take the name in vain, was to act and speak as if there were no such presence, no such Person; as if a man's words were his own, and there was no lord over him. He who did this would not be held guiltless; he would have the sense of guilt in him; he would feel as if the friend whom he had trifled with was pursuing him. To keep the *Name* in the heart as its special treasure, would be to keep this commandment.

The fourth says, '*Remember the Sabbath day to keep it holy. Six days shalt thou labour, and do all that thou hast to do. But the seventh day is the Sabbath of the Lord thy God. In it thou shalt do no manner of work, thou, nor thy man-servant, nor thy maid-servant, nor thy cattle, nor the stranger that is within thy gates. For in six days the Lord made the heaven and the earth, and all that therein is, and rested the seventh day; wherefore, the Lord blessed the seventh day and hallowed it.*' How was an Israelite to keep this commandment? According to the very terms of it, remembrance or recollection was involved in the act of observing it; there could be no sanctification of the Sabbath without this. Merely to do certain things on the Sabbath, or to leave certain things undone, would not be keeping it. Unless the Jew said to himself, 'God has appointed the 'six days, God has appointed the seventh day; I am to 'work because He works, I am to rest because He rests'— he would in vain strive to obey even the letter of the precept. The command is nothing apart from the divine reason for it. The man who thought most of that, who considered most why the Lord his God had ordained rest for him, and work for him; what one had to do with the other; why the man-servant and the maid-servant and the cattle were to share in both; why the ground of both was said to be in the creation of heaven and earth—he would be most filled with delight and wonder at the order in which he found himself placed; he would most devoutly ask God to teach him so to behave himself, that he might not follow his own pleasure and his own foolish notions, either about working or resting, but might conform himself to the divine purpose in each; he would be most afraid of judging his neighbours.

Next comes, '*Honour thy father and thy mother, that thy days may be long in the land, which the Lord thy God giveth thee.*' How was an Israelite to keep this commandment? The very word 'honour' indicates a certain temper or habit of mind. I do not honour a person to whom I make certain presents—on whom I bestow some customary ceremonious respect. The command to honour involves, therefore, a recollection of this father and mother; a recollection of them in this character; a recollection of the bond which unites me to them. It involves too, as the latter part of it shows, a recollection of God as the giver of the soil on which my home is placed; a recollection of Him as the preserver of families on that soil; a recollection of Him as the cause of their continuance upon it from age to age; of my continuance on it from day to day; a recollection of this continuance as in some way inseparable from the reverence to parents.

'*Thou shalt not kill.*' How might a Jew keep this commandment? No doubt he might abstain from taking the life of his neighbour, having either no strong temptation to do it, or being hindered from yielding to the temptation by the terror of the punishment which the avenger of blood would inflict upon him. But how might he keep it as if it were not man's commandment, but God's; as if it were not enforced by man's terrors, but by the thunder and lightning which are in His hand? Only while he thought of God as the author and preserver of life, only while he remembered ' He ' watches over the life of me and of every one of these ' my fellows. I may take their life at His bidding. I am ' not to gratify any instinct of mine.'

'*Thou shalt not commit adultery.*' How was a Jew to keep this commandment? Perhaps, he might never be tempted to pollute the marriage bed; perhaps, he might overcome the impulse by thinking of exposure and disgrace and probable punishment. But, to keep it as God's commandment, to say, as Joseph did, ' How can I do this great wickedness and sin against God!' he must surely recollect that God is the author of wedlock; that He binds man and wife together; that He protects this union; that it expresses some truth in His own nature which I am to be acquainted with. And so obedience to this precept serves the same purpose as obedience to all the others serves; that purpose of which St. John speaks, when he says, ' *We do know that we know Him, if we keep His commandments.*'

Again, '*Thou shalt not steal.*' How might a Jew keep this commandment? He might be a rich man like the young ruler. The motive to rob might be as far as possible from him; or he might be poor, and the fear of the prison might deter him from meddling with that which is not his. But how might it be God's commandment to him? How might it be God's presence which held back his hand? If he thought of God as fixing what was his and what was another's; if he looked up to God to set right what man's fraud or violence had made wrong; if he committed his cause and the cause of all people to Him as the just God, and the upholder of order; then he would delight in this law in his inner man, however strong might be the inclination of his bad nature to break it. And every observance of it and victory over that inclination would be a step in the knowledge of God.

'*Thou shalt not bear false witness against thy neighbour.*' How could an Israelite keep this commandment? Outward and open perjury was dangerous—it might be detected—a righteous recompense awaited the offender. The lies which pass from mouth to mouth in companies of men, slanders and private whispers, are not so easily found out. They may circulate further and further, and each new utterer may keep the last and the original forger in countenance. Still, a man may, through prudence or good nature, abstain even from this kind of false witness. But to abstain, because God has commanded it, how may he do that? Only if he thinks of God continually, as a God of Truth, as the hater of every false way and false word, as pledged to destroy lies as well as to lay them bare. Must not those who kept this thought in their mind, who turned it into act, grow in the knowledge of Him, who was keeping them from that which He hated?

Once more, '*Thou shalt not covet thy neighbour's house; thou shalt not covet thy neighbour's wife; nor his man-servant,* nor his maid-servant, nor his ox, nor his ass, nor anything that is his.' How may an Israelite keep this commandment? Think what it is! Not to covet! What law can take hold of me there? What public or private accuser, what quick-sighted judge, can bring that charge home to me? Surely not one. And, therefore, if it *is* brought home to me, if my inmost heart does confess it, I know who must be saying this to me, ' Thou shalt not covet.' I know it must be an unselfish and uncovetous Being. I know it must be one who desires that I should not covet; who is willing to deliver me from my covetousness; who can impart to me that unselfish, uncovetous life of His. So then, I have to interpret, ' Thou shalt not,' to mean, ' If ' thou trustest thyself to me, I will not let thee do the things 'which I hate.' So then I come to know by that which He would not have me do and be, what He himself is.

But here a question arises, which I must treat before I go further. St. Paul appears to speak of these commandments very differently from St. John. It would seem not from a few passages in his Epistles, but from the whole tenor of them, as if the commandments had been to him great burdens, as if he had turned to the Gospel of Christ that he might find deliverance from them. Especially he says of this last commandment, ' *Thou shalt not covet,*' that it wrought in him all manner of concupiscence; that he was alive before he heard it; that with the commandment sin came to life, and he died. What is the reason of this diversity of language? Were these apostles in very deed at issue with each other? They both taught the Ephesians. Did they bring to them contradictory tidings?

I am certain that they did not preach opposing doctrines;

G

that their lessons are essentially harmonious; that we cannot enter into the one unless we enter also into the other. Saul of Tarsus had reverenced these commandments as the peculiar treasure of his nation; he had considered all other nations accursed, for not possessing them. Saul of Tarsus believed, as the young ruler who came to our Lord believed, that he had kept these commandments from his youth up. Had he kept them as treasures committed to him by a Friend? Had he learnt the nature and character of that Friend by means of them? Had he learnt from the very first of them, that he was to worship a Deliverer, and none else? No such thing. He had read the commandments as letters written in stone, laid up in the Temple; he had read them as the decrees of an arbitrary Being who was determined that they should be obeyed, and who would have his satisfaction in punishing to the death those who did not obey them. And the discovery came to him, with dreadful power, that he himself, the pure Israelite, the strict Pharisee, was at war with the Being who made these laws. He says, 'Thou shalt not covet, 'And I do covet! Yes! I covet more since I have 'been told not to do it than I did before.' What did this mean? These commandments were not condemning others, but him; they were not cursing the Heathen; they were cursing him who had believed himself to be separated from the Heathen, to be the object of God's especial favour. There was no escaping from this conviction. The more he tried to obey the law, the more it forced itself upon him. There was a deep covetousness down in the very depths of his nature; it seemed as if it was a part of his very self. And God was proclaiming this to be evil; this to be hateful in His sight. How did he arise out of this misery, which seemed to draw all the past and the present and the future into it? 'It pleased God,' he says, 'to reveal His Son 'in me, that is, it pleased God to show me the Lord 'of my spirit, the Lord of all men; to show me that 'though in myself there dwelt this deep, radical covetous-'ness,—though in myself there dwelt no good thing,—yet 'that in Him I might claim God as my Father; in Him 'I might claim men as my brethren.' Yes, claim men as his brethren; for this discovery made him no longer a mere Israelite, though he could thank God more than ever for being an Israelite; though he could feel more than ever the responsibility of his calling and his education. But he was raised to be a Man; he had been taught what is the condition and glory of a man; and his calling and responsibility as an Israelite were, to tell all people—to tell those Heathens whom he had hated—that this condition and this glory were theirs as well as his. He could preach to them the Gospel, or good news, that Christ was revealed as their Lord, as the root of their life; that in Him they might call God their Father; that in Him they might renounce their selfish, covetous nature. Therefore, St. Paul having had this terrible experience himself, having this commission to mankind, could say once for all, 'The law shows us our 'sins; the law makes us aware of the evil nature that is in 'us. It is not something to boast of; if we look at it as 'separate creatures, whether we be Jews or not, it simply 'curses us, it simply drives us to despair. But if it is our 'schoolmaster to teach us of one true Lord, of Him in 'whom we are created, of Him in whom we have a new 'and true life, then indeed it is a blessing to us; for then

we give up boasting altogether of ourselves; then we can
'surrender ourselves freely and heartily to God as our Friend
'and our Deliverer; then we can become His ministers to
'carry the news of Him to those whom He knows, though
'they know not Him.'

Well; St. John, we saw, *began* with this revelation of God to men in His Son. It was the ground of all his teaching. He had told the Ephesians already that there was that darkness, that covetousness, in them which St. Paul had found in himself, which had caused him so much horror. But he had told them also, as St. Paul had also told them, that they were not created to walk in this darkness; that they might walk in the light which Christ had revealed, and have fellowship with it. So now, taking this for granted, he can tell them that these commandments might be kept as the commandments of a God who was at one with them in His Son, and that the more they kept them the more they would know of Him.

I have been speaking to you of one of the most difficult of all questions in Christian ethics; one with which some of the greatest troubles in the lives of individuals and in the history of Christianity have been connected. But the confusion is not in the doctrine; it is in us; and it is a confusion out of which we can be delivered, I think, only in the way St. John speaks of here. He says in the next verse, '*He that saith, I know Him, and keepeth not His commandments, is a liar, and the truth is not in him.*' The Apostle uses strong language, for this lie was spreading in the church of his own day, and would spread, he knew, further and further in the times that were coming. There were many in that time who used this very phrase, 'We

know God,' and used it for the purpose of self-exaltation; therefore for an immoral, destructive purpose. 'There are
' a set of common Christians,' they said, ' vulgar people, who
' may learn certain lower lessons; they are capable of
' nothing better. The law is very good for them. But we
' can enter into the divine mysteries; we can have the most
' magnificent conceptions about the spiritual world which
' Christ has opened; we can talk about angels, and ema-
' nations, and divine essences and properties; we can
' give them names, and trace their relations to each other.
' What are the commandments—what is common earthly
' morality—to us?' 'I tell you,' says St. John, broadly and
simply, 'that if they are nothing to you, *God* is nothing to
' you. You may use what fine language you will; you may
' have what fine speculations you like; but it is in practice,
' in that daily vulgar practice of life, in the struggle with
' the temptations to cheat and slander, to be unchaste and
' to be covetous, which beset us all in different ways and
' forms; it is in revering parents, and the name of God;
' it is in heeding God's rest and God's work; it is in
' keeping ourselves from idols; it is in worshipping Him
' as the common Deliverer, that we come to know Him;
' thus, and only thus.' And he adds words which, if understood rightly, were even more crushing to the pride of these
haughty men than those which were aimed at themselves.
'*But whoso keepeth His word, in him verily the love of God
is perfected; hereby know we that we are in Him.*' As if he
had said, ' You talk about the perfect, the initiated man,
' and the mere beginners or novices. I will tell you who is
' the perfect or initiated man. Look at that poor creature
' who is studying hard in the midst of all opposition from

' his own ignorance, to be right and to do right; who is
' trying to hold fast that Word which is speaking to him
' in his heart, though he can form no high notions at all
' about things in earth or heaven. There is the initiated man;
' he is the one who is learning the perfect lore; for God's
' own love is working in him; God's own love is perfecting
' itself in him. He is keeping the commandments, and
' they are teaching him that in himself he is nothing; that
' in God he has everything that he wants.'

It was so then; it is so now. I have seen hard fighters among poor men and rich men; some on sick beds and some in the world, in whom I am sure the love of God was perfecting itself. One longed to sit at their feet and learn their wisdom. But it was the wisdom of life, not the wisdom of letters; and in life it must be learnt. They were striving according to St. John's precept to walk even as Christ walked; to live, by daily trust and daily self-renunciation, as He lived. And since they could not do this by any efforts of their own—since all their efforts only showed them their own weakness—they learned to abide in Him; they learned the deepest of all secrets, by learning more than others of their own shallowness; they came to know God by finding that they could not be honest men without knowing Him.

LECTURE VI.

THE OLD AND NEW COMMANDMENTS.

1 JOHN II. 6—11

He that saith he abideth in Him ought himself also so to walk, even as He walked. Brethren, I write no new commandment unto you, but an old commandment which ye had from the beginning. The old commandment is the Word which ye have heard from the beginning. Again, a new commandment I write unto you, which thing is true in Him and in you: because the darkness is past, and the true light now shineth. He that saith he is in the light, and hateth his brother, is in darkness even until now. He that loveth his brother abideth in the light, and there is none occasion of stumbling in him. But he that hateth his brother is in darkness, and walketh in darkness, and knoweth not whither he goeth, because that darkness hath blinded his eyes.

LAST week St. John was teaching us how very simple people, with no high imaginations and little acquired learning, may know God in the strictest sense of the word *know*. If they keep His commandments they acquire a knowledge of His character and of His ways, of what He is in Himself and of what He is to them, which can be reached in no other method. There are some expressions which he uses in reference to this subject that are very plain in themselves, just what you would suppose the fisherman apostle, writing for people of all kinds and classes and for those hereafter that might speak all varieties of languages, would use, and yet which, for that very reason, often puzzle scholars greatly '*Walk as He walked.*'-

'*abide in Him*,'—they say, 'what can phrases like this signify?' A specially bad name has been found for them. They have been called *mystical*. It has been said that the people who resort to them fancy they have some peculiar affinity with the Divine nature.

It is quite right, as I think, to condemn that self-exaltation which leads one man to fancy he has spiritual privileges to which his brother is not entitled; in fact, all boasting and exclusiveness of every sort and however justified. The more sacred the privileges asserted are, the more dangerous this presumption is; to plume ourselves on wealth, titles, fashion,—even office, even on stewardships for which we must give an account,—is not half so bad as pluming ourselves upon being admitted to intercourse with God. For the more nearly we approach to Him, the more should the sense of difference from other men disappear. And unhappily it is true enough that men were tempted in St. John's days, and are tempted in ours, to this vaunting. It did then, it has since, taken shapes to which this phrase *mysticism* may be lawfully applied. I spoke of them to you last Sunday. I spoke of men who in the early days of the Church exulted in their knowledge of *mysteries*, who identified this with the knowledge of God. I remarked that St. John was probably alluding to them, and was dealing them hard blows, when he connected the knowledge of God with keeping the commandments. And it is just when he is doing this, just when he is vindicating this knowledge for humble people, that he talks of abiding in God, and of walking as Christ walked. I believe the adoption of that language was precisely the best witness he could bear for the universality of the blessing he was announcing.

He will frame no fine, elaborate, out-of-the-way forms of speech, such as the men he complained of were continually inventing. The acts of life which are familiar to every peasant shall be the vehicle for conveying the greatest treasures of God to mankind. He is treating men as a race of spirits,—of spirits with bodies which connect them with this earth. The relations between their bodies and the earth explain the relation between their spirits and Heaven. The power of moving from place to place is one of the most wonderful they have. Without a certain bodily organization, without frames curiously and wonderfully made, they could not do it; but with that bodily organization, with these wonderful frames, they could not do it, if there was not a spirit, a will, which bade the body go in a certain direction, which overcame its natural inertness. This spirit has a motion too. All its thoughts, wishes, impulses, are motions. And all these thoughts, wishes, impulses, *may* move downwards. The appetites of the body may determine which way they shall go. The things of earth, over which they have such a mighty dominion, may acquire a dominion over them. Or they may move upwards. These thoughts, wishes, impulses, may point to a Being from whom they are derived: they may seek for One in whose image they are made. Either course may be described as a walk; but the second is Christ's walk. This upward looking, this perpetual acknowledgment of a Father, describes the course of His Spirit. And if we confess Him to be our Lord and Head, we must confess it to be our course; the course for a man as he is distinguished from a mere animal.

We may confess it; but can we take this course merely because we see it is the right one? Here comes in the other phrase. Our bodies rest as well as move; they abide in a place as well as change their place. Even in our railroad days we cannot quite forget that fact; fatigue and sickness fix it upon our minds, if we are ever so fond of roaming. Our bodies demand rest, and our spirits, our wills, say to them, 'Stop; stay at home.' Our spirits, then, know what rest means; they require a rest too. But what kind of rest? Are they to stop thinking, desiring, hoping? That would be a miserable privilege to a weary spirit! For in its greatest weariness it dreads losing its powers; it dreads death. 'No,' says St. John, 'the 'spirit's rest is to abide in the living Lord. It is weary of 'itself: it is weary of always seeking the objects which the 'body and the earth present to it. It wants to find One 'above itself, and yet like itself. Christ is the object 'which is offered to it. The spirit of man has a home, 'a resting-place, while it trusts Him. And doing so, it 'never can become lazy. It has found its centre, and 'therefore it can move without irregularity. It has found 'Him by whom its powers of life are continually re-'newed; therefore it can move without exhaustion. The 'man that abideth in Him ought himself so to walk even 'as He walked.' As if he had said, 'To confess Christ is 'not merely to confess what is the right way for me. It 'is to confess One who is keeping me in that way; who 'is holding me up that I may not wander from it.' Well! if that is mystical, God make us all mystics; since this is not a high lore for a certain set of wise people; it is emphatically the lore for feeble tempted human beings such as we are.

But though St. John might not be setting up one class

of men in his own day above another, was he not setting up his own day above all previous days? Could men in former generations abide in Christ, seeing that He had not been upon the earth? Could they walk as He had walked, seeing that they did not know what that walk was? The question was one which puzzled many then as it has puzzled many since. It involves a great many questions which are often discussed amongst us, and dismissed rather hastily, before we have sounded the bottom of them. It concerns, for instance, the whole question of progress; in what sense one age is better than its predecessor, in what sense it is worse; in what sense all ages have a common blessing and a common evil. I wish you to see how the Apostle treats it. I do not think we shall find a better way out of the perplexity than that which he points out.

He had been telling them that they were to keep the commandments if they would know God. Now, those people who boasted that they had discovered quite another road to the knowledge of God than this, had an especial dislike to the Old Testament. They were in the habit of setting up the New against the Old, as if they were directly contrary. So they would be sure to turn upon him and say, 'The commandments? what commandments do you 'mean? Not those old commandments surely which were 'given to the Jews! You would not bring us back to the 'law, would you? Has not St. Paul made it clear that we 'are delivered from that yoke? has not he shown us that 'the Gospel has set us free?' He is not afraid of these questions, startling and plausible as they sound. He faces them boldly. 'I do mean those old commandments,' he says; '*I write no new commandment unto you, but an*

'*old commandment which ye had from the beginning.* I
'mean, distinctly, that I look upon those old command-
'ments, if they were faithfully kept, as a way to the
'knowledge of God.' But how? St. Paul had said that
the commandments, written and engraven in stone, only
pronounced man's condemnation. They had no power to
make any man righteous. St. John does not preach any
different doctrine. He does not say for a moment, that
letters written on stone could lead any man to God. He
does not say for a moment, that a person merely regarding the commandments as written on stone could keep
them. But he says,—'*The old commandment is the* WORD
which ye have heard from the beginning.' Here is the secret
of the whole matter. The commandments were not letters
on stone. They were a *word* proceeding from a living
God; they were a *word* addressed to the hearts of human
beings. This was the language which the prophets and
holy men of the Old Testament had always used. If, for
instance, you read the 119th Psalm (I take it merely as a
specimen of what you may read all through the Book of
Psalms), you will find the word of God, the law of God,
the commandment of God, used for each other. Each
is said to give light, each is said to quicken, each is said
to make the heart rejoice. No dead letters, no stones, no
threatenings. The word makes alive; it speaks; it warns
indeed of evils into which the man is ready to fall, but it
lifts him above the evil; it is good, and it is mightier
than evil. The old men knew this to be so; they could
not be mistaken about the fact; it was wrought into all
their experience. But they longed to know the meaning
of the fact; the ground of the fact. They wanted to

know why this word had so much to do with them, so much to do with God. They wanted to know why it reproved them, ruled them as a superior, while it was so closely identified with them. More and more they began to be confident that there was a Person from whom this word proceeded; who was with them and with God; who ruled and reproved them in God's name; who did not the less feel with them and sympathise with them. This was the discovery—the partial discovery—of the great Truth of the universe, of the Word who was in the beginning, who was God, and who was the Light of Men. The full discovery of that Truth was not yet. That could only be when the Word was made flesh, and dwelt among men; when apostles were permitted to see and handle that which was about the Word of Life; when they were sent forth with the message, '*That which was with the Father, and has been manifested, declare we to you, that you may have fellowship with us.*' But when this discovery was made, did it make them look back with pity or contempt upon their forefathers? No; it enabled them to understand their forefathers as they had never understood them before. It made them see why their forefathers had used such strange expressions about the law and the commandments. They had heard that WORD speaking to them from the beginning, who had now dwelt and walked on earth. It was He who had quickened them; He who had given them light. Without Him the commandments on stone would have been curses on their sin and weakness; coming from Him they were blessings unspeakable; a living voice enabling them, in spite of their palsy, to rise up and walk.

And there was more still in this discovery, which I have hinted at already. As long as the commandments were looked at only as written and graven in stone, they belonged to Israelites. When they were regarded as the word which was heard from the beginning, as words proceeding from *the* Word which was from the beginning, it was intelligible how God had been speaking to other nations; how that which was known of God had been manifested in them; how those had the knowledge of God who did not like to retain Him in their knowledge; how though they had not the law, they did by nature the things contained in the law; how they showed the work of the law written in their hearts, their consciences meanwhile accusing and excusing each other; how they as well as the Jews could be contentious, obeying not the truth, but obeying unrighteousness; how they, as well as the Jews, might seek by patient continuance in well doing for glory, honour, and immortality. All these assertions are from St. Paul. They are the foundation of his gospel to the nations. And they receive their fullest illustration and explanation from the teaching, which more strictly, though not exclusively, belongs to St. John, respecting the Word, whose light had been shining always and everywhere, and making men aware of their own darkness.

But was there nothing gained by this revelation of the Word in the flesh? by this gospel of His life? Had the world taken no step in advance of its older self? Was it not a good thing to be born under the New Testament instead of the Old? '*Again*,' says St. John, '*a new commandment I write unto you; which thing is true in Him and in you, because the darkness is past, and the true light now shineth.*' He is a teacher of progress much more truly than those who treated all the past as worthless or evil. He can be thankful for the more advanced wisdom which has been imparted to his generation through the manifestation of the Son of God, partly because that manifestation makes him apprehend more clearly his close relation with the men who lived before it; partly because it lays him under a responsibility which did not attach at all in the same measure to them. The old commandment which they kept, the word which spoke to them from the beginning, is dearer than ever; its worth is more apparent, its influence on them is more clearly divine, because He who was their secret teacher, their invisible king, the hidden light of their hearts, has come forth and been proclaimed as the Teacher of all the Nations; the King of Men, the Light of the World. But by so coming forth, by taking the nature of men, by fulfilling in that nature the very sense of the old commandment, by showing forth the life which that commandment proved to be the only true life, He had brought forth a new commandment, not inconsistent with the old, scarcely an addition to it, rather the very essence of it, which yet it was unable to express. How is that? What is this essence of the law, which the law *could* not declare even to those who received it most dutifully as the word of the righteous and living Lord? You shall hear: ' *He that saith he is in the light, and hateth his brother, is in darkness even until now.*'

What was there new in this statement? There was nothing new in the commandment, ' *Thou shalt love thy neighbour as thyself.*' That was old; that St. Paul declares, that St. John declares, that our Lord declares, is implied in all the commandments. But you will remember what question the lawyer—who fully admitted this doctrine, who even quoted the words out of the book of Deuteronomy which affirmed it—asked of our Lord, 'Who,' he said, '*is* my neighbour?' That was the difficulty. All possibility of self-justification lay hidden in men's hearts till this question was answered. The story in which our Lord replied to it, is perhaps the passage in the whole Bible with which we are most familiar, and partly perhaps from its very familiarity we often miss the point of it, and do not understand the depth of the principle which it embodies. A poor Jew had been plundered by thieves, on the dangerous road between Jerusalem and Jericho. A priest, one of his own countrymen, the one who was appointed to represent the nation and its members before God, and to bless them in God's name, did not recognise him as a neighbour; he left him lying where he was. Another of his countrymen, a Levite, the one who should have known the law best of all, whose business it was to expound the law, did not recognise the wounded man as a neighbour, but passed by on the other side. A Samaritan, who was not his countryman, who did not worship in the same temple with him, who was regarded as cut off by the law from fellowship with him, whom he regarded, and who had been taught to regard him, as an enemy, *did* treat him as a neighbour, *did* behave to him as one of his own kith and kin, of his own flesh and blood. He poured oil and wine into his wounds, he sat him upon his own beast, he took care of him. Why? Because he looked upon him as a *man*, because he confessed his fellow-man to be his neighbour. The lawyer acknowledged that the Samaritan heretic had, by some means or other, found the interpretation of the Jewish law, which he had been unable to find. And he was bidden to go and do likewise.

How was he to go and do likewise? How was he to get the power to go and do likewise? St. John is about to tell us. You see he has introduced us to a new word. He speaks of a man hating his *brother*. ' *He that saith he is in the light, and hateth his brother, is in darkness until now.*' We have been hearing of *neighbours*. Men knew that they ought not to hate their neighbours; that is, men who dwelt near them, who belonged to their own tribe or nation; however often they might do it in spite of their knowledge. The code could not bid them do more than this. We may say it boldly, *No* mere code can. A code should not attempt to bind men as men together; it must fail if it makes the experiment. But there must be a bond between man and man; there must be a power to make that bond effectual, or the law concerning neighbours will be most imperfectly heeded. As we have seen in the case of the Priest and the Levite, the servants of the law may utterly forget the law. As we have seen in the case of the Samaritan, the man without the law may fulfil its commands to the letter, and far beyond the letter. Why? The revelation of Christ explains the secret. When He came forth, when His light shone upon men, then it was seen that there is a common Brother of Men; of men, I say, not of Israelites merely. Jesus Christ, born of the seed of David, circumcised according to the law, enters into the wants of men, the sorrows of men, the death of men. He is the Universal Brother.

'*Therefore*,' says John, '*this thing is true in Him and in you, because the darkness is past and the true light now shineth.*' As if he had said, 'Now we are come into a new
' and higher state; the state not only of neighbourhood but
' of *brotherhood*. When we claim to belong to Christ, we
' claim this new name. But by claiming it, do we escape
' out of the region of commandments? Are we no more
' under an obligation? Nay, verily, we come under a
' new commandment, under a wider and deeper obligation.
' Before, it was a sin to hate neighbours; now, it is a sin to
' hate men; because this brotherhood of men with men is
' made known. It is a sin; a sin which punishes itself.
' For to hate a brother is to walk in darkness. It is
' to hide ourselves from Him who is our great common
' brother. It is to live as if the Lord had not appeared.
' It is to say, I will shut myself in my own dark, evil self;
' though the great blessing and redemption of the world
' is that I am under the Lord of human beings, that I am
' permitted to take up my state and glory as a man.'
Therefore St. John scouts all the pretences of men to illumination, on whatever ground they may be founded, which do not involve the practical acknowledgment of this brotherhood, and the conformity of their actions to it. A man may say he is in the light as much as he pleases; but to be in the light implies, that he is able to see his brethren and not to stumble against them.

You see, then, how it is that the New Testament confirms and establishes the Old; and yet that it takes us into a region so much larger, and higher, and purer than the Old. You see how it is that the commandment which was heard from the beginning retains all its force and grandeur; nay, how it is that it acquires a greater force and grandeur, just because there is a new commandment, grounded on that revelation of Christ the Head and Brother of all men. And you see why it is that St. John at once tells us of the greatest sin which it is possible for us, under the New Testament, to commit, and of the greatest blessing which it is possible for us to inherit. For us to hate our brother— to hate any man—is nothing less than to deny *the* man, the Son of Man; the common light of men. For us to love our brother is nothing less than to walk in the light of Christ's presence, nothing less than to be free from all occasion and danger of stumbling. '*He that loveth his brother abideth in the light, and there is none occasion of stumbling in him.*' He adheres to the language which he has adopted throughout the Epistle. The highest blessing is to walk in the light, and to have fellowship with it; the most terrible curse is to be out of the light, to love darkness rather than light. There is no condemnation, as he says in his Gospel, so great as this; *this* is the condemnation. To be like Christ, that is blessedness; to be in a state of mind that is contrary to His, that is misery.

There are various thoughts which crowd upon me as I advance to this great point of Christian ethics. I must dismiss most of them, lest they should confuse us, and lest I should anticipate what will explain itself more fully hereafter. But this I cannot suppress. I who lecture to you on politics, I who have been lecturing lately on the French Revolution, have often to touch upon this subject of Fraternity or Brotherhood. I hope we none of us merely touch upon it; I hope we wish in our hearts to understand it that we may practise it. I hope we are convinced that a college which has not this basis does not deserve the name. We ought never to hear how this thought was awakened in the minds of the poor people of France in 1789; how it clung to them through all the strange, terrible times which followed; how, even when they were trampling all nations down, they still talked of making them brethren; how the belief that Fraternity was possible, started to life again in 1848; how the outward tokens of it were marked on every building, public and private;—we should never read of these facts which belong to our own times, which have fallen under our own eyes, without being persuaded that a special duty is laid upon us to find out what they mean, and how that of which they speak may become a reality for us. I believe that this Epistle of St. John, this book of Christian ethics, tells us what we want to know; tells us how the idea of brotherhood may become a fact; how a phantom which has been often pursued till it led to deeds of darkness, may be changed into a Person who is the Light of the world, and who can enable us to walk in His light, by enabling us to love our brothers as He loves them.

LECTURE VII.

THE CHILDREN; THE YOUTHS; THE OLD MEN.

1 John II. 12—14.

I write unto you, little children, because your sins are forgiven you for His Name's sake. I write unto you, fathers, because ye have known Him that is from the beginning. I write unto you, young men, because ye have overcome the wicked one. I write unto you, little children, because ye have known the Father. I have written unto you, fathers, because ye have known Him that is from the beginning. I have written unto you, young men, because ye are strong, and the Word of God abideth in you, and ye have overcome the wicked one.

PERHAPS it may occur to some of you, that I did not fairly represent the obligations of Israelites when I read to you the Ten Commandments. You may have thought that the old commandment of which St. John speaks must have included many more precepts than these. For were they not bound to observe all the statutes and ordinances which are contained in the books of Moses? Were they not to circumcise their children, and to keep a number of feasts? were they not to offer sacrifices continually? Did the apostle mean that he and his flock at Ephesus ought still to keep these commands? If not, where was the line to be drawn? And that new commandment about hating the brother, did this also stand alone? Were there no ordinances and institutes which the Christian Church observed as well as this?

To understand this question aright, you should consider what St. John says is the end of keeping the commandment. Throughout, as I have shown you, it is the knowledge of God. Through obedience they would rise to this knowledge. They would become acquainted with His mind and character; they would have the acquaintance of belief and sympathy. But they would also understand one another. The commandments showed how they were bound to each other, as well as how they were bound to God. The commandments warned them of acts by which they separated themselves from each other, as well as of acts by which they separated themselves from God.

Unless then the Israelites remembered that they were united to God, and that they were united to each other, the commandments became unintelligible. They were worse than unintelligible. They were heavy burdens, grievous to be borne. They were letters written on stone, cursing them, not words coming forth from God to do them good, and give them understanding. Now, the precept to circumcise their children was a witness to them that they *were* united to God and to each other. It was a pledge that the Lord of all had taken them to be a people of inheritance to Himself. It was a pledge that He was keeping them at one. This precept was not a hard addition to the Ten Commandments; it laid a foundation for practical obedience to them; it gave them a new character; it changed them from the decrees of a Being who was at a distance from them, into the promises of one who was at hand to keep them in the right way. 'Thou shalt not' meant, 'Trust in me, and I will not suffer thee to go astray.' And this covenant included the child of eight days old, who as yet could read no letter, who could understand no precept, as well as the grey-haired man and the stout warrior. Over all God was watching; even the youngest had parents to bring them up in His faith and fear; and if their father and mother forsook them, He would be their guide; the eldest, who had no earthly guardians, would depend all the more securely and directly upon Him. He would go forth with the younger men in their hard fighting with themselves and with the world. This was the use of circumcision.

Well! and the Sacrifices, were they additional burdens laid upon the consciences of the Jews? They might become so, undoubtedly; they did become so. But when they were received as sacrifices ordained by God, they did not add weights to the conscience, but relieved it of a weight. Each Israelite was sensible that he had transgressed the commandment, that he had not remembered God's dominion over him, and his relation to his fellows. He had not kept his position, but had lived as if he was a separate creature. The sacrifices were witnesses and pledges to him that the king of his land forgave him and received him back. The belief that it was so set his conscience free; he could act as if he was still God's servant, one of a nation. He might again look his neighbours in the face, and be at peace with them; he might again do the work which was given him to do.

The Feasts, again, were witnesses of deliverances which God had wrought for the whole land; of a common law which He had given to Israelites; of His watchfulness over the seeds in the ground, that they might bring forth fruit in their season; of His presence with them when they journeyed and when they were settled in fixed habitations. They were to keep the feasts with joy and thankfulness, that they might grow in the knowledge of Him who was the same from generation to generation, that they might feel they were one people, however they might be scattered in different countries; yea, though some might be upon the earth and some in the unseen world. The feasts, then, gave a meaning to the commandments, they helped to accomplish the purpose of the commandments; if they were forgotten, the commandments were either forgotten or became oppressive.

Besides these institutions, the Israelites required, as every nation does, special arrrangements adapted to the special circumstances of soil and climate in which they were placed, adapted to the special work to which the commonwealth was called, adapted to the pursuits of its different citizens. These precepts were declared to be statutes of the invisible Lord for the well-being and good ordering of His people. While they were so regarded they were not oppressive; they made the Israelites feel that the Highest of all cared for them; that His divine order had respect to all their common transactions, and that they might break through it by neglecting the care of their bodies or of their houses, by tolerating dirt or infection, as well as by graver crimes. Even in these little things obedience led to a deeper knowledge of God.

Did St. John then mean that all these commandments were still to be kept as in the beginning? I am sure that he clung—in fact, all the records we have of him prove that he clung—with the greatest tenacity and affection to the institutions which testified of his relation to the family and nation of the Israelites. He would not have given up circumcision, the pledge of God's adoption of His people and of His care for them, if he had not believed that God had given a wider and more perfect sign of His adoption and His care. But when Christ bade the Apostles go and baptize all nations, He declared that that was a sign that God looked not upon Israelites, but upon men, as more than His servants or people, as His children, and that they might claim to be brothers of each other. Now that was a pledge of the new commandment, of. the commandment which I said pointed not to neighbourhood but to brotherhood, which was granted at the revelation of Christ as the Universal Brother. St. John would not have parted with the sacrifices which were offered day by day and year by year in the temple (for they were dear to him beyond expression), if Christ had not given a sign which Jews as well as the Heathen might receive, that He had made one sacrifice for all; that all were forgiven for His Name's sake. St. John would not have given up the feasts of the Passover, the Pentecost, the Tabernacles, if there had not been an universal feast, which gathered into itself the memory of them all; a feast at which the Heathen as well as Jews might give thanks to God as their Deliverer from sin and death, and all the enemies of man; to God, as enduing men with the Holy Spirit, and with all living powers; to God, as dwelling with them, as dwelling in them for ever. 'The new commandment, 'Thou shalt love thy brother,' required this support, as the old commandment required the support of the Jewish sacrifices and the Jewish feasts. The Eucharist was not a fresh burthen added to that commandment. It enabled the whole society to own the commandment as a living power. If they did not receive this pledge of the new life which God bestowed on them, and of His eternal presence, that commandment would become a weight to them; not, as it was meant to be, the divinest treasure, the way to the highest joy.

You see how the Christian Sacraments, as we call them, must have presented themselves to the mind of an Apostle who was educated as St. John had been educated under the Old Testament. I wish you to see it, because men in our day are often perplexed about them, and are inclined to suppose that we should be lightened of a load if we were excused from them. I am satisfied that no opinion is so mistaken as this; that if we lost the Sacraments, we should lose the pledges of God's relation to us all, of the redemption He has wrought out for us all, and that the duty of loving one another, which we cannot be discharged from, would seem to us an oppressive duty that must be performed, but which we had no strength to perform. I am satisfied that we should then lose the sense of being called to share in a common salvation, and that each would be trying to obtain a salvation for himself by efforts of self-will. This is not what St. Paul calls working out our salvation; that we do, as he says, when we remember that God is working in us to will and to do of His good pleasure.

And thus I think we are able better to understand what the Apostle means when he writes to the little children, to the fathers, and to the young men of his flock. I have shown you how the institutions of the Jews appealed to all these different classes, what a testimony they bore that God cared for the youngest and the oldest in their weakness, and that He did not forget the middle-aged in their strength. St. John feels that we are not in a worse, but in a better condition under the new covenant than under the old; that though that is a wider and more general covenant, it takes not less but more account of all the differences in men, of all the stages of their youth, of all their special necessities. We shall very much mistake the character of Christian ethics, if we suppose that they reduce us all to an indiscriminate mass, because they speak of all as sinful, and of all as redeemed in Christ. The Apostle's favourite language respecting the Light may tell us that this is not so. It is darkness which obliterates all distinctions; the light brings them all forth.

When men are struggling together as rivals, each tries, as card-players say, not to show his hand; he wishes to pass for having some of the qualities which appertain more properly to another; he will have credit for being able to do just what those who are contending with him can do. But in a united family each finds out by degrees what he is fit for, and what each of his brothers and sisters is fit for. Each learns some lesson which the other could not learn. The child is glad to be led by those stronger and more experienced; they gain as much from the simplicity of the child. The Apostle does but apply these truths to a larger family: to God's Church. He does but hint to different degrees in the Church what wisdom they are most in need of, and are most competent to receive. He tells them how the witnesses or sacraments of God's love in Christ, which are for all, may yet assume a different aspect and bear a different message to them, according to their preparations, and capacities.

1. '*I write unto you, little children, because your sins are forgiven you for His Name's sake.*' Many interpreters are careful to tell us that the Apostle does not mean actual children, but only children in faith or knowledge; young converts. I do not think this distinction is necessary. I like to take words in their simplest sense, if I can. I dare say the Apostle had in his mind some of those who had newly been baptized, even if they were adults. But I suspect he had also in his mind those sons and daughters of Christian parents who were receiving their earliest lore respecting the things of earth as well as of heaven. To both, I apprehend, the same language was suitable. *Trust* is the great necessity of a child. It wants to feel that it may go to those who are over it with confidence. It wants to feel that it may go to them when it has done wrong. It has many impulses which urge it to stay away from them then. It has been told to do what it has not done; it has done something which it has been told not to do; how natural to avoid the person who has given the precept, to seek any society rather than his! The concealment once practised is more difficult to break through; the eye which is to be met looks more lowering; shall it be encountered? There is a sense of guilt within; guilt and guile are closely allied, if they are not the very same. The simple child becomes insincere; it parts company with truth. The story is a very sad one; experience, the experience of ourselves and of children, explains it to us; the secret of education lies in knowing how to turn the experience to profit. Let the child expect to find a friend in the lawgiver; one in whom it may confide; one to whom it may make known its offence more safely than it can to any

other. Let it be assured that the lawgiver means to have his laws performed; and that *because* he means this, he is ready to receive back the transgressor of them. Let *him* by his habitual conduct, destroy the barrier of suspicion which sets the child and himself at a distance. And so he will free its conscience, he will make it stronger after its falls than it was before them; stronger because more aware of its weakness, and more trusting. He will make it willing to bear any punishment which he may think good to inflict as a remembrance of the past and a warning for the future. But all this treatment of a particular child will be far more effectual for its cure and its education, if it sees others treated in the same way; if it perceives that this is the principle upon which its father and lawgiver acts in all cases; that it is his character to act so.

St. John would have us to understand that this course is right for men who are made in the image of God, because it is His course. He tells us that the first lesson of all to be learnt concerning God, is that He remits or sends away sins; for that is the force of the word. He would have all Christian children know this; he would tell it to the Heathen, who had been dreaming of gods altogether different, gods that had no delight in remitting sins at all. He does not expect that they will advance further in knowledge, if they do not get this lesson well into their hearts. But how were they to get it into their hearts? How was each particular child to feel, ' I may go ' and tell what I have done wrong, every time I have done ' it; I may get my conscience set free; I may rise up in a ' right state after I have been in a wrong one' ? It could not be unless the child felt that thus God was dealing with *all;* that there was a law of remission or forgiveness under which all were placed. We are very apt to think thus, 'We 'belong to a guilty race; God looks upon us all as sinners. 'But perchance *I* may get Him to treat me differently; *I* 'may procure a separate pardon.' No! that will not do. There is selfishness, there is separation from *thy* brother, there is the very essence of sin in that thought. St. John strikes at the root of it when he says, '*Your sins are forgiven you for His Name's sake.*' You are not looked upon as a sinful race; you are looked upon as a race of which Christ the Son of God is the head. When He offered Himself to God, He took away the sin of the world. We have no right to count ourselves sinners, seeing that we are united in Him. We become sinners when we separate from Him, when we forget His Name, and resume our own miserable separate name. But He does not forget, though we forget; He does not change, though we change. And therefore we may arise and go to our Heavenly Father in that Name which He has put upon us, and may have our consciences set free, and our sins sent away.

This, St. John treats as an early, fundamental lesson in Christian ethics, one in which we should be instructed from the first. But he does not mean that because it belongs to the elements of our instruction we must not continually go back to it, assure ourselves that we have hold of it, recollect what is the ground of it, what is the sign and pledge of it. I think experience must show most of us how little grasp we have of this truth; how apt we are to let it slip. I do not know any one that it is so hard thoroughly to retain, especially when we have most need of it for the actual struggles of life. It seems to me, sometimes, that we want a new reformation in our country, to make our people understand the length and breadth of this child's truth; how it applies to all our most complicated circumstances, and yet how heartily the youngest could embrace it if we did not contradict it in our conduct and invent theories that are at variance with it. I will tell you plainly that it is the consideration of Baptism and of its meaning as it is set forth in our Child's Catechism, which has given me the little apprehension I have of this truth, and that I would not part with that testimony to it, to obtain the wisdom of the greatest doctors in the world.

The Jewish nation is spoken of in the Old Scriptures as a holy nation, consecrated and sacrificed to God. Every Jew was to claim to be a holy, devoted, sacrificed man. When he confessed his sin, and presented the sacrifice, he was restored to his right position. St. John justifies the language, and extends it. The Jewish nation was holy in Christ its King. When that King was manifested as the Son of Man, not the nation, but mankind, was shown to be holy in Him. When He sacrificed Himself He offered up the race as a living sacrifice acceptable to God. Each man is to claim that privilege, to consider himself as sacrificed to God, as one of a redeemed body. When he confesses his sins,—*i.e.* his separation from Christ and His sacrifice,—he asks that he may be restored to the blessing of that sacrifice; he asks that he may offer himself again as a sacrifice in Christ's name. This is the very meaning of Christian devotion. All our prayers and services have this ground: 'Children, your sins are remitted for His Name's sake.' They imply that His Name is the only bond to God; that to lose hold of it is to fall back into our selfishness; that nothing else can raise us out of our selfishness. The other Christian sacrament is a pledge of this remission of sins and redemption for the whole body. It is our thanksgiving for the sacrifice of Christ's death, which has bound us to God and to each other, and so has released us from sin. It is our confession how each of us has had some way or scheme of his own which has been inconsistent with our union to Him. It is the acceptance of God's continued forgiveness and remission in His Name.

II. Why does St. John pass at once from these children to those who appear farthest from them?—'*I write unto you, fathers, because ye have known Him that is from the beginning.*' I do not think that aged men are those who are least able to sympathise with children, or who most discard the lore of children. I think that the sight of the human as well as of the natural spring is a special delight to those who are feeling the winter—frosty but kindly. I think that what they heard and committed to memory in their earliest days comes back to them with a sense of its meaning and its power which men in the intermediate time do not possess at all in the same degree, and which they do not possess respecting the intermediate period in their own histories. St. John may have felt something of this himself. There seems to me a great beauty in his way of connecting the child's belief in forgiveness with the aged man's knowledge of Him who was in the beginning, as if one lay beneath the other, and as if the experience of each new year had been drawing it forth. The child receives forgiveness as a gift to himself. To be sure it makes him forget himself. It makes him think of the person who has bestowed it. But yet the blessedness of it springs out of the sense of having found a friend where he had deserved an enemy. The old man more and more sees this forgiveness as coming from the very nature of Him who was in the beginning. All the successive revelations of God discover to him the same unchangeable Will. In that he rests. The revelation of what God has done leads him to what He is. It is a delightful vision of a calm, clear old age. We need not desire to have it in this earth. The old Apostle must have entered far more fully into its joys himself, when his eyes were closed on the earth.

III. And now he comes to a class which we know better than either of these, though perhaps it may not have the same charm for us as either. '*I write to you, young men.*' We take it for granted that he is going to speak of hard, tough fighting, when he introduces these young men. How strange that he should add, '*for ye have overcome the wicked one!*' 'Overcome!' we say; 'they cannot be much 'like us, then. We are at best but able to keep ourselves 'from being overcome; and that by no means always. And yet I am confident he would not have wished us, any of us, not to receive his writing as addressed to ourselves. I am confident he would have been greatly grieved if any one of the young men of Ephesus had said,—' Yes! ' that applies to me; I can take it home to myself, but my ' neighbour here has no part or lot in it.' I believe that just as he told all the children to believe that their sins were forgiven for Christ's Name's sake, so he meant all the young men to understand that the Evil One had been overcome for them in the same mighty Name. That is the meaning of our Lord's Temptation. It was a victory over the power of evil, not for Himself only, but for those whose nature He had taken. '*Man*,' He said, '*shall not live by bread alone, but by every word of God.*' He would not tempt God by casting Himself from the pinnacle of the Temple, that we might not tempt God by casting ourselves from any position that is given to us. He said, '*Get thee behind me, Satan; thou shalt worship the Lord thy God, and Him only*,' that we might be sure we owe no worship to the Devil; that we might know he is not our master; that we might mock and defy him. St. John, therefore, could say to these young men, in the midst of all the toil and war of the world, '*Ye have overcome the Evil One.* Treat him ' as one that is overcome. Refuse him homage, and he will ' flee from you.' And this is a truth, which we, too, must lay fast hold of; however strange and incredible it may sometimes appear to us. We must say, fearlessly, ' The ' Devil is not the king of the world, though he may feign ' to be so. The good God is the King; whatever sets ' itself against Him will be found weak and contemptible ' at last.'

IV. There is, however, a danger even in these blessed and necessary testimonies, if others are not joined to them; they must not be qualified, that we cannot afford,—that would have been unworthy of our Apostle's truthfulness,— but another aspect of them may be needful that this aspect may be clearer, and that we may be delivered from any false impressions which the first may have produced on our weak eyesight. You will observe that the Apostle travels over the same ground again, not fearing the charge of repeating himself, if he can make his position more evident. '*I have written to you, little children*,'—not now, because your sins are forgiven, but—'*because ye have known the*

Father.' Christians have often exulted in the thought that their sins were forgiven, till an incredible conceit has taken possession of them, and the very belief that their sins are blotted out, has led them to commit fresh sins. Therefore he tells these children that the blessedness of being forgiven was, that it brought them to trust in a Father, and be acquainted with a Father; that it gave them confidence to approach Him and have fellowship with Him. This is not merely the correction of a possible (and a too probable) error. It is the enlargement and full illustration of the doctrine he had declared before. It shows how the forgiveness of the family is the foundation of the forgiveness of the individual. To draw nigh to God by that name of Father,—to understand how He thinks, feels, acts as a Father,—this is, indeed, the privilege of children.

The reason for writing to the fathers is the same as before; that deep-grounded knowledge of Him that was from the beginning, excludes false and self-conceited notions; nothing can be added to it which can make it more perfect. But the address to the young men undergoes a very important alteration: '*I have written unto you, young men, because ye are strong, and the word of God abideth in you, and ye have overcome the wicked one.*' He gives them credit for strength. It belongs to their age. They have it even if they are misusing it; they have it, even if they are priding themselves on it, and require to be taught their weakness. But this is the secret of their strength. The Word of God abideth in them. It is not their own power which is struggling against all the temptations to evil within them and around them. It is the Word of God who is the source of all light and wisdom and power in man; it is the Word who took flesh and dwelt among them that He might overcome the Evil Spirit. These young men are engaged with a conquered enemy, but with one who will seek to persuade them that he is almighty. Only while they give up their own strength and depend upon that living Word who is sustaining them at every moment, will they be able to prove that they are not the slaves of the enemy.

All young men of this day, all that are now struggling against their own enemies and God's, have a right to this same confidence. It is only dangerous when it becomes confidence in themselves. It is only dangerous when they forget that Christ's victory in the wilderness was not the end but only the beginning of the conflict in which He was engaged for the deliverance of them and the glory of God

LECTURE VIII.

THE WORLD AND THE FATHER.

1 JOHN II. 15—18.

Love not the world, neither the things that are in the world. If any man love the world, the love of the Father is not in him. For all that is in the world, the lust of the flesh, and the lust of the eyes, and the pride of life, is not of the Father, but is of the world. And the world passeth away, and the lust thereof: but he that doeth the will of God abideth for ever

You remember the words of which I spoke to you last Sunday, '*I write unto you, little children, because ye have known the Father. I have written unto you, young men, because ye are strong.*' I think it is especially for these young men that St. John designs the precept, '*Love not the world,*' which I have just read to you. But we shall not understand that precept, nor the reason of it, nor the place which it holds in Christian ethics, if we do not recollect also what he has said to the children.

We talk of sons going out into the world. Hitherto they have been dwelling in the house of their father. Day by day they have had experience of his care and government. They have had experience of it when they have been right, and when they have been wrong; when they have done the things which he commanded them, and when they have disobeyed him; when they have confessed their faults, when they have received his forgiveness, when they have suffered the punishments he has appointed for them.

This going out into the world we speak of as if it were a loss of some of these blessings. It *may* be a loss of them altogether; the father and the father's house may be altogether forgotten. We may come into an atmosphere as unlike that as possible, and we may prefer it because it is unlike. The world may seem to us a good world, because it sets us free from the restraints of the family in which we have been brought up.

But, on the other hand, all children look forward to this time of going out into the world. Their fathers encourage them to look forward to it. They tell them that it is what is appointed for them; they tell them that they are to work in the world, and make their way in the world; they tell them their discipline in the nursery has been intended to prepare them for the world. This is not the language of inconsiderate, or mercenary, or ambitious parents. It is the language of parents who remember that their sons are to have a life of their own, that they are to shift for themselves, that they will not fulfil the purpose of their existence, unless they fall in with evil men as well as with good men, with things that may do them hurt as well as with things that may profit them. It is the language of men who reflect, that though there are a number of disorders in the world, yet that the world itself is an *Order*. That is what the word means; at all events, the Greek word which St. John uses, if not the English word which we use.

Well, as I have shown you already, St. John is regarding all those Ephesians to whom he is writing, as members of one family, in different stages of their growth. The children, the young men, the fathers, are all treated as sons of God, and as brothers of each other. Christ has revealed to them their Father; Christ has revealed to them their brotherhood in Him. These are not fantastic titles; they belong to real human beings. So St. John would have them understand that what is true in particular families, is true also of this great family. There is a time of childhood, a time when the name of a Father, and the care of a Father, and the forgiveness of a Father, are all in all. It seems as if nothing was wanted, but that name, and the belief that we are under that eye. This is a genial, blessed time, which may last longer with some than with others. Numbers who die in their early years, numbers, perhaps, who have been awakened in their later life to a sense of their Father's forgiveness and goodness, may go to their graves without having any other belief than this, without having needed any other. Sometimes we may count them fortunate, we may be inclined to envy them. But we are not to envy them. If another state is provided for us, that is the state which is best for us. If we are to be thrown upon the world, there is a lore which will be given us for the world, which is an advance upon the lore that we had in our childhood, though it need not be the least inconsistent with that, though it need not drive that out of our minds.

St. John, therefore, has not condoled with these young men who had lost the smooth cheeks of infancy, who had acquired a strength which does not belong to infancy. He has not treated them as unhappy for having made this exchange; he has given them assurances of the victory which had already been won for them, the recollection of which was to fit them for their own battles. He has told them what the particular wisdom is which they want and which they can now enter into, because they want it. They must believe that they have the *Word of God* dwelling in them; they must learn that there is One who is speaking to them in their consciences, who is quickening their hearts, who will go with them where they go, and stay with them where they stay; who knows what they are thinking, wishing, doing at every moment; who can give them the right thoughts, the right wishes, and guide them to the right acts. To make this discovery, to find that they have such a Friend, such a Teacher with them continually, is a compensation for a thousand losses; it is worth while to know a thousand evils which they did not know in infancy, if they may know also of this Deliverer from evil, this Director to all good.

But while he looks thus encouragingly and hopefully upon these youths, while he sees in them the strength of the time that is, as well as of the time that is to come, he is also fully alive himself, and he wishes them to be alive, to the danger of their new position. They may forget their heavenly Father's house, just as any child may forget his earthly father's house. And the cause will be the same. The attractions of the outward world, the attractions of the things that are in this world, these are likely to put a great chasm between one period of their life and another; these may cause that the love of the Father shall not be in them.

But are the cases parallel? The family of my parents is manifestly separated from the general world; to pass from one to the other is a great change indeed—like the crossing an ocean, like entering into another hemisphere. But is not the world GOD'S world? Is not the order which we see, His order? Did He not look upon it and say, '*Lo! it is very good*'? Does not our own Apostle speak of His loving the world; of His so loving it as to give His only-begotten Son for it? The word is the same here as there. How then can these young men be told that they are not to love that which He, in whose image they are created, is said so earnestly to love? How can they be told, that if they have this love, the love of the Father is not in them?

Assuredly, it is God's world, God's order; assuredly, He did form it and pronounce it good; assuredly, that love of which St. John speaks, includes every fowl of the air, and insect, and flower of the field; but is especially directed towards that creature who has wilfully erred and strayed, who has brought disorder into God's order. All this we must remember. We shall not understand St. John's precept unless we do. And *how* has disorder come into this order? for that it is there, we all confess. It has come from men falling in love with this order, or with some of the things in it, and setting them up and making them into gods. It has come from each man seeing the reflection of himself in the world, and becoming enamoured of that, and pursuing that. It has come from each man beginning to dream that he is the centre either of this world, or of some little world that he has made for himself out of it. It has come from the multiplication of these little worlds, with their little miserable centres, and from these worlds clashing one against another; and from those who dwell in them becoming discontented with their own, and wishing to escape into some other. All these disorders spring from that kind of love which St. John bids these young men beware of. They are to beware of it, because if it possesses them, and overmasters them, they will assuredly lose all sense that they ever did belong to a Father, and that they are still His children. They are to beware of it, because if they have this love, this disorderly, irregular love for the world, they cannot have that love of it which their Father has; they cannot *so* love it that for the sake of putting down the disorders that are in it, and making it indeed a true order, and bringing it to revolve about its true centre, they would be ready to give up themselves. This selfish love is the counterfeit of that self-sacrificing love; the counterfeit, and therefore its great antagonist. The Father's love must prevail over this, or it will drive that Father's love out of us.

St. John is never afraid of an apparent contradiction when it might save his readers from a real contradiction. Of course, the thought which suggests itself to us would have suggested itself to the men in his day. 'How can he 'tell us that God loves the world, and yet that *we* are not 'to love it?' The opposition which is on the surface of his language may be the best way of leading us to the harmony which lies below it. The Father's love to the world which He has created is never absent from the Apostle's mind. He does not wish it to be ever absent from the minds of the young men to whom he is writing. If they keep up the recollection of it, they will in new circumstances and amidst new trials retain the freshness of their childish feelings; the home and the family will be dearer to them than ever. They will find the world an order indeed; they will find in it the most wonderful adaptations to their own natures, each sense having something which answers to it; each power and energy having something on which to exercise itself. They will find adaptations in the world not to their own uses only, but to the uses of all the creatures which dwell in it. And beyond all this,—as we were told in that beautiful lecture which was delivered here some weeks ago,—the student will perceive a typical form in the different kinds whereof the world consists, which he cannot explain by any adaptations, which recals,—that, I think, was the lecturer's phrase, and I doubt if he could have found a better or a more devout one— the work of a human artist who makes his picture or statue after a form that was present to *him*, though the observer may only rise by slow degrees and by long study, to apprehend what it was. How delightful the contemplation of the world in this sense is to one who has been taught that he is a child of God, our poet Cowper tells us in these lines of his ' Winter Morning Walk : '—

> ' His are the mountains, and the valleys His,
> And the resplendent rivers, His to enjoy
> With a propriety that none can feel,
> But who, with filial confidence inspired,
> Can lift to heaven an unpresumptuous eye,
> And smiling say,—"My Father made them all !" '

But we must not disguise it—there is a tremendous power in these objects when we first come into close converse with them. Another English poet has described it in his splendid poem on the ' Intimations of Immortality from Recollections in Early Childhood : ' *Wordsworth*

> ' Earth fills her lap with pleasures of her own ;
> Yearnings she hath in her own natural kind,
> And even with something of a Mother's mind,
>   And no unworthy aim,
> The homely Nurse doth all she can
> To make her Foster-child, her Inmate Man,
> Forget the glories he hath known,
> And that imperial palace whence he came.

In another passage of the same ode he speaks in even a more melancholy strain :—

> 'Heaven lies about us in our infancy!
> Shades of the prison-house begin to close
> Upon the growing Boy;
> But He beholds the light, and whence it flows,
> He sees it in his joy;
> The Youth who daily farther from the east
> Must travel, still is Nature's Priest,
> And by the vision splendid
> Is on his way attended;
> At length the Man perceives it die away,
> And fade into the light of common day.'

Wordsworth testifies from his own experience to the truth of St. John's doctrine. He explains how the earth, by its very loveliness, by its very harmony, may turn the man, who has a higher origin and a higher destiny, into its victim and slave. And he explains as truly what the result is. The beauty of the world becomes fainter and dimmer to us as we give up our souls to it. When heaven was about us, earth looked very lovely; when we came down into earth and believed that we had to do with nothing but that, earth became flat and dull; its trees, its flowers, its sunlight, lost their charms; they became monotonous, more wearisome each day because we could not see beyond them.

Here, then, are good reasons why the young men shall not love the world, neither the things that are in the world. For if they do, first, their strength will forsake them; they will give up the power that is in them to the things on which the power is to be exerted; they will be ruled by that which they are meant to rule. Next, they will not have any real insight into these things or any real sympathy with them. It may sound strange to say so, but it is true. Those who love the world, those who surrender themselves to it, never understand it, never in the best sense enjoy it; they are too much on the level of it,—yes, too much below the level of it,—for they look up to it, they depend upon it—to be capable of contemplating it and of appreciating what is most exquisite in it. You have proofs of this continually. The sensualist does not know what the delights of sense are; he is out of temper when he is denied them; he is out of temper when he possesses them. Nothing is exactly to his liking; he expected what he cannot procure; gout or a liver complaint comes in to make the gratification impossible. That is a single instance; you may multiply the instances in all directions. The lover of praise and reputation is continually baulked of the flattery that has become necessary to him. He detects something disagreeable in that which is most highly flavoured; a rough word is a torment to him. In one of these cases the man is dependent chiefly upon material things, though men are needed to dress and prepare them. In the other, he is dependent upon the words that go out of men's lips. Both belong to the world; both are parts of the order which God has created; both therefore in themselves are good. But the man who yields up his heart to them—who, as we say, falls in love with them—makes himself in the judgment of all, even of those who commit the same error, a poor creature. Heathen philosophers had pronounced sentence upon such as he is, long before St. John said, '*Love not the world, neither the things that are in the world.*' They had pronounced the sentence partly from observation of the results to which such devotion led, partly from a consciousness that they were men and must have some kindred with beings higher than themselves, with another world than this.

But they were not able to explain satisfactorily the facts of which they took notice, because they could not tell what that kindred was of which they dreamed. When St. John said, '*If any man love the world, the love of the Father is not in him,*' he interprets this judgment of the wise heathens; he shows what was the warrant for it. At the same time he takes the harshness out of it. Men become the slaves of the world because they do not know that they have a Father of their spirits; because they do not know that He created this order, and put them into it, and that He sustains them in it. They do not know that all the love which is seeking to satisfy itself in these things flows from Him; that the love is nearer to them than it is to these things; that all the beauty which they see in these things is a sign and pledge of it; and a message to them concerning Him from whom it has been derived. '*For,*' the Apostle goes on, '*all that is in the world, the lust of the flesh, and the lust of the eyes, and the pride of life, is not of the Father, but is of the world.*' These words require some thought before we can take in the full force of them; but one remark is obvious. That which the Apostle is condemning here is no part of the order of nature; it is not Sun, or Moon, or Stars that he finds fault with; it is something in *man*, something which belong to his flesh, his eye, his inward character. Is it, then, the order of human society that he is finding fault with? Is he complaining of family life, national laws, the bonds of fellowship between the members of the same nation or between different nations? Is it not rather that which disturbs family life, draws down the vengeance of the laws, tears the bond of fellowship asunder? The appetites which must be indulged whatever is sacrificed to them; the eye which must have its idol, however poor that idol is, and however much that is noble is cast down for the sake of it; the pride of wealth, place, character, which must be pampered on whomsoever it tramples;—are not these the curses of mankind, do not they bring a curse on the world?

But if they bring curses upon the world and proceed from man, why does he say they are '*of*' the world? Because he contemplates men as occupying a position *between* God and the world. All that constitutes them, truly and properly comes to them from God, who has made them in His image. Their social impulses are from Him; their sense of law is from Him; their love is from Him. But their eagerness to get things for themselves is not of Him; their recklessness of obligations is not of Him; that lust which, as Milton says, is hard by hate, is not from Him. These come from their putting the world in His place; from the turning the world into their God. Then it becomes their torment, and they become its torment. That which is best in it often proves the source of the greatest covetousness and pride; this covetousness and pride turn the order upside down, and convert it into confusion. The world, then, though altogether good to the man who refers it to a Father, is the provocative of all evil in him when it becomes separated from his Father, and is substituted for Him. Then it changes what is highest and noblest in man into that which is lowest and basest.

Some will say, 'But these young men to whom St. John 'wrote were godly young men, to whom he gave credit for 'all right and holy purposes.' I believe it; and therefore such words as these were all the more necessary for them.

It is an idle fashion of preachers to bid people who have sold themselves to the world, not to love it. They do not love it; their love is all dried up and exhausted. They tell you so. They say, 'It is a dreary business altogether; 'we wish we were fairly out of it; only, we do not know 'what is to come after; that may be worse.' Talk not to such men of giving up love. Try whether there is not some object which even in the midst of their weariness,— yes, even because they are so weary,—they may be tempted to embrace. Tell them of a Father's love which is seeking them out; which has allowed them to wander away from home, and to feel famine and to feed upon husks, that they may be driven to seek Him—that so the yoke of the world may be broken from their necks; it never can be broken by exhortations about the vanity of enjoyments which they know much better than the preacher does, to be insipid and insincere. It is the man who is full of the highest, bravest, most godly impulses, who rejoices in the belief that he has a Father in heaven, and that He is good, and that the world is overflowing with His goodness,—it is just he who needs this warning, '*Love not the world*'—needs it not that the fire in his heart may burn less vehemently; not that he may be chilled with prudential notions; but precisely that the fire may not die out and leave only a few smouldering ashes behind; precisely that he may not sink into a dry, withered, heartless creature, a despiser of all youthful aspirations and hopes. '*Love not the world*,' St. John says. For there is a love in you that the world did not kindle, that your heavenly Father has kindled; love it not, lest you should be turned into worldlings, whose misery is their incapacity of loving anything He uses the general phrase, '*world*,' though these young men might perhaps be taken into very different regions of the earth and into very different societies. He does not draw lines, and say, 'That 'is the world you are to shun; here is a region where you 'may dwell safely.' They were to shun no place and no men; they were to love all places and all men; but in all places and among all men, there would be a world which they were not to love. They would carry that world about with them, for they would carry the lust of the flesh, and the lust of the eye, and the pride of life about with them. They were to fear the world; but their chief fear was to be of themselves: they were to fear the world, but their fear was to be lest the world's love should separate them from the love which was blessing and renovating the world.

I think these distinctions, the lust of the flesh, the lust of the eye, and the pride of life, prove themselves to be very accurate and very complete distinctions in practice, though an ordinary philosopher may perhaps adopt some other classification of those tendencies which connect us with the world and give it a dominion over us. To the lust of the flesh may be referred the crimes and miseries that have been produced by gluttony, drunkenness, and the irregular intercourse of the sexes; an appalling catalogue, certainly, which no mortal eye could dare to gaze upon. To the lust of the eye may be referred all worship of visible things, with the divisions, persecutions, hatreds, superstitions which this worship has produced in different countries and ages. To the pride or boasting of life,—where you are not to understand by life, for the Greek words are entirely different, either natural or spiritual life, such as the

Apostle spoke of in the first chapter of the Epistle, but all that belongs to the outside of existence, houses, lands, whatever exalts a man above his fellow,—to this head we must refer the oppressor's wrongs, and that contumely which Hamlet reckons among the things that are harder to bear even than the 'slings and arrows of outrageous fortune.' In these three divisions I suspect all the mischiefs which have befallen our race may be reckoned, and each of us is taught by the Apostle, and may know by experience, that the seeds of the evils so enumerated are in himself.

Against the ripening of these seeds the young man is to watch. So far as he sells himself to the world, so far, he may be sure, they will ripen and bear fruit. But the Apostle gives him an aid against this prostration of soul which, if he uses it, will be very effectual. It is the recollection that all that his flesh lusts after, that his eye lusts after, that he is boasting of as his, passes away, is even now in the act of passing away.

These sensual pleasures, these gods of our creation, these lusts which we are feeding, have their death doom upon them; they are here to-day and will be gone to-morrow. The world, the order which is fashioned out of these, is not God's order, but a perversion of God's order,—that which we have substituted for His. Therefore it has no subsistence, no endurance. '*But he that doeth the will of God abideth for ever.*' He has attached himself to the Unchangeable, the Eternal. He belongs to an order which cannot disappear. It is the order of Him Whose children we are; of Him Who created the world and all that is in it; of Him Who loved the world, and sent His Son into it to claim as His.

Here a deep and grand subject opens upon us at which I can but glance, though I must glance at it. That Word Who is said to be dwelling with these young men, to be upholding them against the lust of the flesh, and the lust of the eye, and the pride of life, that Word Who is to keep them at one with the forgiving Father they knew in childhood, and Who has promised to be with them till the end; that Eternal Word is declared in St. John's Gospel to be the same by Whom the worlds were created, and without Whom was not anything made that was made. He is affirmed to be that form or type after whom the Divine Artist fashioned the whole universe. And He it is Who, as St. John speaks again, '*was made flesh and dwelt among us.*' He is that '*only begotten Son which taketh away the sin of the world.*' Therefore the young men, who by this Word are kept from that false selfish love of the world which is so dangerous to their faith and their freedom, may look for a blessed reward. They may come now or hereafter to know the world, not in its fleeting fashions, which pass away, but as it is constituted in Him who is to abide for ever and ever. They may know it with a true divine knowledge; they may love it with a true divine affection. I have quoted some lines from Cowper already. I will quote one more passage from the same poem. It is in a higher measure, I think, than that of his ordinary song. I wish that all divines, and all naturalists, and all artists would ponder it. I would commend it to you as containing truths in which every human being has a right to share:—

'So reads he nature, whom the lamp of truth
Illuminates. Thy lamp, mysterious Word!

Which whoso sees, no longer wanders lost,
With intellects bemaz'd in endless doubt,
But runs the road of wisdom. Thou hast built,
With means that were not till by thee employ'd,
Worlds, that had never been hadst thou in strength
Been less, or less benevolent than strong.
They are thy witnesses, who speak thy power
And goodness infinite, but speak in ears
That hear not, or receive not their report.
In vain thy creatures testify of thee
Till thou proclaim thyself. Theirs is indeed
A teaching voice; but 'tis the praise of thine
That whom it teaches it makes prompt to learn,
And with the boon gives talents for its use.
Till Thou art heard, imaginations vain
Possess the heart, and fables false as hell,
Yet deem'd oracular, lure down to death
The uninform'd and heedless souls of men.

or "Luck"

We give to Chance, blind Chance, ourselves as blind.
The glory of thy work, which yet appears
Perfect and unimpeachable of blame,
Challenging human scrutiny, and proved
Then skilful most, when most severely judged.
But Chance is not; or is not where thou reign'st.
Thy Providence forbids that fickle power
(If power she be, that works but to confound,)
To mix her wild vagaries with thy laws.
Yet thus we dote, refusing while we can
Instructions, and inventing to ourselves
Gods such as guilt makes welcome, gods that sleep,
Or disregard our follies, or that sit
Amused spectators of this bustling stage.
Thee we reject, unable to abide
Thy purity, till pure as thou art pure,
Made such by thee, we love thee for that cause
For which we shunn'd and hated thee before.
Then we are free: then liberty, like day,
Breaks on the soul, and by a flash from heaven
Fires all the faculties with glorious joy.
A voice is heard, that mortal ears hear not
Till thou hast touched them; 'tis the voice of song,
A loud Hosanna sent from all thy works,
Which he that hears it with a shout repeats.

And adds his rapture to the general praise.
In that blest moment, Nature, throwing wide
Her veil opaque, discloses with a smile
The Author of her beauties, who, retired
Behind his own creation, works unseen
By the impure, and hears his power denied.
Thou art the source and centre of all minds,
Their only point of rest, eternal Word!
From thee departing, they are lost and rove
At random, without honour, hope, or peace.
From thee is all that soothes the life of man,
His high endeavour, and his glad success,
His strength to suffer, and his will to serve
But oh thou bounteous Giver of all good,
Thou art of all thy gifts thyself the crown!
Give what thou canst, without thee we are poor:
And with thee rich, take what thou wilt away.'

LECTURE IX.

THE LAST TIME; THE CHRIST; THE ANTI-CHRIST; THE CHRISM.

1 John II. 18—23.

Little children, it is the last time: and as ye have heard that antichrist shall come, even now are there many antichrists; whereby we know that it is the last time. They went out from us, but they were not of us; for if they had been of us, they would no doubt have continued with us; but they went out, that they might be made manifest that they were not all of us. But ye have an unction from the Holy One, and ye know all things. I have not written unto you because ye know not the truth, but because ye know it, and that no lie is of the truth. Who is a liar but he that denieth that Jesus is the Christ? He is antichrist, that denieth the Father and the Son. Whosoever denieth the Son, the same hath not the Father: [but] he that acknowledgeth the Son hath the Father also.

How could St. John say that his time was the last time? Has not the world lasted nearly one thousand eight hundred years since he left it? May it not last yet many years more?

You will be told by many that not only St. John, but St. Paul and all the Apostles laboured under the delusion that the end of all things was approaching in their day. People say so who are not in general disposed to undervalue their authority; some adopt the opinion practically, though they may not express it in words, who hold that the writers of the Bible were never permitted to make a mistake even in the most trifling point. I do not say that; it would not shake my faith in them, to find that they had erred in names or points of Chronology. But if I supposed they had been misled themselves, and had misled their disciples on so capital a subject as this of Christ's coming to judgment, and of the latter days, I should be greatly perplexed. For it is a subject to which they are continually referring. It is a part of their deepest faith. It mingles with all their practical exhortations. If they were wrong here, I cannot myself see where they can have been right.

I have found their language on this subject of the greatest possible use to me in explaining the method of the Bible; the course of God's government over nations, and over individuals; the life of the world before the time of the Apostles, during their time and in all the centuries since. If we will do them the justice which we owe to every writer inspired or uninspired,—if we will allow them to interpret themselves, instead of forcing our interpretation upon them,—we shall, I think, understand a little more of their work and of ours. If we take their words simply and literally respecting the judgment and the end which they were expecting in their day, we shall know what position they were occupying with respect to their forefathers and to us. And in place of a very vague, powerless, artificial conception of the judgment which we are to look for, we shall learn what our needs are by theirs; how God will fulfil all His words to us by the way in which He fulfilled His words to them.

It is not a new notion, but a very old and common one, that the history of the world is divided into certain great periods. In our days, the conviction that there is a broad distinction between ancient and modern history has been forcing itself more and more upon thoughtful men. M. Guizot dwells especially upon the unity and universality of modern history, as contrasted with the division of ancient history into a set of nations which had scarcely any common sympathies. The question is, where to find the boundary between these two periods. About these, students have made many guesses; most of them have been plausible and suggestive of truths; some very confusing; none, I think, satisfactory. One of the most popular, that which supposes modern history to begin when the barbarous tribes settled themselves in Europe, would be quite fatal to M. Guizot's doctrine. For that settlement, though it was a most important and indispensable event to modern civilization, was the temporary breaking up of a unity which had existed before. It was like the re-appearance of that separation of tribes and races, which he supposes to have been the especial characteristic of the former world.

Now, may we expect any light upon this subject in the Bible? I do not think it would fulfil its pretensions if we might not. It professes to set forth the ways of God to nations and to mankind. We might be well content that it should tell us very little about physical laws; we might be content that it should be silent about the courses of the planets and the law of gravitation. God may have other ways of making *these* secrets known to His creatures. But that which concerns the moral order of the world and the spiritual progress of human beings, falls directly within the province of the Bible. No one could be satisfied with it if it was dumb respecting these. And, accordingly, all who suppose it is dumb here, however much importance they may attach to what they call its religious character, however much they may suppose their highest interests to depend upon a belief in its oracles, are obliged to treat it as a very disjointed fragmentary volume. They afford the best excuse for those who say, that it is not a whole book as we have thought it, but a collection of the sayings and opinions of certain authors, in different ages, often not very consistent with each other. On the other hand, there has been the strongest conviction in the minds of ordinary readers as well as of students, that the book does tell us how the ages past and the ages to come are concerned in the unveiling of God's mysteries, what part one country and another has played in His great drama, to what point all the lines of His providence are converging. The immense interest which has been taken in Prophecy, an interest not destroyed or even weakened by the numerous disappointments which men's theories about it have had to encounter, is a proof how deep and widely spread this conviction is. Divines endeavour in vain to recall simple and earnest readers from the study of the Prophecies, by urging that they have not leisure for such a pursuit, and that they ought to busy themselves with what is more practical. If their consciences tell them that there is some ground for the warning, they yet feel as if they could not heed it altogether. They are sure that they have an interest in the destinies of their race as well as in their own individual destiny. They cannot separate the one from the other; they must believe that there is light somewhere about both. I dare not discourage such an assurance. If we hold it strongly, it may be a great instrument of raising us out of our selfishness. I am only afraid lest we should lose it, as we certainly shall, if we contract the habit of regarding the Bible as a book of puzzles and conundrums, and of looking restlessly for certain outward events, to happen at certain dates that we have fixed upon as those which Prophets and Apostles have set down. The cure for such follies, which are very serious indeed, lies not in the neglect of Prophecy, but in more earnest meditation upon it; remembering that Prophecy is not a set of loose predictions like the sayings of the fortune-teller, but an unfolding of Him Whose goings forth are from everlasting; Who is the same yesterday, to-day, and for ever; Whose acts in one generation are determined by the same laws as His acts in another.

If I should ever speak to you of the Apocalypse of St. John, I shall have to enter much more at large on this subject. But so much I have said to introduce the remark, that the Bible treats the downfal of the Jewish polity as the winding-up of a great period in human history, and as the commencement of another great period. John the Baptist announces the presence of one '*Whose fan is in His hand, and He will throughly purge His floor and gather His wheat into the garner, but He will burn up the chaff with unquenchable fire.*' The Evangelists say, that by these words He denoted that Jesus of Nazareth, who afterwards went down into the water of Jordan, and as He came out of it, was declared to be the Son of God, and on Whom the Spirit descended in a bodily shape.

We are wont to separate Jesus the Saviour, from Jesus the King and the Judge. They do not. They tell us from the first, that He came preaching a Kingdom of Heaven. They tell us of His doing acts of judgment as well as acts of deliverance. They report the tremendous words which He spoke to Pharisees and Scribes, as well as the Gospel which He preached to publicans and sinners. And before the end of His Ministry, when His disciples were asking Him about the buildings of the Temple, He spoke plainly of a judgment which He the Son of Man should execute before that generation was over. And to make it clear that He meant us to understand Him strictly and literally, He added,—'*Heaven and earth shall pass away, but my words shall not pass away.*' This discourse, which is carefully reported to us by St. Matthew, St. Mark, and St. Luke, does not stand aloof from the rest of His discourses and parables, nor from the rest of His deeds. They all contain the same warning. They are gracious and merciful—far more gracious and merciful than we have ever supposed them to be—they are witnesses of a gracious and merciful Being; but they are witnesses, that those who did not like that Being, just because this was His character—who sought for another being like themselves—that is, for an ungracious and unmerciful being—would have their houses left to them desolate.

When, therefore, the Apostles went forth after our Lord's Ascension, to preach His Gospel and baptize in His name, their first duty was to announce that that Jesus whom the rulers of Jerusalem had crucified, was both Lord and Christ; their second was to preach remission of sins and the gift of the Spirit in His name; their third was, to foretel the coming of a great and terrible day of the Lord, and to say to all who heard, '*Save yourselves from this untoward generation.*' It was the language which St. Peter used on the day of Pentecost; it was adopted with such variations as befitted the circumstances of the hearers by all who were entrusted with the Gospel message. It was, no doubt, peculiarly applicable to the Jews. They had been made the stewards of God's gifts to the world. They had wasted their master's goods, and were to be no longer stewards. But we do not find the Apostles confining this language to the Jews. St. Paul speaking at Athens—speaking in words specially appropriate to a cultivated, philosophical, heathen city—declares that God has '*appointed a day in the which He will judge the world by that man whom He hath ordained;*' and points to the Resurrection from the dead as determining who that man is. Why was this? Because the Apostles believed that the rejection of the Jewish people was the manifestation of the *Son of Man;* a witness to all nations who their King was—a call to all nations to cast away their idols and confess Him. The Gospel was to explain the meaning of the great crisis which was about to occur; to tell the Gentiles as well as the Jews what it would imply; to announce it as nothing less than the commencement of a new era in the world's history— when the crucified man would claim a universal empire, and would contend with the Roman Cæsar, as well as with all other tyrants of the earth who should set up their claims against His.

This Scriptural view of the ordering of times and seasons entirely harmonizes with that conclusion at which M. Guizot has arrived by an observation of facts. Our Lord's birth nearly coincided with the establishment of the Roman empire, in the person of Augustus Cæsar. That empire aspired to crush the nations, and to establish a great world supremacy. The Jewish nation had been the witness against all such experiments in the old world. It had fallen under the Babylonian tyranny; but it had risen again. And the time which followed its captivity was the great time of the awakening of national life in Europe—the time in which the Greek republics flourished—the time in which the Roman republic commenced its grand career.

The Jewish nation had been overcome by the armies of the Roman republic; still it retained the ancient signs of its nationality; its law, its priesthood, its temple. These looked ridiculous and insignificant to the Roman emperors, even to the Roman governors who ruled the little province of Judæa, or the larger province of Syria, in which it was often reckoned. But they found the Jews very troublesome. Their nationality was of a very peculiar kind, and of unusual strength. When they were most degraded, they could not part with it. They would stir up endless rebellions, in the hope of recovering what they had lost, and of establishing the universal kingdom which they believed was intended for them, and not for Rome. The preaching of our Lord declared to them that there was such an universal kingdom, that He, the Son of David, had come to set it up on the earth. The Jews dreamed of another kind of kingdom, with another kind of King. They wanted a Jewish kingdom which should trample upon the nations, just as the Roman empire was trampling upon them: they wanted a Jewish king, who should be, in all essentials, like the Roman Cæsar. It was a dark, horrible, hateful conception; it combined all that is narrowest in the most degraded exclusive form of nationality, with all that is cruelest, most destructive of moral and personal life in the worst form of imperialism. It gathered up into itself all that was worst in the history of the past. It was a shadowing forth of what should be worst in the coming time. The Apostles announced that this accursed ambition of the Jews would be utterly disappointed. They foretold that the ambition of the Romans would also be disappointed. They said that a new age was at hand— the universal age—the age of the Son of Man—which would be preceded by a great crisis that would shake not earth only, but also heaven; not that only which belonged to time, and the condition of man as related to time, but also all that belonged to the spiritual world, and to man's relations with it. They said that this shaking would be that it might be seen what there was which could not be shaken, which must abide.

I have tried thus to show you what St. John meant by the last time if he spoke the same language as our Lord spoke, and as the other Apostles spoke. I cannot tell what physical changes he or they may have looked for. Physical phenomena were noticed at that time; famines, plagues, earthquakes. Whether they or any of them supposed that these indicated more alterations in the surface or the substance of the earth than they did indicate, I cannot tell; these are not the points upon which I look for information from them; I should probably not understand their information if they gave it. That they did not anticipate the passing away of the *earth*—what we call the destruction of the earth—is clear from this— that the new kingdom they spoke of was to be a kingdom on earth as well as a kingdom of Heaven. But their belief that such a kingdom had been set up, and would make its power felt as soon as the old nation was scattered, has, I think, been abundantly verified by fact.

I do not see how we can understand modern history properly till we accept that belief.

Hence you will understand what St. John says in the next verse, '*You have heard that antichrist shall come.*' We are told by St. Luke, that when Jesus went into the synagogue of Nazareth, where He had been brought up, shortly after the commencement of His public ministry, He opened the book of the prophet Isaiah, and read these words, '*The Spirit of the Lord is upon me, because He hath anointed me to preach the Gospel to the poor; He hath sent me to heal the broken-hearted, to preach deliverance to the captives, and recovering of sight to the blind, to set at liberty them that are bruised; to preach the acceptable year of the Lord.*' He added, '*This day is this Scripture fulfilled in your ears.*'

Now all in that Synagogue, and throughout Galilee, had heard that a Christ was to come. By the word Christ, they meant one who would be anointed by God—one who would be marked out by God as a king. Here Jesus declares what kind of anointing this king would receive, and how all might know that he had received it. He would not require some visible oil or unguent poured upon his head, but he would require a Spirit, the very Spirit of God Himself, to enable him to do the works of God.

What these works of God are, the same passage declares. One who healed the broken-hearted, preached deliverance to the captives, opened the eyes of the blind, would be proved to have the true anointing, the true Spirit. One who wanted these characteristics, whatever others he might possess, would be proved not to have the true anointing, not to be endued with the Divine Spirit. On this ground Jesus rested His own claim. On this ground the Jews rested their denial of Him. They did not want such a Christ as this. This was not the anointing they had dreamed of. When the Apostles went forth, declaring '*Jesus is the Christ*,' to the Jews, they testified that this was the kind of Christ their prophets had spoken of. When they delivered the same message to the Gentiles, they testified, 'This is ' the kind of King, the kind of Christ you are wanting; ' this is the true Desire of Nations.' Those who gave heed to them, whether Jews or Gentiles, confessed, 'We have ' been looking for such a Person, He fulfils our cravings. ' Such an One we believe to be the Head of human beings.' In His name, therefore, they fraternized; in His name they became a Church.

Our Lord had clearly intimated in His last discourse to the disciples, that before the end came, false Christs should arise, and should deceive many. Such an announcement could not surprise His disciples, if they seriously reflected upon it. Unless the Jews had a false idea of a Christ, an idea of some being wholly unlike Jesus the Crucified, what did their treatment of Him mean? Unless the Gentiles had the idea of a Christ wholly unlike Jesus the Crucified, why did they look up to any tyrant, to any sophist, with more reverence than to Him? No doubt their notions were in many respects different; 'The Jews,' said St. Paul, 'require ' a sign, the Greeks seek after wisdom.' One set before themselves the image of a great ruler who should do strange signs to establish his dominion, and make men tremble. The other set before themselves the image of some being of profound sagacity, who should make them fear him for his wit and wisdom, who should rule over their souls, as well as their bodies. Might not these two different conceptions, some time or other, come into one? Might not some emperor support his pretensions by alleging that he had spiritual powers to work out his ends; or might not some priest claim to have temporal as well as spiritual power combined in him? Might there not be some one person to whom men would pay homage as their king or Christ, who should be in all respects the opposite of Jesus; who should not heal the broken-hearted, who should not be a deliverer, who should not proclaim a jubilee to the captives, who should bind the world with new and more terrible fetters?

Such an one the Apostles looked for, before the end of the age. '*Ye have heard*,' says St. John, '*that antichrist shall come.*' He is far from contradicting the opinion; no one, perhaps, was so fully possessed with it. But he says, '*Even now are there many antichrists, whereby we know that it is the last time.*' There might be some one person hereafter, in whom *all* the features should be combined, which did not belong to Jesus—all that were most exactly the reverse of His; but in the meantime there were many who were exhibiting *some* of these features, who were showing themselves to be possessed by the spirit which was not in Him, by such unclean, lawless, spirits as He came to cast out.

'*These antichrists*,' St. John says, '*have gone out from us, because they were not of us.*' We can understand very well what he means, by the facts of Church History. The belief of spiritual powers was strong in that age. The Gospel strengthened and deepened it, but it existed before the Gospel. The Gospel declared what *manner* of spirit it was that men were to receive. It said that Christ would baptize them with the *Holy* Spirit; this was their distinguishing peculiarity: not the exercise of power; not the possession of an inspiration; but the exercise of powers for a *holy* end,—the receiving of an inspiration from a *Holy* Being. But many of those who had joined the Church exulted in the gifts for their own sake, in the inspiration for its own sake. These became enchanters and impostors of the worst kind. The spirit of which they boasted, instead of uniting them to their brethren, was merely a ground for self-exaltation. What they *were*, signified nothing. The wonders they could *do* was all they thought of, or wished others to think of. Such persons often described themselves as Christs. They used the very name. But whether they did or did not, they were assuming the powers of Christ, for the ends which were the contraries of His ends. They were therefore antichrists. *Their* chrism or anointing was to set them in high places; *His*, made Him the servant of all. Theirs, was to make men wonder at them, and be their tools; His, was to make them free, and to give them life. Such persons, therefore, St. John pronounces, were not *of them;* they did not choose to belong to a brotherhood; what they cared was to assert their independence of others, their superiority to their fellows. It was far better, he intimates, that such men should not continue in the Church, to be its disturbers and tormentors; that they should go out from it, and become its enemies. It was far better that they should not belie the name of Jesus, by acts that were directly the reverse of His; but should at once avow that they renounced Him.

But, continues the Apostle, in words which have surprised many: '*Ye have an unction from the Holy One, and ye know all things.*' You will see at once upon what word the emphasis in this sentence rests—they had an unction, of anointing from the *Holy* One. God had given them His *Holy* Spirit. If they believed they had that Spirit, if they submitted to His teaching, these antichrists would not and could not deceive them. A divine instinct would tell them, 'This is not the kind of being we need; this is not the per-'son to whom we owe allegiance; this is not God's anointed 'one.' They could trust to this instinct much better than to any cleverness of theirs in finding out, by collating passages of Scripture, whether such a pretender was or was not the Christ. They might be deceived in their interpretation of a *book* ; their intellects might fail to discern the force of sentences; but if they were simple and childlike, if they yielded to the guidance of that Spirit who was to make them simple and childlike, they would not be deceived about a *man*, they would know whether he was true or a liar.

I do not wonder that many should think such confidence very much misplaced, seeing that the persons to whom St. John wrote must have been, many of them, ignorant people, or in his own language, little children. But that fact, I suspect, gave good warrant for his confidence. The most experienced people will tell you that they had rather trust the judgment of an innocent woman, even of a child, about character, than their own. The surest divination of a rogue and of an honest man lies in those who are guileless, and who do not boast of their own sagacity. St. John tells us the reason: 'They have an unction from the Holy One.' A better wisdom is guiding them; they lean upon that wisdom, not finding they can rely upon their own. They know all things, even what seems the most inscrutable, unfathomable thing of all—a human soul.

He adds, therefore, '*I have not written unto you because ye know not the truth, but because ye know it, and that no lie is of the truth.*' There is the modesty and the sound philosophy of an Apostle! Many of us think that we can put the truth *into* people, by screaming it into their ears. We do not suppose they have any truth *in* them to which we can make an appeal. St. John had no notion that he could be of the least use to his own dear children of Ephesus unless there was a truth in them, a capacity of distinguishing truth from lies, a sense that one must be the eternal opposite of the other. He can write to them about those antichrists, because they have a chrism, because there is in them a power of listening to his words and of understanding them. The presence of that power does not make the words unnecessary, any more than the fitness of the ground for receiving the rain makes the rain unnecessary. An Apostle can help them to reject those men who would blind them and lead them captive, because they have in them an anointing which shows them that only He Who brings light and freedom is the anointed of the Father.

These Ephesians had learnt '*that no lie is of the truth.*' 'Common-place learning enough!' some will say. 'Most 'people know as much as that.' Do they, indeed? Alas! half the doctors in Christendom have not known it. They have thought that some lies *are* of the truth, that some lies may serve the truth. Their cleverness has led them to think so. Their notion that the truth was left to them to take care of and keep from harm, and to defend against impugners, has led them to think so. 'Just a *little* 'fraud, a pious fraud, will help us here. The people 'cannot take in truth; spice it with falsehood, and it will 'go down.' These have been the sage conclusions of divines and men of God. And so Christ has been mixed with antichrist; so the way has been prepared for antichrist to come in and claim the whole ground which Christ once occupied. It is for the latter days of an age that such a catastrophe as that is reserved. There is a mingling of the false and the true, of the foul and the fair, till then. At length the false appears in its falsehood; the foul asks homage because it is foul. And then they who will not bow down to it, perceive that *no* lie is of the truth; that they must purge their hearts of every base mixture. And since they cannot depend upon their own truthfulness, they ask the Spirit of Truth to guide them into all truth.

Now he comes directly to the point: '*Who is a liar but he that denieth that* JESUS *is the* CHRIST?' He appeals to them as men seeking truth and loving truth, and endowed with a capacity for discerning truth. He says, ' These men that I am speaking of, these men that have
' gone out from us, affirm very loudly that Jesus, the humble
' man, He Who went about doing good, He Who was cruci
' fied, is not at all the Christ for human beings. They will
' only honour one who is *not* a humble man, one who does *not*
' go about doing good, one who has *not* been crucified. They
' especially scorn that last characteristic. They say that
' that defeats all the pretensions of Jesus to be a king. He
' could not have submitted to death if He had been. You
' Ephesians have heard these words uttered; you have known
' the people who spoke them. Yes, and the words *had* an
' attraction for you. The men did look like men who had
' high spiritual pretensions. But what was it in you that
' their words attracted? What was it in you that was in-

150   LECTURE IX.

'clined to receive these men? Do you not know that it was
'the lying temper in you which went along with their boast-
'ing? Do you not know that so far as you yielded to them,
'you were yielding to a lying temper? And were you not
'prevented from doing this altogether by a Spirit of Truth
'which forbad you to obey the false inclination within you?
'Here then is a clear witness in yourselves, that to say
'Jesus is not the Christ, to set up another Christ who is
'unlike Him, is to be a liar.'

I have hinted already that the grand distinction between Jesus and these antichrists was, that He said He came from a Father, and received His anointing from a Father; and that they came in their own names, boasting of themselves as great ones. This is the contrast which St. John pursues in the following verses: '*He is antichrist, that denieth the Father and the Son.*' In his Gospel St. John illustrates this point at great length. All our Lord's discourses with the Jews at Jerusalem which he records, have reference to His Father and His relation to the Father. All their misunderstandings of Him, their rage against Him, their condemnation of Him as a blasphemer, have reference to His language on this point. *Ultimately* He was put to death as a rebel against Cæsar; as a rival king. But the dislike of the *Jews* to Him, that which prompted *them* to deliver Him to the Gentiles, was gathered up in the complaint, '*He calleth God His Father, making Himself equal with God.*' Was He proud; or were they? Was this the height of exaltation, or the depth of self-humiliation? Was it, as the Jews said, that He made Himself equal with God, or, as He said Himself, that He could do nothing without His Father, that what He saw His Father do, He did likewise;

that He came down from the Father to become in all things like the meanest of men? All the difference between Christian ethics and antichristian ethics; between the ethics which treats it as the highest glory of God that He can stoop to us, and the ethics which makes it our highest glory that we can lift ourselves to be as Gods,—is latent in this question.

I will not press it further upon you now. It will come before us again in connexion with the beautiful verse which opens the next chapter. But I cannot conclude without saying that I am not so far as I may seem from those who speak of this day as one of the latter days. I cannot tell how close we may be to the end of *our* age, to *our* judgment. If we are very close to it, the hints which St. John gives us respecting the end of *his* age, respecting the judgment which was approaching then, will be all the more precious, and should be all the more earnestly pondered. God gives us what we need for our necessities. We may require to be warned of antichrists, and to be told what they will be like, as much as the Ephesians. Certainly we want to know the characteristics of the true Christ as much as they did; certainly we cannot know them unless that same anointing Spirit who abided with them, who is truth and no lie, has been assured to us and to our children for ever.

LECTURE X.

THE PLACE OF THE DOCTRINE OF THE FATHER, THE SON, AND THE SPIRIT, IN CHRISTIAN ETHICS.

1 JOHN II. 23—28.

Whosoever denieth the Son, the same hath not the Father: [but] he that acknowledgeth the Son hath the Father also. Let that therefore abide in you, which ye have heard from the beginning. If that which ye have heard from the beginning shall remain in you, ye also shall continue in the Son, and in the Father. And this is the promise that He hath promised us, even eternal life. These things have I written unto you concerning them that seduce you. But the anointing which ye have received of Him abideth in you, and ye need not that any man teach you: but as the same anointing teacheth you of all things, and is truth, and is no lie, and even as it hath taught you, ye shall abide in Him. And now, little children, abide in Him; that, when He shall appear, we may have confidence, and not be ashamed before Him at His coming.

OUR translators appear to have doubted whether the last clause of the 23d verse is genuine; for they have taken the very unusual course of printing it in Italics, as they print words which they insert to fill up the sense of the original. Modern scholars, I believe, do not share in this suspicion; they suppose the words ' *He that acknowledgeth the Son hath the Father also,*' to be St. John's as much as those which precede them. Certainly, they make his meaning somewhat clearer; but it would not be obscure, I think, if they were absent.

One peculiarity you must notice in each of these clauses.

He says, '*He that denieth the Son* hath *not the Father. He that acknowledgeth the Son* hath *the Father.*' A person writing a paraphrase of the Epistle would probably render the Apostle's meaning in this way: 'He that denieth the 'Son, virtually or by implication denies the Father. He 'that acknowledges the Son, virtually or by implication 'acknowledges the Father.' One who ventured this alteration would think that he made St. John much more intelligible. I cannot tell how others may find it; but I do not find the expressions 'virtually and by implication' half so intelligible as the little words for which they are substituted. I do not mean merely that an ignorant person might be puzzled by these logical expressions, *virtually* and *by implication.* I mean that they do not convey to *any one* the full sense which, if I am not mistaken, St. John did convey to his little children at Ephesus by his own words. He is writing to them,—I have told you so before, I shall have to tell you so again and again,—as members of a family, as sons of God. He is writing to them just now about certain persons who had been members of their family, but had thrown off their fellowship. Why had they done so? He says, because they did not believe Jesus to be the Christ. Because they believed in a Christ who claimed high powers for himself. Because they did not believe in a Christ who was *a Son*. Therefore he says, they *have* not the Father. They refuse for *themselves* the title of sons of God. He in whom they suppose the highest glory to dwell, is not one who looked up to a Father. He is not one who has come from a Father, and gone to a Father. He has not come to be a brother of men, and to claim His Father as your Father.

Slight as this difference may appear, I believe it is very important for the understanding of St. John. The message which he and all the Apostles brought to the Jewish and Heathen world was, 'You are not separate creatures, as you 'have taken yourselves to be. You have one Lord and Head; 'He being the Son of God has come into our world, stooped to 'our weaknesses, died our death, that He might make us one 'body in Himself, as we were created to be.' They could not therefore say to those who separated from them, and set up another Christ, ' You are committing an error of *doctrine.*' They were obliged to say, ' You are choosing not to have a ' Father. You are choosing not to own us common men ' as your brethren.' It was no unfair charge. It was this which all their words and acts imported. They revolted from Jesus because He was lowly and meek; because He made Himself one with the most abject. They said that in so far as He wrought miracles, He had the signs of a divine anointing; but that when He died on the cross, if He died actually, He must have ceased to be the Christ— the Spirit must have forsaken Him. Whereas St. John holds that He never so thoroughly proved Himself to be a Son – that He never so entirely showed forth GOD—as in that death.

We sometimes suppose that the temper of mind which these teachers exhibited belonged only to *their* age. I cannot think so. There is a disposition in many of us to hold that Jesus proved Himself to be the Christ by doing great and startling miracles, by showing that He had power to break through laws which men generally are obliged to obey. This, we affirm, was the sign that He came from God. Now, the Gospels, it seems to me, represent the mighty acts of Jesus,—His healing the lepers, raising the dead, casting out devils,—in a light which is very unlike this. They say that He came to do the *will* of His Father; they speak of these acts as showing forth that Will, as accomplishing a part of that Will, by overcoming the enemies which had assaulted men, by breaking the fetters with which men were bound. They speak of these acts as acts of sympathy with human beings. '*Himself*,' they say, '*took our infirmities, and bare our own sicknesses.*' These acts, then, revealed the *lowliness* of Jesus, the *submission* of Jesus, just as His Cross and Passion revealed them. Did they not also reveal the *power* of God? Wonderfully, I think. They revealed that power to be a gracious, loving power; a calm power; a health-giving, life-giving power. They revealed the very mind from which laws have proceeded, the very might by which laws are executed and enforced. They are not breaches of laws, they are assertions of laws against irregularities and disturbances. Jesus vindicated laws as no one ever did. Obedience is the characteristic of His whole life upon earth.

This is what all the Evangelists report concerning Him; this is the honour, they say, that He claimed for Himself. St. John is especially occupied throughout his Gospel in setting forth the ground and principle of this obedience. '*The Son can do nothing of Himself*,' thus he speaks in the fifth chapter of his Gospel; but '*what things soever He seeth the Father do, these also doeth the Son likewise.*' It is *filial* obedience. It is the obedience of a Son to a Father, in whom He delights, and who delights in Him. And so He reveals the Father. And the Apostles receiving Him as the Christ, learnt from Him not to think of the Godhead as self-willed power or sovereignty. They thought of a Father and a Son. They could not see the Will of the Father except in the submission of the Son. They could not dwell on the submission of the Son without finding its ground and root in the Will of the Father. They were Jews; they had a greater horror of dividing the Godhead, of setting up two gods, than any of their countrymen had. But it was precisely this belief in the Unity of the Father and the Son which kept them from dividing the Godhead. If they had reverenced and loved Jesus as they reverenced and loved Him, and had not believed that He was one with the Father, they *would* have worshipped two gods, or they would have set a man above God.

St. John perceived that the preachers of a new Christ were guiding their disciples back into the old idolatry. The heathen gods each expressed some conception which men had formed of the Divine Being; some relation which they had seen must exist between them and Him, or some quality which they supposed must belong to Him, because they found it in themselves. The Name of God which the Christian Church proclaimed was, the Apostle believed, that Name which the heathens had been seeking after. It was the full revelation of Him Whom they had divided. If that Name were forgotten, Jupiter, Apollo, Minerva might not return in their old forms, but there would come in a multitude of vague conceptions and notions that would be far less real and personal than the demigods they displaced.

Therefore he says, in the next verse, ' *Let that, therefore, abide in you which ye have heard from the beginning. If* that which ye have heard from the beginning shall remain in you, ye also shall continue in the Son, and in the Father.' They had heard from the beginning that God had sent forth His Son made of a woman, that they might be the sons of God in Him. They had heard from the beginning that God had sent forth the Spirit of His Son, that they might be able to cry to God as their Father. This was the groundwork of the Apostolical teaching. Those who accepted it as true, those to whose consciences it came as a word sent to them from Heaven, were baptized. They might come from the East or the West, they might be Jews or Greeks, they might be rich or poor, they might be freemen or bondsmen. This baptism was for all nations. The Name of the Father, the Son, and the Holy Spirit embraced all. Each man had a right to say, 'It is put upon 'me. I am sealed with it. The God in Whom I am living, 'and moving, and having my being, has written His 'Name upon me, has made me a partaker of His life and 'blessedness.' Therefore St. John says, 'I do not tell you 'something different from that which I told you at the 'first. All I say is, do not forget that. Let it dwell in 'you. Let it enter more and more deeply into you.'

What would be the result? The two blessings which men want most; perseverance and growth. They would continue in the Father and the Son. The spirit wants a home and a dwelling-place as much as the body. It as truly *abides* in a person or friend whom it trusts, as a body abides in a house. But the more it abides, the more it expands. It discovers more to trust, more to love in Him to Whom it is attached. It grows wider as it knows more of Him. St. John says to them, 'Abide in Him, Who has

'united you to Himself, Who has died your death, that you
'might share His life; then every day will reveal to you
'more of that Father from Whom He came, Whose perfect
'image He is. It will not be dry, hard knowledge; it will be
'the knowledge you acquire of the home in which you have
'been brought up; it will be the knowledge you acquire of
'the brother upon whom you are leaning daily for succour
'and support; of a parent whose character is coming forth
'to you more and more through His affection to you and
'His care of you. You will *continue* in the Son and the
'Father. You are united to them already. God has esta-
'blished bonds between you and Him which cannot be broken.
'You will find how blessed these bonds are. You will learn
'more of their nature. You will see how all outward
'events, sorrowful and joyful, how all your inward struggles
'may be means of fastening them more closely about you.
'The thought of some other Christ, who is not a brother of
'man, who is not a Son, who exults in his power not in his
'obedience, will become utterly loathsome and intolerable
'to you. You will cry out in your hearts, "How long, O
'Lord, faithful and true, wilt Thou suffer these false Christs,
'these oppressors of the earth, these counterfeits of Thy
'loving power, to deceive men by their lies, and to trample
'upon them with their cruelties?"' And every judgment
upon the nations, every fresh morning that rises upon the
earth out of the dark night, every tempest that sweeps the
air, will be an answer from the throne of God Himself.
'Wait a little; I come to scatter all who divide and rend in
'pieces my heritage. I come to establish the throne of
'Him Who is the Prince of righteousness and peace.'

This is but one part—a small part—of the promise, ' Ye

shall abide in the Son and in the Father.' How can I even dream what is the length and breadth of it? How could I express in words what I have seen among poor bed-ridden men and women of that which they were learning, as they kept up a continual trust in Jesus Christ their Lord, and so rose more and more into an apprehension of His Father and their Father? How could I guess at the glimpses which were afforded them of a love which passes knowledge, a love which comprehends all men and all things within its grasp? One can only judge of what was passing within them by the patience, hope, gentleness, self-sacrifice, which they shed forth around them. These were tokens, not to be mistaken, that they were drinking into a divine life; that it was the life of Him Who bore the Cross and denied Himself; that it was the life of that Father Whom He trusted, and Who dwelt in Him.

For St. John goes on, '*And this is the promise that He hath promised us, even eternal life.*' In my second Lecture I dwelt on these words, *eternal life*. I endeavoured to make you see that the life which Christ manifested, the life of perfect truth, justice, charity, cannot belong to time; that it would be the greatest absurdity to measure it by hours and days and years. Our consciences and reasons utterly repudiate such a contradiction. How, then, shall we speak of it? St. John supplies us with the word. He calls it the *eternal* life. If it is the life of God, it must be that; if it is not the life of God, we deny his first proposition, that Jesus Christ, the Son of God, came to set forth the life of God. What St. John would have us feel is, that there can be no promise to compare with this; that we should share the eternal life, the life of God — every other must look pale and paltry beside it. This might appear a self-evident proposition, and yet there is none which we are so apt to set at nought in practice. We often speak as if people were to be paid for being good; not as if the being good were itself God's highest gift and blessing. Such an opinion comes from our not thinking of God Himself as the good and the true Being, or else from our not thinking that He has made us capable of entering into His goodness and knowing His truth. The Bible from first to last is proclaiming that it is possible to know Him and to be like Him, that this is the end which men are to desire and expect, and that they cannot be content with any lower end. '*When I awake up after Thy likeness, I shall be satisfied with it,*' says the Psalmist. St. John is unfolding to us the meaning of that verse, and is telling us in Whom it is that we may see God's likeness; Who is opening the eyes of our spirit that we may see it.

'*These things,*' he continues, '*have I written to you concerning them that seduce you.*' He had written to them concerning the Father and the Son, because the new teachers were drawing them from their allegiance to Jesus, Who had glorified His Father, and had set up Christs, who came in their own name, and sought their own glory. He had written to them about that which they had heard from the beginning, because these teachers said that their early lessons were obsolete, and that grown men must discard them. He had written to them of their abiding in their family fellowship, because these teachers, under pretence of giving them sublimer lore, would have led them to separate themselves from each other, and not to claim the blessing of a common life. And he had written to them concerning the promise of eternal life, because, in refusing the common life of men, he was sure they were also refusing the eternal life of God. They would not have the jewels which shall shine for ever in God's crown, graciousness, self-sacrifice, sympathy. They would have those counterfeit jewels which glitter in the world's twilight, and which will be shown to be worthless when the day appears.

'*But the anointing*,' says St. John, '*which ye have received of Him abideth in you, and ye need not that any man teach you: but as the same anointing teacheth you of all things, and is truth, and is no lie, and even as it hath taught you, ye shall abide in Him.*' I spoke, the last time we met, of that '*unction from the Holy One, by which*,' as he says in the 20th verse, '*they knew all things*.' I maintained that this language, which sounds so strange to some of us, was strictly true language; language not belonging to that time more than to ours; language, the force of which we recognise every time we speak of the discernment which simple and pure women and men have of what is good and evil, of what is sincere and artificial. Nevertheless, I cannot pass over this verse, for it presents the subject in a new light, and it has a peculiar application to the seducers and antichrists whom he has been exposing. They boasted to be anointed with a spirit which separated them from other men, which endued them with such a power and a wisdom as God had not been pleased to bestow on other men. St. John speaks of an anointing which all had received, which abided with the whole Church; which every member of it might trust in if he did *not* seek to be

M

anything in himself, if he did not wish to be above his brethren. In a Psalm with which St. John had been familiar from his childhood, we read these words, '*Behold, how good and pleasant a thing it is for brethren to dwell together in unity! It is like the precious ointment upon the head, that ran down upon the beard, even unto Aaron's beard; that went down to the skirts of his garments. As the dew of Hermon, and as the dew that descended upon the mountains of Sion, for there the Lord promised His blessing, and life for evermore.*' I dare to say this Psalm has sometimes puzzled you. What has the unity among brethren to do with the ointment that was poured upon Aaron's head? Why is that comparison joined to another that seems so much more beautiful, about the morning dew on the hills? How is any illustration of the nature of unity to be derived from that? The writer of the Psalm regarded the anointing oil which was poured upon the high priest as a symbol and pledge that God had adopted and consecrated the whole nation of Israel. He was sure that the priest was not to be looked upon as a separate being, set up in *contrast* to the rest of the people. The running down of the ointment to the skirts of the garments was a sign that the great gift to the priest was a gift also to the people. It was a *greater* gift to them than if it had not been bestowed first upon him, for now they could feel that it was for all; that it united them; that it denoted them to be one nation. The thought of this unity fills the Psalmist's heart with joy. He is sure it is God's unity, not man's. Oils and unguents in the East had a virtue which we do not commonly attach to them. They were associated with life and strength of limb, with the energy to run and to fight. All these the Psalmist connects with unity. The nation is crippled, helpless, dead, when it is disunited. God's oil is to quicken and restore each separate member of it, and the whole body. And then the natural emblem comes in to assist and expand his contemplations. How dry and dead these hills would be if it were not for the dew which comes down every morning to moisten them! What life, what continually renewing life, there is in that! How all things spring up and flourish together under its influence! Is God's dew for grass and flowers? Is there not a more precious dew for the dry and thirsty spirits of men? Is not that what must bind them into one?

So the old Psalmist thought and sung. How could St. John apply his words now that the office of the high priest at Jerusalem had become utterly degraded, if it had not ceased altogether; now that there was no unity, but the most frightful division and hatred in the Jewish Church, if it had not actually been deprived of its capital and its temple? He believed that Jesus being the Son of God and the Son of Man was the real high priest of the universe; that He had received the true anointing, the Divine Spirit of His Father; that this Spirit had not been poured on Him alone, but had run down to the skirts of His garments; that He was raised on high that men on earth might be filled with it. Because this Spirit of Christ, the anointed one, was present with them; because God had promised that it should be renewed in them day by day, as the dew fell every day upon the hills; therefore they could, as brethren, dwell together in unity; therefore the Church could live on amidst all the powers, seen and unseen, which were threatening to destroy it.

You see, then, the force of the Apostle's words. 'Ye 'have received this anointing; this Spirit does abide in 'you; and you have the highest, most perfect of all teachers 'with you at every moment. He can enable you to dispense 'with other teaching. He alone can make other teaching 'profitable to you. For He does not deceive you. He is 'the Spirit of Truth. He does not pretend to dwell with us 'and then desert us. The more you are willing to be under 'His guidance, the more you will be guided by Him, the 'more you will find that peace of God which the world 'cannot give, and which all its tribulations and all its 'temptations cannot take away.'

Some people will maintain that these words about an anointing, a Divine Teacher, a Spirit of Truth, were very suitable to the apostolic age, but do not concern us. I believe that the apostolic age was simply the witness of the treasures that are bestowed upon all ages. It was a witness that all powers of healing, of speech, of government, by whomsoever they are exercised, proceed from the Spirit of God, and are the signs of His presence with men. It was a witness that this Holy Spirit of God is greater than all other gifts, and that we, in our ignorance, feebleness, and despondency, may call Him to our aid, and may be sure that we do not call in vain. The men of the apostolic age had the same difficulty that we have in believing this; signs and wonders could not make them believe it; signs and wonders could not make us believe it; they were led to this faith by the perplexities of their consciences, by the confusions of their understandings, by the weariness and longings of their hearts: that same experience will lead us to it also.

I know not who want it so much as we do. For when were people so divided? When was there less of that dwelling together in unity which the Psalmist pronounced to be so good and comely? And surely all the arguments and arrangements in the universe will not bring it one whit nearer to us. We shall become more and more separate, each man will shut himself more closely in his own notions, conceits, and selfish pursuits, until we all own that we require the Spirit of God, of Unity, to keep us one. Then we shall find that He who has breathed into our nostrils the breath of life, does not deny us this more needful breath, this deeper life.

The two last verses of this chapter belong, I think, to a new subject, and are more properly connected with the opening verse of the following one. They are, no doubt, also closely connected with these of which I have spoken to-day; for the Epistle is a continuous work, and each doctrine in Christian ethics leads on to the next. But there is a pause, it strikes me, at the 27th verse, and I shall stop there. Many would say that I have not been occupied to-day with a question of morals at all, but with a question of theology. To speak of the union of the Father and the Son, and of an Anointing Spirit who testifies of both, is to speak, they would tell me, of a topic which has occasioned more controversy than any other, which has given rise to greater divisions. Perhaps they will quote against me the lines of Pope—

> 'For forms of faith let graceless zealots fight,
> He can't be wrong whose life is in the right.'

And I, for my part, should be very glad to hear those lines produced, and to accept them as the utterance of a great truth. For, if I have not failed wholly to express the mind of St. John, I have shown you that it is Life we want; that everything is worthless except that. He denounces those who had separated from them only because they refused the humble life of Jesus, and preferred a proud, self-exalting life of their own. It is the life of a Son, a filial life, which he desires we should all possess; it is a life which does not exclude one human creature from its blessedness. That we rise into theology when we seek for this life, I have confessed from the first; for theology means the teaching or word concerning God; and St. John's teaching or word concerning God is, that this loving universal life is His; and that He has made us partakers of it. But if we rise into theology, it is not that we may bring ourselves into a circle of notions, opinions, dogmas; it is that we may escape from them; it is that we may drop the forms and conceits of our mind, as the butterfly drops the chrysalis in which it has been buried. I know that there have been endless controversies about the Unity of the Father and the Son in the Spirit. These controversies have, I think, all served to show what a deep, all-embracing unity it is; how it takes up our different thoughts and conceptions into itself; how we enter into it most when we are most seeking for union and fellowship with all our brethren; with the God who in His well-beloved Son adopts them and us as His children. He who is proud and contentious, *i. e.* whose life is in the wrong, will certainly never acknowledge the Son and the Father as St. John acknowledges them, however accurately he may pronounce the creed respecting them. For he will have another spirit than that uniting reconciling Spirit, to which St. John declares that God in Christ has anointed us. And he who is humble and earnest, *i. e.* whose life is in the right, will find the Father and the Son, and will at last abide in them, however much he may be perplexed about the Articles of the Creed, because the Spirit of the Father and Son has bestowed that true mind upon him, and will guide him into all truth.

LECTURE XI.

HOPE; ITS GROUND, OBJECT, AND EFFECT.

1 John II. 28 29 · III. 1—6.

And now, little children, abide in Him; that, when He shall appear, we may have confidence, and not be ashamed before Him at His coming. If ye know that He is righteous, ye know that every one that doeth righteousness is born of Him. Behold, what manner of love the Father hath bestowed upon us, that we should be called the sons of God: therefore the world knoweth us not, because it knew Him not. Beloved, now are we the sons of God, and it doth not yet appear what we shall be: but we know that, when He shall appear, we shall be like Him; for we shall see Him as He is. And every man that hath this hope in him purifieth himself, even as he is pure. Whosoever committeth sin transgresseth also the law: for sin is the transgression of the law. And ye know that He was manifested to take away our sins; and in Him is no sin. Whosoever abideth in Him sinneth not: whosoever sinneth hath not seen Him, neither known Him.

ST. JOHN is speaking to his little children as to human beings. He wants them to exercise their proper human privileges. What are these? To eat, to drink, to sleep? or, to remember, to trust, to hope? The first belong to us as animals; the others belong to us as men. The first support the life which each of us has apart from his neighbours; the others are exercises of the life which we have in common, which bind us as man to man. Are these exercises then to be less habitual, less substantial than those? Have they not much more to do with our own very selves? Do they not require as much direction that they may not miss their proper object?

May they not have *many* objects? May I not remember many friends; trust many promises; hope for many blessings that I have not yet? Assuredly, the more memory, the more trust, the more hope the better. The fear is lest they should wither and perish, not lest they should expand too much or find too many outlets. And we know from bitter experience that they do wither and perish, that there is a tendency in us all to forget, to be distrustful, to despair. Disappointments which we meet with from other men, and still more from ourselves, the loss of the spring of youth that was once in us, the presence of petty cares, the anticipation of coming evils, the sense of evils committed, all are stealing away hour by hour something of our human life. You have seen, perhaps, a man surrounded by all possible outward comforts and luxuries; he has grown old in the midst of them; they have become necessaries to him, of which he does not think, but complains bitterly if he misses any of them. You have seen him girt round by comforts, yet he is altogether without comfort; his heart is dried up within him; his countenance exhibits a vague, vacant longing for something that he has not; everything that he has is weariness and vexation to him; he cares for nothing and no person. The man seems to be gone. Yet he had a mother, who nursed him and watched over him; sisters; perhaps a wife, and children. He may even have friends, who remember him as a cordial companion, full of merriment, intelligence, wit; and who still cleave to him, now that he is only the shadow of what he was. Such a man is a spectacle and a warning to us all. There is nothing in us which there was not in him; he may have had more glow of heart, more of benevolence and geniality than we can boast of. Medical men, who meet with a multitude of such cases, often ask how we can reconcile them with our belief in man's immortality; 'for do we not 'see here,' they say, 'an end, not of the body's life, but of 'the soul's life, of all that is worth preserving in this world 'or any other?'

To such questions I should be unable to make any answer, or to the still more awful questions which present themselves to me, when I think of the spiritual death which I have found in myself, if I did not receive that message which St. John delivered, respecting a Fountain of Life—a divine life from which human life is derived, by which its springs may be renewed, in which it can find its full repose and satisfaction. The words '*Little children, abide in Him*,' are the simplest encouragement to remember that Christ is this Fountain of Life for every man, to trust in Him, to hope in Him. The word '*abide*' denotes that we are united to Him; but that it is in our power to deny that we are, and to act as if we were independent of Him. In the fifteenth chapter of St. John's Gospel that truth is illustrated with great fulness. Our Lord says to His disciples, as they walk towards the Mount of Olives, after the last Passover, '*I am the Vine, ye are the branches. As the branch cannot bear fruit, except it abide in the vine; no more can ye, except ye abide in Me.*' The branch has no power to sever itself from the vine; but it may be severed by some accident; then it withers and dies. That is the condition of a natural thing. The man has power to sever himself from the Being who is the spring of all his memory, trust. hopes; he *can* say, 'I will try to live by myself and to 'myself.' That is the condition of a voluntary or spiritual being. But he *need* not say this. He may abide in his true proper state. And if he has not done so, if he has struggled to be independent, he may give up that struggle; he may discover that it is a vain struggle; he may learn from the pricking of his conscience that there is One mightier than himself whom he has been fighting against. He may learn what that Friend is; he may turn to Him and say, 'I desire to abide henceforth in Thee, for I have ' no strength, no life or goodness of my own.' This is what St. Paul did when he found, on his way to Damascus, that the Jesus whom he had persecuted was his true Lord. All who received the message of the Gospel from the Apostles, whether Jews or Greeks, did this. They were told that the Lord of their spirits had taken their flesh and had come amongst them, that he might deliver them from their tyrants, and claim them as His subjects and liegemen. They were told that they might turn to Him, and trust in Him, and abide in Him. They had wanted such a Deliverer, such a Lord, such a Brother. They were sure it was not a delusion that they had one. The more they acted on this faith, the more they were sure that it was not.

Every exhortation, then, of their teachers—if those teachers were true to their calling—had this burden: 'Abide ' in Him. Do not forget what you are. Do not forego your ' rights. Do not sink back into the condition of animals.' This exhortation is strengthened here by the argument:

'That when He shall appear ye may have confidence, and not be ashamed before Him at His coming.' I said that the Apostles expected a speedy appearing or manifestation of Jesus as the Judge of their nation and of all nations. I said also that they regarded every judgment upon their own nation or upon any nation in that age, or any age, as a manifestation or appearing of Jesus Christ. They believed Him to be the King of the World; they could not doubt that what we describe as crises or revolutions in the condition of society were, in very deed, discoveries of His purposes, the destruction of something which had interfered with them. Such a doctrine was involved in the belief which they had in Him as the Son of Man. But that same belief obliged them to suppose that a very thin veil is interposed between us and Him, and that when we shut our eyes upon this world that veil is removed. Then the outsides of the world which present themselves to our senses will vanish; the substantial principles and realities which the eye cannot see, but which the spirit confesses and believes in, will stand forth. Christ the Lord of our own selves will appear, when those things that have only been surrounding us disappear. When He does so appear, must it not be a terrible shock to those who have dwelt in the things which are fading away, whose hearts have known no home except them? Must there not be a sense of strangeness, of utter dissonancy, when He of whom we have thought nothing here, whom we have put away as far as we could, is known to be the ground of our being, the Life apart from which there is no life? What words can be used to describe that awakening? St. John's are the best words and the simplest and truest—though they are not those which a rhetorician would make use of. He speaks of being '*ashamed*' at His appearing. 'He has been 'with us ever since we began to exist, and we knew it not! 'He has been doing us good, and we turned away from 'Him! He has been tempting us into the light, and we 'chose the darkness.' Yes! infinite shame, the remorse for a self-chosen alienation,—does not that exceed all the mere outward horror which the fancy pictures to itself; do we not feel *that* is no picture—*that* is reality?

But St. John speaks to his disciples of their *not* being ashamed before Him at His coming, of having confidence in Him. This would be the effect of that abiding in Him to which he has urged them; so they would acquire a growing trust in Him to whom they were attached. Every step in their experience would deepen it. The accidents of the world which seem contrived to alienate them from it, would drive them to it. Their own weakness, ignorance, sinfulness, would be a perpetual excuse and warrant for it. They would be sure that God Himself was grafting them by all His discipline into that root which alone could cause them to bear fruit. What is there, in the event of death, to shake that confidence? What is the truth to which they awaken, but that which has been every hour becoming more certain to them? It is but the full life of which they had been sipping draughts from time to time. It is but the light to which they had been continually turning from their own darkness.

But our Apostle is never satisfied with emblems, not even with such beautiful emblems as that of the vine and the branches. His meaning is altogether practical. He wants men to be doing righteous, honest acts. He knows it is very hard to do such acts, that there are ten thousand temptations not to do them, but to change them for mere words or professions. So he explains in the 29th verse what he has been saying before, by adding, '*We know that if He is righteous, every one that doeth righteousness is born of Him.*' Righteous acts spring from a righteous person, as sound healthy branches proceed from a sound healthy root. When he speaks of Christ as the root in which we are to abide, he means that He is the righteous Lord, by fellowship with whom we may be able to do righteousness. He has no notion of divine knowledge which does not lead to this result. As I have said so often, he never separates knowledge from life.

But you observe, he changes his form of expression in the last verse. He leaves natural symbols; he begins to talk of human relations. 'He that doeth righteousness is *born* of Him.' Such a man has the signs of a heavenly parentage; he has a birth from above. Is it that he has earned his relation to God by doing righteous acts? Has he made himself God's child by some services which he has rendered to Him? No! these are the world's ethics; in these lies that self-righteousness which the Bible denounces, and which the conscience in us revolts against. Christian ethics proceed on the opposite principle. We do not attach ourselves to Christ by performing righteous acts. We are able to perform righteous acts because we are attached to Him. We do not become God's children because we are good; but being the children of a good God, we can be like our Father in heaven.

You see, therefore, how the first verse of the next chapter is connected with this: '*Behold, what manner of love the*

Father hath bestowed upon us, that we should be called the sons of God: therefore the world knoweth us not, because it knew Him not. 'Born of Him,' — think what that means. It means nothing less than this: — 'God, of ' His own free and infinite love, calls you His children, ' claims you as His children, in His only begotten Son. ' Wonder at that announcement as much as you can. Refer ' your state to God altogether, not the least to yourselves. ' See in it the proof of what He is. But do not deny it; ' for so you deny that you can do what is right, what the ' righteous God would have you do. Say not that it is ' impossible; for so you say that it is impossible for you ' not to be unrighteous; untrue men. And remember ' always that this relation is one between God and your ' spirits; hidden, therefore, from the world; not to be ' recognised by those who see with the world's eyes. If ' you have ever been disposed to complain that you are not ' understood when you are acting as God's children, seeking ' to obey His will, nay, that the very notion of your being ' connected with a spiritual family and a spiritual Father ' is scouted as ridiculous; then remember that He who was ' called the Only Begotten Son, the well beloved Son—that ' elder brother in whom we are united, and through whom ' we claim our filial rights—was unknown to the world, ' mistaken by the world, for precisely the same reason, be-' cause He spake of a Father, trusted a Father, lived in a ' Father.'

That, as St. John shows us in his Gospel, was not merely *a* cause why the Pharisees, the leaders of the Jewish religious world, misunderstood Him and reviled Him, but *the* cause. '*They knew not*,' he says, '*that He* 'spake of the Father.' ' They have hated,' Christ says, ' both me and my Father.'

'*Beloved*,' the Apostle continues, '*now are we the sons of God, and it doth not yet appear what we shall be, but we know that when He is manifested, we shall be like Him, for we shall see Him as He is.*' It was a continual temptation to men in the first age, as it is now, to think that they were not the sons of God, that they had no right to claim so high a title. Every time they committed any transgression against God's law, every time they forgot the duties which they owed to their brethren, the thought would arise in their hearts, ' Our state is changed; we have no ' longer a right to that name which betokens a resemblance ' to God, or sympathy with Him; it may be recovered, but ' for the present it is lost.' There was the greatest plausibility in this opinion; it seemed to savour of a becoming humility; it might be justified by the words of holy men, even of St. John himself. And yet it was fatal to all morality; for as I have been saying, to do righteous acts we must be in fellowship with the righteous God; it ministered to the greatest pride and self-righteousness, for it was by the man's own acts, done when he was in an evil state, that he must entitle himself to God's favour, and recover His gifts; whatever texts might be twisted into the support of it, practically it condemned the whole Gospel which the Apostles had preached, the baptism with which they were sent to baptize the nations. Therefore he presses the assurance upon them, '*Now are we the sons of God.*' This faith we must hold fast, for this is the ground of all the good works which God would work in us. We must not suffer any to persuade us, that this is a future or possible blessing, and not one that has been conferred on us already. Not as if there were *no* future blessings; not as if the love of the Father had exhausted itself in the act of adopting us. There are good things behind the veil, which eye hath not seen, ear hath not heard, it hath not entered into the heart of man to conceive. We are to be raised to a higher and nobler condition of being; how high, how noble, doth not yet appear. But we do know the kind of good that is in reserve for us, though we do not know the measure or extent of it. *'We know that when He is manifested, we shall be like Him; for we shall see Him as He is.'* That is included in our being God's children; the promise of beholding Him in whose image we are made; the promise of really reflecting that image, instead of any meaner or baser image.

St. John, you see, has not forgotten the subject of Christ's appearing, whilst he has been reminding the Ephesians of their sonship to God. That appearing is to give them the inheritance which is consequent on their divine birth; that is the manifestation which is to make them what they are intended to be, by showing them what God is. He regards this appearing or manifestation of Christ as not less certain than the appearing or manifestation of the sun in the morning. One he holds to be just as much implied in the constitution of the moral world as the other is in the constitution of the physical world. One, therefore, may be hoped for just as much as the other. When we say at night, 'We hope the sun will rise to-morrow,' we do not express any doubt that he will rise; we merely mean that at present he is set. When I say, 'I hope I snall see the sun to-morrow,' I speak more doubtfully, for my eyes may be closed on the earth which he illuminates. But in speaking of Christ's manifestation, the Apostle has no occasion to make this distinction. He believes that Christ rules here and everywhere; that He is the Light of men on this side of death and on the other; but that there His Light will be confessed, not hidden; that there none will be able to shut it out, if they dislike it ever so much.

According to the Ethics in Pope's 'Essay on Man,'—

> 'Hope springs immortal in the human breast,
> Man never is, but always to be blest.'

There is a truth in that statement; the experience of the world shows how it has been kept alive by hope; how men have always been pursuing some object or another; how it seems always to be a little in advance of them, like the end of the rainbow of the boy who is in chase of it. The poet is right in speaking of hope as immortal. It is he very witness and pledge of immortality; to be without it is the sign of death. And yet there is something unspeakably sad in such a view of human existence; that we are cheated into the only good which is possible for us; that what is, has no worth; that shadows have more power over us than substances; that if we could only know the truth of things, we should fold our hands and give over all earnestness and enterprise. Alas! I sometimes think we are not very unlikely to make that experiment. When I see the listless faces of some of our young men, and hear them declare that they have exhausted all sources of enjoyment, almost before the down is off their cheeks, it seems as if we might be permitted to try whether we shall be more sincere and less frivolous, when we no longer anticipate good from anything to come; when we have armed ourselves against disappointment by giving up hope.

Depend upon it, there is no frivolity, there is no insincerity, like that into which a nation falls, when this kind of exhaustion overtakes it; there is no such terrible curse for a man. The only resources left for either are the dicebox and the bottle; one to keep up that excitement which is the bastard form of hope; the other to produce unconsciousness and torpor. But how can these perils which are threatening us so very nearly, be escaped? I believe we must turn from Pope's or Bolingbroke's Ethics to St. John's, that we may find why 'hope springs immortal in the human breast;' that we may perceive how the blessedness which is to be, has a ground in the blessedness that is. '*Now are we the sons of God*,' is the revelation of that ground. That is the true glory of man, the glory which Christ has vindicated for him by taking his nature; a glory which overshadows prince and beggar; a glory which, ever since the Gospel has been received in our land, we have declared to be the possession of little children. But that possession is the commencement of a long hope. The discovery of a Father is not like the discovery of a bag of gold, which we can hold fast against all claimants, and which enables us to eat, drink, and be merry. It is the opening of worlds which that Father has called into existence, which He invites us to explore, of which each may investigate some little portion; of which, after ages upon ages, the wisest will only know a little. It is the opening of wonders deeper than these worlds contain; the wonders of His mind and purpose who created them; depths of love, in which men and angels must be content to be lost. '*We shall see Him as He is,*' is the short summary, the only one that can be given of this future revelation; with which man can never say that he is, but always that he is to be blest, because there will be something beyond what he has apprehended, for which what he has apprehended makes him long.

This hope, then, is infinite; but it never can be disappointing, because it is the hope of conversing more with realities, of escaping more from what is fantastic and unreal. St. John attributes to it another, even a higher virtue: '*He that hath this hope in him purifieth himself even as He is pure.*' In the Ethics of the world, especially in those which Christian men have borrowed from the world, hope is often treated as dangerous. 'We must 'beware,' it is said, 'of encouraging men to hope too 'much; when they have attained a higher standard of 'moral purity and excellence, then we may speak to them 'of the rewards which God has prepared for those who 'love Him; till then we should keep them in doubt and 'uncertainty.' There is so much truth sprinkled over the outside of this language, as to hide the subtle poison which is within it. St. John makes hope the means, the only means, of purification. Without hope, he intimates, we cannot be pure. And why? All purity comes from the God of Purity; the more we aspire to be like Him, the more we aspire after purity; we cannot aspire unless we believe that it is His will we should be like Him; unless we believe that this is the end and fruition to which He is leading us. What harm can it do any human being to tell him that he may hope to rise out of evil; that he may hope to be a righteous man? 'Oh,' you say, 'but

' that is not what he hopes for; he is expecting quite a
' different reward from that.' Then, the sooner you tell him
what reward is prepared for him—what reward he may
be sure of, if he does not refuse to desire it, the better.
That is the way to cure him of his delusions. Yes! and
whatever experienced people may say to the contrary, that
is the way to meet the inmost longing of his heart. He
may not be conscious of it; he may think he wishes
for a stone, but in very deed what he wishes for is bread.
The hope that is springing immortal in his heart—the
hope that he has been unable to quench, though he has
tried to quench it, at many a sweet and many a bitter
water, is the hope of being himself better; of some day
casting his slough; of some day rising up a real man. You
answer what he means, though not perhaps what he says,
when you tell him of this hope which maketh not ashamed,
when you tell him that he may and shall find all in God
which he has failed to find in the world or in himself.

No doubt men exclaimed then, as they may exclaim now,
'What! you would invite transgressors—people who have
broken God's law—to hope! How audacious!' St. John
anticipates the objection: '*Every one that doeth sin transgresseth also the law. And sin is the transgression of the law. And ye know that He was manifested to take away our sins, and in Him is no sin. And every one that abideth in Him sinneth not. He that sinneth hath not seen Him, neither known Him.*' As if he had said, 'If I want to
' hinder transgression, that is the breach of law, I must get
' rid of *sin*, for that leads to all breaches of law; that is *the*
' departure from God's eternal law. Well! Christ was
' manifested for this very end; that He might deliver us

'from sin, from the very root of transgression; from the inward disease of which my transgression is the outward symptom. *And in Him is no sin.* When, therefore, I bid men hope to see Him, I bid them hope to be free from the principle which issues in the offences that the law condemns. Not to see Him, not to know Him is the cause of sin. To see Him, to know Him, is the emancipation from it.'

A very deep and wide-spreading principle, which St. John enunciates in the most fearless manner. At first it sounds alarming to be told that *'Every one that sinneth hath not seen Him, nor known Him.'* For he said before, *'If we say that we have no sin, we deceive ourselves, and the truth is not in us.'* And again, *'If any man sin, we have an advocate with the Father, Jesus Christ the Righteous.'* But he is not contradicting himself. What he is saying is that sin and the sight or knowledge of Christ are antagonistic. The act of sin is the act of shutting our eyes to the true Lord and Deliverer; if we had kept our eyes open, if we had seen and confessed Him, we should not have sinned. This is a truth, and it is an universal truth. It cuts away the pretences of those who call themselves Christians or believers, and make that an excuse for committing sins, because they say God does not treat sins in them as He does in other people. St. John destroys lies and blasphemies of this kind. He affirms once for all, that a man is not a believer, not a Christian, who does any unrighteous and foul acts. But he in nowise hinders any man whatsoever from confessing his sin and betaking himself once more to that hope in God which makes pure.

There is no part of Christian Ethics more profoundly

important than this; none on which we are more liable to make mistakes. I have tried to follow St. John step by step, and not to put my own foolish thoughts and interpretations between you and him. I cannot tell you how many of these foolish thoughts and interpretations his words have laid bare in me, and I trust have scattered. If I did not know how much I am inclined every day to doubt whether I have a right to call God my Father, I should never have found how necessary that faith is to you and to all men; if I had not learnt in myself how hard it is to hope, and how much impurity follows from the loss of hope, I should never have had courage to press it upon you and upon all as at once the divinest privilege and the most sacred duty.

LECTURE XII.

THE DEVIL AND HIS WORKS.

1 JOHN III. 7—11.

Little children, let no man deceive you: he that doeth righteousness is righteous, even as He is righteous. He that committeth sin is of the devil; for the devil sinneth from the beginning. For this purpose the Son of God was manifested, that He might destroy the works of the devil. Whosoever is born of God doth not commit sin; for his seed remaineth in him: and he cannot sin, because he is born of God. In this the children of God are manifest, and the children of the devil: whosoever doeth not righteousness is not of God, neither he that loveth not his brother. For this is the message that ye heard from the beginning, that we should love one another.

I HAVE spoken to you already of the teachers who boasted that they had a knowledge of divine mysteries to which vulgar Christians could make no pretensions. They were the initiated; the rest were novices. Simple people, the little children of the flock, were likely to be much staggered by such lofty words. Their humility made them think that they deserved the contemptuous treatment which was bestowed on them; they could not tell that the others might not have the profound insight for which they gave themselves credit. The old Apostle speaks to them with a confidence which they felt he at least had a right to assume. '*Little children, let no man deceive you: he that doeth righteousness is righteous, even as He is righteous.*' 'Knowledge, you are told, is the thing to be chiefly de-

'sired. Even so. Knowledge of the Righteous One;
'knowledge of Him who makes us righteous. And doing
'righteousness—sincere, just, truthful acts,—are the results
'and signs of this knowledge. They show whether we
'have this knowledge or are without it.' He comes back
to the test which these self-exalting doctors wished to get
rid of; the severest test; the most levelling test. But by
coming back to it, he vindicates a higher knowledge for the
humblest disciples than that which those who refused to be
reckoned among mere disciples could claim for themselves.
The knowledge of Christ, as the standard of all righteousness, he declares to be the heritage of them all; a knowledge involving practice, and advancing as it advances.

He has told them what will make them righteous; fellowship or intercourse with a Righteous Lord of their spirits. He goes on to tell them how they become sinful; viz. by holding intercourse with an unrighteous spirit, by submitting to him as their Lord. '*He that committeth sin is of the Devil, for the Devil sinneth from the beginning.*' The word 'Diabolos' means Accuser or Slanderer. What he says, giving his words their most literal sense, is, that one who sins or goes astray from God does so by listening to the voice of a spirit who accuses or slanders God. I have often been told by persons whose learning I respect, that this is the doctrine of an old Jew, which we in the nineteenth century have long outlived. They speak, no doubt, for themselves; they mean that there are no facts in their own experience, to which this doctrine of the old Jew corresponds. If it were so with me, I should be silent. For I have found so much in my own mind which his teaching has explained, which I could not have understood without it, that I should think he was probably right where I could not follow him, and that hereafter he might discover something to me which was now hidden from me. But I cannot pretend that this is the case. What he said to the Ephesians about this Accuser does answer to the inmost witness of my conscience.

I know that I did not learn this doctrine by the precept of men. I was not taught it in my childhood; those I reverenced, and still reverence, considered it a fable. As I grew up, I felt the same motives to retain that opinion which act upon many of my contemporaries. The notion of a Devil was associated in my mind with many superstitions which science had confuted; it was held by vulgar people among whom I did not wish to be reckoned. It was quite possible, if I cared for that, to pass muster with the orthodox and respectable, though I was sceptical on this point. But there are some things which are more terrible than being confounded with vulgar people. It is more terrible not to be honest with oneself. It is more terrible to think that one is given over hopelessly to work iniquity. It is more terrible to be cut off from all fellowship with human beings, if they are vulgar.

Now there come to me every day whispers not received through the ear but heard in the heart, that God is not the Being whom Jesus Christ manifested; not a Righteous and True Being; not one whom I may trust; not one who means good to me and to my brethren; not one who cares that I should do right, or who will give me strength to do right. With these whispers come others also very strange, against persons whom I know, persons, possibly, who have done me wrong, quite as likely persons who have done me nothing but good; suspicions of their kindness; doubts of their character; hints that they may be plotting something very evil. Then there are whispers more directly affecting oneself; incitements to think foully and to feel foully; to be malicious against those to whom one owes only forgiveness, affection, gratitude.

It may be that this experience is a peculiar one; but I do not believe it is. I find people of the most opposite characters, living in the most different circumstances, who report the same things of themselves. I read of horrible thoughts of jealousy coming over this mind, horrible thoughts of ambition into that,—and of murder being the result of both. It is, of course, the most natural solution in the world to say, 'Oh! these suggestions proceeded from some ' vile servant or companion.' Possibly they did; but like words from that servant and companion might have gone in at one ear, as we say, and out at the other; they might have been repulsed indignantly; how did they get the dominion over *me*, over my spirit? 'Oh! that was your ' own fault; that shows that *you* were to blame.' There is no question that I was to blame wherever the suggestion came from. I know that well enough. No one who has had such thoughts, unless he is a miserable self-deceiver, can shift the blame from himself; he must take it home to himself. But did the thoughts originate with me? I could not say so to please any theorist, or to get credit for ever so much liberality and wisdom. I might have rejected the thoughts, but they were presented to me. I may bewilder myself—all men have bewildered themselves at some time or other, by saying, ' I shuffled the cards, I played both hands;' but it will not do; it is not a fair representation of the facts: to a man in earnest, it is a quite maddening explanation of them. Did they, then, originate with some other mortal? It is the same story again. If he is making his confession on his death-bed, he too will speak of the thought having been in some way offered to him. He knows then that this does not make the case better for him; but he uses the language because it is the only natural language; the only language which sets forth the thing as it was.

Let me repeat what I have said once again. St. John never for a moment says or dreams that he who commits sin, commits it because the devil or the accuser *obliges* him to do it. The thought of being obliged or forced is not only not implied in his words; it is contradicted by them. The names Tempter and Accuser do not indicate it; the word *Sin* excludes it. That must belong to the man himself. I have shown you in a former Lecture how inseparably it is connected with *choice* and with *conscience, i.e.* with the man's own self. What the Apostle does say, is that sin comes from contact or fellowship between our spirit and a sinful spirit; that to commit sin is to become his liegemen, his bondsmen. Do you think I shall assert my responsibility for my own acts more strongly if I throw St. John's doctrine overboard? It seems to me that I shall *then* be in the greatest danger of denying my responsibility. I shall fancy that sin is so much a part of me, so much implied in my existence, that I cannot escape it Under the words, *my inclination, my tendency, my disposition*, there will lurk all excuses for wrong doing, and at the same time the most utter despair of reformation. And *they* must cut me off from my fellow creatures.

The inclination, tendency, disposition, which is strong in some of you, is perhaps weak in me; that which is strong in me, is weak in you. Each tries to make out a case for himself; each pleads that *his* infirmity is irresistible; each looks hardly upon his neighbour's of which he knows nothing. It is no fancy—you know that it is what we are all tempted to do continually. It is the secret of the intolerance and want of sympathy among us; it is the secret of our hugging our own vices till they destroy us. But if we heartily believed that we had a common enemy plotting against us all, making use of every man's peculiar gift or characteristic which is meant for his blessing, to work his ruin, accusing our Father in heaven to us all, accusing every brother to another; persuading each of us that he is not a child of God, that he does not belong to a family of brothers; should we indulge this miserable tenderness of that which is preying upon our own vitals, should we indulge our cruelty by mocking the diseases and derangements of our brothers? Should we not feel that we had a common fight; that each man who stood his own ground firmly was doing something for all that each might aid some other, even by his wounds and his falls?

He says, '*for the devil sinneth from the beginning.*' Does that mean that sin was from the beginning; that Evil is as old as Good? Think whether that is possible! Does not the very word *sinneth* show that it is impossible? Does not that indicate the departure from an object—the transgression of a Law? There *was* the Object then, there *was* the Law. Whoever sinned first, confessed Good to be; he said that a law was binding him, and that he wished to shake it off. All, then, which can be intended by this expression, '*the devil sinneth from the beginning*,' is that there is a spirit who sinned before man sinned, one who tempted or seduced—(I beseech you to use these words in their common every-day sense, and not to put another sense into them which shall connect them with some kind of compulsion)—one who tempted or seduced men to make the experiment of separating themselves from God, of asserting their independence. The phrase '*from the beginning*' intimates that there has been no period of the existence of human beings in which they have not been liable to the assaults of this Tempter; that accusations against God, reasons for doubting and distrusting Him, have been offered to one man after another, to one generation after another. This is just what the Scripture affirms; just the assumption which goes through the book from Genesis to the Apocalypse.

But though this is true—though the fact of Temptation is implied throughout the Bible, and though its histories signify nothing, if that is not a fact for all men—it is not true that there are frequent allusions to a *one* Tempter, to an Evil Spirit, in the Old Testament. It is not true that St. John speaks so confidently of a Devil because he was a Jew, and was filled with Hebrew opinions. For once that the Devil is introduced into the Law, the Psalms, and the Prophets, he is spoken of twenty times in any single Gospel or Epistle. How is this? St. John tells us in the next clause of this verse: '*For this cause the Son of God was manifested that He might destroy the works of the devil.*' This is the characteristically Gospel or New Testament doctrine. The Son of God has been manifested to answer the accusations against God, which all men have heard and believed, which sorrow, sin, and death, have appeared to confirm; He has manifested them to be slanders; He has shown forth God as He is; the Light in whom is no darkness. He has been manifested to answer the accusations by which man has been separated from man, the cruel whispers and suspicions which are infused into our hearts one against another. He has been manifested as the common Head of our race; in Him only we can see it; in Him only we can know how blessed and glorious a race it is; in Him each man may honour and reverence every other man. He has been manifested to refute the accusations which each of us hears from the Evil Spirit against himself; accusations which cannot be refuted, which our consciences affirm to be true, while we live apart from Christ and try to have a righteousness and life of our own; accusations which we can throw aside as false and calumnious, when we learn to say with St. Paul, 'We are dead indeed unto sin, but alive unto God through Jesus Christ our Lord;—we live, yet not we, but Christ liveth in us.'

Seeing then that it is the New Testament which sets forth the Son of God, *the* complete justifier of God, it is the same New Testament which sets forth the Evil Spirit as *the* accuser of God. Seeing it is the New Testament which sets forth the Son of Man as the complete justifier of Man, it is the New Testament which sets forth the Evil Spirit as the accuser of Man. Seeing it is the New Testament which sets forth the Son of Man as the justifier of each of us from the torments of his own conscience, it is the New Testament which sets forth the Evil Spirit as ever seeking to darken and disturb our consciences. The one revelation confronts the other. The revelation of an author of death would be intolerable if it was not met by a revelation of the Prince of Life. Contemplating them together, they deliver us from that awful question by which the men of the old world were agitated, whether there might not be something of wrong—something to be avoided and fled from—in the character and purposes of the Creator; whether our race might not after all be given up to the curse which it had drawn upon itself; whether any one could dare to say, '*I am not bound and sold to my enemy; for is not that enemy myself?*' If we accept the message which St. John brought to the Ephesians and lay it up in our hearts, we can solve these questions when they present themselves to us in all different and frightful shapes; we can feel that our most personal and inward struggles are yet human struggles; we can rise up and do God's work, knowing that whoever is against us He is on our side.

Then follows the sentence,—'*Whosoever is born of God*,' or rather every one that is born of God, '*doth not commit sin*,' or doeth not sin, '*because his seed abideth in him, and he cannot sin because he is born of God.*' 'How,' you will ask, 'can this be, if what you said last week is true, ' that it is the duty of every man to believe that he is ' born of God; if what you have said now is true that he ' yields to the evil spirit, when he gives up that faith? ' If this is the test of being born of God that a man does ' not sin; can any one of us—(not to say all), claim such ' a dignity?' Exactly; that is the right way of stating the difficulty. This sentence cuts off *all* from that title, if it cuts off *any*. As I reminded you last Sunday, it is not some one else but St. John himself, who tells us that if any man say, he hath no sin, he deceiveth himself, and the truth is not in him; it is St. John himself who says, '*If any man sin, we have an advocate with the Father.*' What he says here—what he was bound to say, unless all his former teaching respecting God was to be void — is, that no evil thought, word, act whatsoever can have God for its author. But the evil acts which I do, proceed from *me*. I cannot shift them upon any one else. How then can I say that *I* am born of God? I do *not* say it; that evil act is a disclaimer of my heavenly birth; here is the greatest proof that it is a lying act. I make myself another man. I choose another parent. Your common language justifies this teaching. You say to a child or a friend, ' It was not your own true self which came out in ' those words and acts. It was a vile counterfeit. Send ' away the changeling! Let me see him whom I love ' again.' St. John gives us the *rationale* of these common expressions. That man, he says, who does the sinful act, is not God's child; *he* cannot sin; the seed out of which *he* is formed is altogether good. What is the practical inference? That every one who has *disclaimed* his true birth by an evil act should *reclaim* it; when ' he comes to ' himself,' this is our Lord's expression, he will remember his true Father; he will say, I will arise and go to Him; he will find His Father on the way to meet him. Before that, he was not himself, he had lost himself.

And now the next verse will explain itself to you without much effort of mine. '*In this the children of God are manifest, and the children of the devil. Whosoever doeth not righteousness, is not of God, neither he that loveth not his brother.*' Sinful acts, words, thoughts, he has declared, cannot have a divine origin. To refer them to the divine seed in a man, is to commit the greatest of all contradictions. But they must have *some* origin; they must spring from *some* seed. What must that be called? It must be called, he affirms, a devilish seed. If, therefore, you see sinful acts and righteous acts coming from the same person, you must say that there is in that person a heavenly seed and a hellish seed. And you must say that a man identifying himself with that hellish seed makes himself a child of the devil, though he ought to count himself a child of God. No fear of a contradiction must lead you to shrink from such a statement as this. The contradiction exists; you cannot destroy it by shutting your eyes to it. But you can produce a most fatal confusion of things eternally distinct, eternally opposed, by refusing to state the case as it is, to whatever perplexity of phrase you may be driven. Herein, and herein only, the children of God and the children of the devil are manifest. Nothing but good comes from good; nothing but evil comes from evil. If you declare that nothing but good comes from any man you meet with on this earth, some startling wrong in him will confute your assertion. If you declare that nothing but evil comes from any man you meet with on this earth, some good which you did not expect will confute that assertion. Be honest, then; do not invent theories to explain away facts. Do not hide the facts under delusive formulas which will stand no searching examination. But let all wickedness, without respect of persons, be assigned to the devil as its parent; let all good, without respect of persons, be assigned to God as its parent. And let each person be encouraged to say, I have no right whatever to acknowledge the evil spirit as my parent. If I have done so, it has been under a dark and horrible infatuation. For in very deed nothing in me is of him, but that which is destroying me. No living powers, energies, affections are from him; only that which extinguishes my powers, energies, and affections, only that which is making me not a man. I have a right to say that God is my parent. For every power, energy, affection, that is awake or slumbering in me, I have received from Him. Jesus Christ has said that He is *His* Father. He has bidden us say, ' *Our* Father.'

St. John is sometimes called the Apostle of Love. That they might give us that impression of him, painters have chosen to represent the last of the Apostles—who must have written all his books in his old age, perhaps in extreme old age—as a beardless youth, with a delicate complexion and a feminine expression. I hope Mr. Ruskin has warned us in this College sufficiently of departures from fact, of false ideals, such as these, by whatsoever great names they have been sanctioned. This mode of conceiving St. John is especially misleading and mischievous. Hitherto in this Epistle he has spoken much of righteousness; only once about men loving each other, and that in connexion with keeping a commandment; only once about God's love to us, and that in connexion with our doing righteousness. His language has been simple and broad; not sentimental at all. He has told us in plain terms of men who lied and did not the truth. His discourse has been that of a father; of a father who would encourage his children, but who, from his care for them, would rather reprove than fondle them. It has been that of a man deeply experienced, not the least of one whose countenance was not furrowed by thought and sorrow. It has been that of one who has known temptations, and has been out in rough weather, not the least of one who has kept himself from contact with evil lest it should spoil his innocence.

I make these remarks here for two reasons. One is that we are coming to that portion of his Epistle in which he does dwell with great particularity upon the love of men for each other and upon the love of God for man; to that portion of it therefore which has won for him this special reputation. I could not enter upon the passages on this subject without warning you that in them, quite as little as in those we have gone through, shall we hear of anything answering to that sentimental love which the artists suppose that he wished to glorify. Love of the brethren, we shall find, is with him a habit or state of mind which leads directly to practice, and is treated as utterly worthless apart from practice. The love of God to man is manifested not in any tenderness to his evil ways, but in bringing him into the right way. The two indications of the offspring of the evil spirit he gives us here are, (1) he doeth not righteousness, (2) he loveth not his brother. We shall find that the two are never separated. Love does not interfere with the strictness of right, but establishes it. Right does not make love less deep, or less universal; apart from right it would be superficial and partial.

These principles are some of the most vital and essential in Christian ethics, and there are none which we are in greater danger of forgetting. If you say to me, 'But what 'do you mean by Right, and Love? how do you distinguish 'one from another? how do you determine when one or 'another is outraged?' I reply, 'These are, indeed, the

'most needful of all inquiries; I hope that I shall not—I
'am sure that the Apostle St. John will not—evade them,
'even if they take the most searching form.' They do *not*
take the most searching form, as I have tried to shew you
before, when you crave for *definitions* of Right and Love.
These it is easy enough to give; different schoolmen could
provide twenty or a hundred at a short notice. What we
want is some help for discerning right from wrong in
the business of every day and hour. What we want is
to know when love or hatred has possession of *us* and is
ruling *us*. When you hear great words like these, words
that are wrought into the heart of every language under
heaven, you know, you positively know, that there are
realities corresponding to them. You cannot take a step
without that assumption; if you try to do it, you will find
that you are unawares thrusting in a notion of right, a
notion of love, which you have framed for yourselves, and
are making *that* the reality. These notions are, indeed,
poor things; we must try to get clear of them in moral
studies as we do in physical, by a steady experimental
pursuit of the truths which are hidden beneath them. I
hope we have gained some help from this Epistle in learning
what that method is, and in applying it; I hope we shall
gain still more hereafter.

I can testify for myself, that no part of it has been of
more use to me, than that of which I have spoken to-day.
And this was my second reason for alluding to the supposed fondness of St. John, for the softer and tenderer side
of morality and of the Gospel. His teaching about the
devil is not at all agreeable to those who dwell exclusively
on the sunny aspects of the world and of life, and would

shut their eyes to whatever is dark and terrible. They like to hear of a Being who is all-gracious and loving; the vision of one who is the enemy of all that is gracious and loving shocks them: they wish to suppose that it belongs to the world's infancy, and that it disappears as we know more of optics, and can distinguish between real forms and the shadows that are thrown from ourselves. Now, I am quite sure that men in other days did confound shadows which were cast from themselves with objects in Nature; that they saw spectres coming towards them which their own fancy—generally their own guilty fancy —had raised; that they feared where no fear was. I am thankful to any natural philosopher who assists in dispelling any of these phantoms; I believe that, in doing so, he is a useful fellow labourer with the moralist and the theologian. For the moralist and the theologian, if he understands his own business, if he follows St. Paul and St. John, asserts, what all these natural discoveries confirm, that it is not among God's works one is to look for shapes and forms of evil; that they are very good; that the sorrow and death which have mingled with them and overshadowed them, come from some other source than themselves; that they are groaning to be delivered from these; that their day of emancipation is coming. Moralists and theologians therefore are driven to account for the evil which they see—and which natural philosophers see— affecting the world and affecting themselves by spiritual not material agencies. I must think of evil as spiritual, as present, as appealing to my spirit, as appealing to me. I cannot deny its presence, or its influence. But if I believe that the spirit who tempts me to be unrighteous is a deceiver and a liar; that he seeks to make me deny a truth which has been manifested, to distrust a goodness which has come forth to redeem and to unite my race,—then I can maintain, hour by hour, the good fight of faith; I can say to the accuser, 'Get thee behind me. I know ' that the Son of God *has* appeared to destroy thy works, ' I know that He *will* appear to make Good and Truth ' triumphant for ever.'

9. Nov. 42.

LECTURE XIII.

RELATION OF LOVE TO RIGHTEOUSNESS.

1 JOHN III. 11—23.

For this is the message that ye heard from the beginning, that we should love one another. Not as Cain, who was of that wicked one, and slew his brother. And wherefore slew he him? Because his own works were evil, and his brother's righteous. Marvel not, my brethren, if the world hate you. We know that we have passed from death unto life, because we love the brethren. He that loveth not his brother abideth in death. Whosoever hateth his brother is a murderer: and ye know that no murderer hath eternal life abiding in him. Hereby perceive we the love of God, because He laid down His life for us: and we ought to lay down our lives for the brethren. But whoso hath this world's good, and seeth his brother have need, and shutteth up his bowels of compassion from him, how dwelleth the love of God in him? My little children, let us not love in word, neither in tongue; but in deed and in truth. And hereby we know that we are of the truth, and shall assure our hearts before him. For if our heart condemn us, God is greater than our heart, and knoweth all things. Beloved, if our heart condemn us not, then have we confidence toward God. And whatsoever we ask, we receive of Him, because we keep His commandments, and do those things that are pleasing in His sight. And this is His commandment, That we should believe on the name of His Son Jesus Christ, and love one another, as He gave us commandment.

I HAVE taken more verses to-day than I am wont to take for the subject of a single Lecture, not certainly because I think any of them unimportant, but because I do not know how to separate them without injuring their sense. The passage may seem at first sight to include many different topics which might be easily considered apart. But when we have carefully examined it, we perceive one principle unfolding itself gradually through the different clauses, which we might fail to apprehend, if we did not observe how each contributes to the illustration of it.

What that principle is, I hinted at the close of my last Lecture. St. John had joined together two signs of the birth which is not from above, but from beneath; of the birth that is not of God, but of the devil. Not doing righteousness, was one sign; not loving the brethren, was another. We often set these two signs in opposition. That man, we say, is rigidly just; he holds to the law; but he is not affectionate, not loving. *That* man, we say, is one of the kindest, most charitable, most tender-hearted creatures in the world; but he is sadly wanting in justice; he will always overlook evil rather than punish it. There may be a plea for such language; there are men, doubtless, who have cultivated the sterner virtues, and who have crushed what they think interferes with them; there are men who have been driven by the sight and experience of this severity into the temper which is most directly the reverse of it. But the contradiction is solely the effect of our imperfection; it has no existence in the nature of things. The proof that it has not, is that it does not last, even in those who appear to present the most remarkable specimens of it. The just man becomes unjust from the want of that sympathy which enables him to understand the degrees of criminality in different men; the merciful man becomes unmerciful, because he is without a standard to which he can refer his own acts, and to which he can raise those whom he spares. So it is shown that there is and must be a radical union between these two great human characteristics. And so it becomes a most important question in ethics to ascertain the ground of this union, and how it may bear upon our practice.

I spoke to you in my sixth Lecture of the contempt which some had thrown upon the Old Testament, as if it were set aside by the New, and of St. John's assertion, that the word which they had heard from the beginning was that which he was declaring to them. I showed you, at the same time, how he justified the reverence for the New Testament as a higher revelation than the Old, on the ground that the true Brother of men had appeared; that the commandment that each man should love his neighbour as himself had become *true in Him and in us;* a law actually fulfilled; a law which could be obeyed. The question presents itself here under a new aspect. It is not whether the New Testament has superseded the Old; but whether, if the New Testament sets forth Love as the principle of human action, it does not contradict the Old, in which Righteousness and Law are so prominent. You shall hear St. John's answer. He does not now speak of the commandments which were given on Sinai. He goes back to an earlier record still. '*This,*' he says, '*is the message which ye heard from the beginning, that we should love one another. Not as Cain, who was of that wicked one, and slew his brother.*'

Here is the oldest story almost in the Bible. You call it the story of a great transgression. A transgression implies something to be transgressed. What was that? There were no decrees then; no tables of stone. But there was God's message to men in the very fact of these two men being brothers. '*Ye shall love one another*' is involved in the very constitution of the universe, in the very existence of a family. Cain proved himself to be '*of that wicked one,*'—to be the servant of the rebel against Right and God, —by this act against his brother. Are Righteousness and Love, then, hostile principles? Is one the mitigation or softening of the other? Is not Love presupposed in Righteousness? Is not an outrage upon Love an outrage upon Righteousness?

He enforces his argument in the second clause of the verse, '*And wherefore slew he him? Because his own works were evil, and his brother's righteous.*' The story represents the dislike of Cain to Abel as originating in anger against God, because his sacrifice had not been accepted. The Epistle to the Hebrews affirms the sacrifice of Abel to have been good, because it was offered in faith; the sacrifice of Cain to have been evil, because it was offered in unbelief or distrust. St. John asserts the same doctrine in different language. The righteous man of the Old and New Testament equally is the man who trusted in a righteous God; the unrighteous man is the distrustful man. The story represents God as arguing the case with Cain's conscience, as saying, '*If thou doest well, shalt thou not be accepted?*' He refuses to listen to that voice. He turns from the righteous Lord; he hates Him; then he begins to hate his brother, *for* his faith, *for* his righteousness. What was the Gospel doctrine but the expansion of this primary history? What was it but the unfolding of a LAW which that history had indicated? What were the experiences of those who accepted it, but this first experience multiplied?

But here was the perplexity. If there were only an

Adam and an Eve, a Cain and Abel, it might be easy enough to say that the loving man was the rule, and the unloving man the exception. How could this be said in an age when the majority—the world at large—was full of hatreds and murders, when there were only a few protestants on behalf of unity? St. John does not blink this difficulty. '*Marvel not, my brethren,*' he says, '*if the world hate you.*' Do not let this fact stagger your faith, that the proportion of haters to lovers seems so enormous. '*We know that we have passed from death unto life, because we love the brethren.*' It is not a question to be decided by a poll. It is a question which each man may decide for himself. Is it not the state of Death to hate? Is it not the state of Life to love? Did we not hate because we had been separated from the life of God? Are we not able to love, because we are in communion with the life of God? What then if a frightful number are hating each other? '*Whosoever hateth his brother, abideth in death.*' He is cutting himself off from the universe; he is at war with its law; at war with its Creator and Lawgiver. He goes on: '*Every one that hateth his brother is a murderer; and ye know that no murderer hath eternal life abiding in him.*' The thought of the 'primal eldest curse' is still present to him. Murder, he says, as that story indicates, is hatred developed into act. Hatred is murder in the heart. But he has been occupied through his whole letter, with telling us that the life of God, the Eternal Life, which was implied in the divine code, but which no divine code could adequately express or make effectual, had been manifested in Jesus Christ. As the code fights with the act, this life fights with the principle. As the code deals out vengeance on the crime which is perpetrated by the murderer's hand, this life is the contradiction of the hatred in the murderer's heart. With that it cannot abide. What, then, must this life, this Eternal life, be?

Last week the question was raised, What does he mean by the Love of which he discourses so much? I said I felt sure that he would not cheat us of an answer, though I doubted whether it would take the form of a definition. In the first verse he produces the answer even in a more direct and formal manner than you would perhaps imagine from our version.

'*Hereby perceive we Love*,' (the words *of God* are added): '*Because He laid down His life for us; and we ought to lay down our lives for the brethren.*' He has been tracing the operation of the law of love, and the transgression of the law of love in former ages. He has fully vindicated the Old Testament from those who say that this law of love is not the one which it recognises. But he agrees with those who exalted the New Testament above the Old, to this extent: he admits that the love which was involved in every true act that had ever been done, which had been the hidden principle of every true life, which was seen in Joseph's tenderness for the brethren who had sold him, in the care of Moses for the people who were ready to stone him, in the burning patriotism of every prophet whom his countrymen put in the stocks or the prison, or doomed to death,—had not yet fully revealed itself. A man of the old time could not say 'I know it.' He longed to know it; he looked forward to a time when it should be known. The time, says St. John, has come. The blessing is ours. The Son of God '*has laid down His life for us.*' By this we know Love. This is the Divine interpretation of it; for Divine interpretations come in acts, not words. I might call it a Divine *definition*. So far as a definition *excludes* all that does not belong to the nature of that which it explains, Christ's death is a definition of Love; for it shows what love is *not;* how unlike it is to that tolerance of evil which men have confounded with it. So far as a definition *includes* all that belongs to the nature of the thing which it explains, Christ's death is a definition of Love. For there is no possible element of Love which men in their right minds have felt that they have need of, which they have recognised in the most heroic and the most sympathizing acts of their fellow men, that is not found in this act. Why, then, do I shrink from using that phrase, *definition?* Why would you feel it to be inappropriate? Because you must attach some notion of what is finite to definition. Because your conscience tells you that the Love which you see here is infinite. There can be no measure found for it in earth or Heaven. I am sorry that our translators inserted any words that are not in the original. It was both wrong and weak to do so. They left room for the thought, that we may learn what Love *itself* is somewhere else than at the Cross of Christ. They anticipated what St. John will tell us in better and fuller language hereafter. But I do not admit for an instant that they introduced any false doctrine. The Love, the infinite Love, must be God's Love. If the death of Christ showed us what the infinite Love is, it showed us what God's Love is.

He goes on—'*And we ought to lay down our lives for the brethren.*' The taking away the life of a brother was proved, by the earliest experience of the world, to be the result of departure from the law on which God had formed His world. The laying down a life for others is proved, by the latest experience in the history of the world, to be the principle, the essence, of that law. The life of the Lawgiver—the life eternal—which had never been manifested till Christ was born, which had never been completely manifested till Christ died, was now shown to be the life of self-sacrifice. Love cannot exist apart from sacrifice; therefore he says, '*We ought to lay down our lives for the brethren.*' It is startling language. We are wont to say, that one who lays down his life for another performs a transcendant deed of virtue, for which he may give himself credit. The Apostle says, 'This is our ordinary duty.' We are not to count it heroic at all; but simply obedience to the law under which we exist. And surely the conscience of mankind confirms his judgment, however the pride of men may rebel against it. The action in the heathen world, which has always inspired most of admiration in true minds, is the death of the 300 Spartans who guarded the pass of Thermopylæ against the army of Xerxes; and it was recorded on the graves of these 300, that they died in obedience to the laws of their country. They felt that it was their business to be there; that was all. They did not choose the post for themselves; they only did not desert the posts which it behoved them to occupy. Our countrymen heartily respond to this doctrine. The notion of dying for glory is an altogether feeble one for them. They had rather stay by their comfortable or uncomfortable firesides, than suffer for what seems to them a fiction. But the words, ' England expects every man to ' do his duty,' are felt to be true and not fictitious words.

There is power in them. The soldier or sailor who hears them ringing through his heart will meet a charge, or go down in his ship, without dreaming that he shall be ever spoken of or remembered, except by a mother or child or an old friend. So it is in private experience. Women are found sacrificing their lives, not under a sudden impulse of feeling, but through a long course of years, to children and their husbands, who often requite them very ill; whose words are surly; who spend what affection they have on other objects. The silent devotion goes on; only one here and there knows anything of it; it is quite as likely that the world in general spends its compassion upon those to whom they are ministering; none count their ministries so entirely matters of course as themselves. Christian ethics explain these facts by which so many are puzzled. There is a law of sacrifice throughout the universe. Some submit to it reluctantly. They try to set up another law, the law of self-pleasing. They try to accommodate all things to that. They cannot succeed. They do *not* please themselves. Earth and Heaven are at war with them. For the mind of the Ruler of Heaven and Earth is a mind of self sacrifice; it is revealed in the Cross of Christ. Some submit to the law of sacrifice cheerfully. They feel it to be a good law. They allow it to shape their acts. These are consciously or unconsciously yielding to Christ, confessing Him as their king, bearing His Cross. It is the privilege of those who live in Christian countries to yield to Him consciously. So they are freed from self-consciousness. Their acts may be perfectly simple. They need not be proud of their humility, tor their humility is His. They need not glorify themselves upon the giving up of themselves, for they look upon no sacrifice as satisfactory but His; every other only derives its virtue from His.

St. John might have good reason to fear that his words, carefully as they were guarded, would still suggest some notions of a special martyrdom, such as many were permitted to undergo in that day for the name of Christ. An Ephesian might say, 'Oh, yes, of course, I must lay down 'my life for the Church, if a persecution should arise, and 'I should be called either to renounce my profession, or 'endure the axe, the cross, or the fire. But I hope I may 'escape that alternative.'

The next verse shows that the principle he had asserted had no such limited application, and was reserved for no extreme case. '*If any man hath this world's goods, and seeth his brother have need, and shutteth up his bowels of compassion against him, how dwelleth the love of God in him?*' As if he had said, 'The law of sacrifice is not a law for 'moments and crises of our existence; it is the law for 'the whole of it. The pettiest events and occasions will 'be tests whether you are subject to it or at war with it. 'You may have very extatic feelings about the Christian 'brotherhood at large; but are you ready to help that par-'ticular brother, who is lying destitute there, not with feel-'ings, but with a little of the actual food and raiment that 'he is in need of?'

This would be a searching question. I do not know which of us might not sometimes quail at it. But what does St. John mean by putting it in this form: '*How dwelleth the love of God in you?* Does he wish us to understand that the very love which is in God, is communicated to us, is to dwell in us? Does he blame us for not allowing

P

this love to dwell in us? That must be what he is saying. It is impossible to explain his words in any other sense. You will see as we proceed, that he repudiates the other sense which is sometimes given to them, as if by the love *of* God he signified the love we bear *to* God. And without anticipating future passages of his discourse, I think we have read enough already to see that his whole method would be changed if he taught that we climb to Heaven by acts of love, and not Heaven comes down and declares itself to us in acts of love.

'*My little children, let us not love in word, neither in tongue; but in deed and in truth.*' That easy way of loving, by talking about love, was a way into which Christians might fall in Ephesus as well as in London, in the days of the Roman emperors as well as in the days of Queen Victoria. St. John warns his children of it with fatherly gentleness; but there is a sting in that very gentleness. He would not tell them not to commit this hypocrisy if he did not know that they were likely to commit it. No; nor would he tell them of it, if he could not also tell them how they might avoid it. If they had no love to draw upon but their own, I do not see how it could fail to run dry very soon, or what would be left but a sediment of word love and tongue love, which never clothed any human body or comforted any human soul yet. But if he could assure them that they were under a law of love, that God's love was burning clearly and brightly always, and that it was their fault if it did not burn in them,—he might well add, ' Why ' should we cheat ourselves of the greatest of all blessings ' by not yielding to the power of this love, by not allow- ' ing it to express itself in our acts?'

'*And hereby,*' he adds, '*we know that we are of the truth, and shall assure our hearts before Him.*' This verse, like the last, seems to break down the barrier which separates the Apostle's world from ours. How often we hear persons say, ' Well, I hope I believe as I ought to believe. I hope
' I am holding the truth. But there is great uncertainty.
' Some people think one thing, some another. I should like
' to have some security. I wish I knew some one who
' could tell me, That is the opinion you should hold, that
' is the opinion you should reject; that is the thing you
' should do, that is the thing you should not do.' Those who speak thus generally ask for some external dictator who shall relieve them of their responsibility. There are others who are craving for an inward assurance. They want to be able, as the hymn says, ' to read their title clear to mansions in the skies;' to have some authentic token that they shall be blessed hereafter.

These anxieties which are at work now, have been at work always, though they may have presented themselves in different aspects. St. John addresses himself to them, and turns them to the most practical account. You want to know that you are of the truth? Ask the God of truth to keep you from loving in word and tongue, and not in deed and in truth. You want to assure your hearts respecting your relation to God? Ask the God of love Himself to dwell in you, and to direct your thoughts and acts according to His will. You will not need dictators to tell you what the truth is, if the Source of all truth is leading you into it. You will not need assurances about a future heaven, if you have heaven within you now.

' *For if our heart condemn us, God is greater than our*

heart, and knoweth all things.' What tricks that we have all practised upon ourselves does this sentence lay bare! What webs of theological and ethical sophistry does it cut through! A man wants some comfortable assurance that he is right with God. And yet his heart is not right with itself. There is uneasiness and bitterness in his conscience. He feels that he has not been loving in deed and truth, but only in word and tongue. His heart tells him so. 'Well,' says the Apostle, ' you must be right with that heart, if you ' wish to be right with God. You are not at peace with ' yourself, because you know that you are wrong. Do you ' really think God does not know you are wrong? What is ' this verdict of your heart but His verdict? Can you get ' Him to reverse it, if it is, as you feel it is, a true verdict?'

The argument is very plain, the doctrine indisputable. And yet by practically admitting it, by accepting it as the rule of our lives, what trouble, what a multitude of complicated calculations, what infinite distress, we shall save ourselves! At first, perhaps, it begets a kind of despair. ' Whatever my heart says, God says first, and with greater ' emphasis. He knows more against me than I know ' against myself. How terrible to encounter His scrutiny! ' Hills and mountains, fall on me, and hide me from Him!' But look again. ' *God is greater than my heart, and knoweth* ' *all things.* He knows what has set me wrong, as I do ' not know it. He can set me right, though I cannot set ' myself right.' This is the comfort of not merely believing in a conscience, but in a God who speaks through my conscience; this is the comfort of not thinking that *it* is my lawgiver, but that *He* is my lawgiver; this is the comfort of being able to say to Him who is my Judge,

Search me, and see if there is any wicked way in me, and lead me in the way everlasting.

And so we are brought to peace with the adversary who is within us. When we turn round to the light from which we have been turning away, our heart no longer condemns us; it tells us we are right. '*And if our heart condemn us not, then have we confidence towards God.*' We can look cheerfully up to Him who has reconciled us to Himself, and wishes us to be at one with Him. We can be sure that His will is the right will, the blessed will, and that to be in subjection to it is our right and our blessedness. Or, as St. John expresses it more fully and satisfactorily, '*And whatever we ask, we receive of Him, because we keep His commandments, and do the things that are pleasing in His sight.*' I have endeavoured before to explain that phrase, '*keep His commandments.*' What we have heard to-day has thrown further light upon it. To keep God's commandments is to remember what that law is which He has established for the universe; what the law of His own mind, of His own life, is. When we submit to that law, His life acts upon our life. As St. John says, ' He dwells in us, and so we are able to do the things that ' He would have us to do, " *the things that are pleasing in* ' *His sight.*" '

But a question might still occur to some person who had been used to hear the doing or keeping of the commandments set in opposition to faith in Christ, ' All you want us, then, ' is to *do* right. You do not care so much what we *believe*.' Nay, he says, ' If you ask me what God's first command-' ment is, I should say, *that we should believe in the name of* ' *His Son Jesus Christ.* For have not I told you that the

'perfect law of God, because the perfect life of God, is set
'forth in Him; specially in His death? Have I not said
'that there we see Love, and how inseparable it is from the
'giving up of self? How, then, can we keep God's com-
'mandment, how can we come under His law so com-
'pletely, as by acknowledging this Son as the brightness of
'His glory, the express image of His person; by trusting
'in Him as our elder brother and Mediator and Advocate?
'For by doing so we are able to keep that command-
'ment which He Himself gave us, which He gave us because
'He had fulfilled it and embodied it in His life, *that we
'should love one another.*'

Thus we arrive at the two counter-signs to those of the devilish birth with which we began. Doing righteousness and loving the brethren are the signs of the heavenly birth. They denote the adopted child of God; because they denote the only-begotten Son of God. He was perfectly righteous, for He perfectly trusted His Father, and would not glorify Himself. He perfectly loved men. That love came forth in the sacrifice of Himself. But this sacrifice set forth, as nothing else could, the character, the righteousness of God. When we come into this region, all the seeming contradiction between Righteousness and Love disappears. They must be one if the Father is one with the Son; they must be one if the Son is the perfect image of the Father; they must be one if the Son is He in whose image Man is created.

I reserve the last verse for the next Lecture. It might be a very beautiful conclusion to the subject which we have been considering to-day. I think it is still more important as an introduction to the subject of the fourth chapter.

LECTURE XIV.

SPIRITUAL POWERS IN OLD TIMES AND IN MODERN TIMES.

1 JOHN III. 24; AND IV. 1—9.

"*And he that keepeth His commandments dwelleth in Him, and He in him. And hereby we know that He abideth in us, by the Spirit which He hath given us. Beloved, believe not every spirit, but try the spirits whether they are of God: because many false prophets are gone out into the world. Hereby know ye the Spirit of God: every spirit that confesseth that Jesus Christ is come in the flesh is of God: and every spirit that confesseth not that Jesus Christ is come in the flesh is not of God: and this is that spirit of antichrist, whereof ye have heard that it should come; and even now already is it in the world. Ye are of God, little children, and have overcome them: because greater is he that is in you, than he that is in the world. They are of the world: therefore speak they of the world, and the world heareth them. We are of God: he that knoweth God heareth us; he that is not of God heareth not us. Hereby know we the spirit of truth, and the spirit of error. Beloved, let us love one another: for love is of God; and every one that loveth is born of God, and knoweth God. He that loveth not, knoweth not God: for God is love. In this was manifested the love of God toward us, because that God sent His only begotten Son into the world, that we might live through Him.*"

WE are again reminded, by the first of these verses, that the expression, *Abide in me*, is characteristic of St. John, and that we could not change it for any more formal or artificial phrase without enfeebling, perhaps destroying, the truth which he is imparting to us. If I call your attention very often to these peculiarities in his language, it is partly because I believe *we* have an especial interest in vindicating them from the contempt which has been cast upon them, and in restoring them to the place which the language of the schools has usurped. Mr. Carlyle used to talk about an 'Age of Work' which is at hand. Such an age, I conceive, will be very impatient of technicalities; will greatly prize all forms of speech which are drawn from realities, and which can be interpreted by the sights and sounds of the common world, by the business of life. Men of business have never made a greater mistake than when they have complained of St. John's mode of thinking, and of uttering his thoughts, as fantastical. They *have* a good right to complain of many of the thoughts and of the discourses that pass current in religious circles, as very fantastical. Many of *us* they have a right to call dreamers. There is a flightiness about our talk as if we disdained the earth, and were always trying to mount above it, though we are continually dropping down to it by the force of an irresistible attraction. It is too true, that religious men often scorn the obligations which hold other men to fair and honourable dealing, without acquiring any stronger obligations. Therefore, they are often observed to be less scrupulous in their outward transactions, less consistent in their habitual morality, than those who rarely confess the influence of spiritual fears and hopes. I cannot wonder that practical men, who notice these facts, should strive diligently to clear their minds of what they call the phantoms of an invisible world, and to occupy themselves only with the present and the palpable. But it is not easy to do that, supposing it was desirable. Have you ever known any one who quite succeeded in the effort?

any who did not feel somewhat restless when his hold on what is present and palpable seemed to be growing feebler? But would it be desirable if it were easy? Would it be honest? Are there not as many facts—facts of ordinary experience—which point to things that we cannot see and touch, as to things that we can? Are there not abundant proofs that we have at least as much to do with the one as with the other? Is there not some evidence that we cannot deal bravely with the things which our senses tell us of, that we must be subject to them,—unless we have some standing ground from which we can overlook them?

This is the ground on which St. John would have us 'abide.' He at all events has no notion of flying into the air for the sake of shunning the earth. What he affirms is, that the true centre of our human life, of all its thoughts, energies, hopes, is in the unseen world. What he says is, that there is an attractive force drawing us to that centre which is no less potent than the force which draws bodies to the earth as their centre. He affirms that we are created to abide or dwell in God; that in Him, not in our own aspirations or dreams, is the foundation of our life and purposes; that our morality is derived from His morality; that we may have dominion over the things which He has created, because we are related to Himself.

The words so often repeated, '*He that keepeth His commandment, abideth in Him*' are a death to dreaming; they maintain the *practical* character of St. John's teaching. But the *scientific* character of it would be lost and it would be entirely inconsistent with itself, if the words, '*And He in him*' had not been added. Wonderful and awful as the idea of God abiding in a man is, you cannot read any portion of the Old Testament, without perceiving that prophets and seers expected a covenant, the ground of which should be, '*I will dwell in you;*' any portion of the New Testament without perceiving that this is the Covenant of which the Apostles and Evangelists believed themselves to be the heralds. After St. John's exhortation to the young men respecting the Word of God who dwelt in them and enabled them to overcome the wicked one; after his assurance to his little children that they had an unction from the Holy One, which would enable them to know all things; it would have been strange if he had shrunk from the boldest statements on this subject. To have maintained that we can dwell in God without asserting the converse of the proposition, would have been to change the whole method of his discourse; to have laid a human and not a divine foundation for his ethics.

We are upon very sacred ground. To approach so near the inmost sanctuary of a human soul would be dreadful, even if we were not also approaching Him before whom angels veil their faces. My impulse would be to leave the subject in the mist which commonly surrounds it, and not to encounter questions which may easily become profane. But this course is not possible for us, if it was for our forefathers. The unseen world has been invaded. We cannot help hearing the most frivolous talk about spirits and their doings, and their intercourse with men. The most sturdy materialism has not been proof against what seems the most inconclusive evidence of spiritual powers and presences. But the acceptance of that inconclusive evidence by persons so little likely to be moved by it is *conclusive* evidence that the spiritual is necessary to man, that he must have it under some conditions. To determine what these conditions shall be, must be of the highest moment. Let us see whether our Apostle will not assist us, and whether we may not walk safely under his guidance in a road which we could not travel without the greatest risks by ourselves.

'*By this we know that He dwelleth in us, even by the Spirit which He hath given us. Beloved, believe not every spirit, but try the spirits whether they are of God; because many false prophets are gone out into the world.*'

I have joined these two verses together, though they have been placed by those who divided the New Testament in separate chapters, because I think it is very important that you should understand what the Christian doctrine respecting a Spirit given to us by God, and dwelling with us, has to do with those notions respecting spirits, spiritual influences, spiritual communications, which have been so prevalent in other times, and are so prevalent in ours. The Apostle leads us directly to this inquiry. He speaks first of *the* Spirit by which we know that God dwells in us; then of other spirits that were in the world, which might or might not be of God. He is evidently not alluding here to that Tempter or Accuser, of whom and his progeny he said so much in the third chapter. He is not pronouncing upon the good or evil of these spiritual influences. But he says they require to be tried. And he intimates very distinctly that there were men in his day who were turning the faith in spiritual influence to an immoral and mischievous account.

He does not then discredit the fact that spiritual influences were widely diffused; he does not monopolize such influences for the Christian Church. How could he discredit this fact? How can we? Are there not myriads of influences about us continually, which do not act upon our senses but upon our spirits, which do not proceed from things that may be seen and handled, but from the spirits of men? Are not the influences that you come under in our College of this kind? I do not say whether they are good and evil; but they must be spiritually good or spiritually evil. And an institution for education is not different in that respect from what we call political institutions. People talk of the electors of Mayo having been subjected to spiritual influences, because they were exposed to intimidation by the denunciations of certain priests. This language is correct, but we must not limit it to such cases. The electors of Oxford who vote for Mr. Thackeray in consequence of any speech he may make to them, are just as much under spiritual influence. He says very truly that there are week-day preachers as well as Sunday preachers; preachers in newspapers as in pulpits. And I say that on week-days as on Sundays, you cannot escape from spiritual influences, if you take ever so much pains to escape from them.

If we once understand this statement, we shall listen, I conceive, with far less of vague astonishment than we sometimes do, to the reports of those who say that we may receive communications from the unseen world, from those who do not speak to us with mortal lips and look at us with mortal eyes. Receive communications from them! Why, are we not doing it every day and hour? If a person gives me some doggrel, and tells me that it was sent from Shakespeare or Milton, I may use my discretion whether I shall believe him or not. But if I do not, one main reason will be, because I *have* received and *am* receiving spiritual communications from these very persons which do not at all resemble in character or style those which reach me through the new media; because words of theirs written long before we were born, and called by such names as Hamlet and Paradise Lost, are fresh and living communications to us every day, and beget thoughts in us which the recent verses said to proceed from them are quite incapable of begetting.

Writers are for mankind. We are told also that communications come to individuals from those whom they have known and cared for, and who were acquainted with circumstances interesting to them, though perhaps indifferent to the world. Here, again, we have to complain of the exceeding poverty and worthlessness of the messages which are brought to us from the unseen world, not of the assumption that it is right and natural that such should be sent. Are they not sent to us? Is not every recollection of a departed friend in some hour of sadness and temptation—confirming us in a right resolution, restraining us when we would do something wrong—a message from he world of spirits? I speak literally, not figuratively. It is easy to talk of such recollections as only acts of memory. But what is an act of memory? The ancients thought Memory a most wonderful and mysterious power; they called it the Mother of all Arts. I cannot think they were wrong: certainly they did not exaggerate the seriousness and awfulness of that act which brings back to us words that have been spoken, deeds that have been done, our own states of mind, in years that are gone; which brings them back to us as present realities. The more we consider what is implied in such an exercise, the more we must tremble at the greatness of our own being; the more we must feel in what close relation we stand to eternity. And if, instead of saying, 'I remember a friend,' 'I call back his image to me,' I say, 'He is actually conversing with me; he is suggesting thoughts to me; he is sympathising with me and upholding me when I am weak;' there is an increase of awe, perhaps of joy. But I do not feel that I have introduced a more difficult or incredible kind of speech. I am not sure that it is not a more simple one, more accordant with experience, even more like what men in all ages have felt *must* be true; more like what the analogies of science would lead one to expect.

I do, indeed, feel for myself that there is a veil between me and those with whom I should most wish to hold converse. It is the veil of my own baseness and corruption—not one that exists, so far as I can perceive, in the nature of things,—not one that need be if one's pride were exchanged for humility, and one's suspicion for trust. And the sense of *this* hindrance makes me regard with more revolting and disgust the sort of intercourse which is carried on through our modern media in England and America; an intercourse which demands no moral purification; which has reference to the idlest topics; which may be carried on in drawing-rooms amidst whispers and talking and the shuffling of cards; which keeps alive all the vanity, restlessness, and folly from which we most need to be delivered. In Mr. Wordsworth's beautiful poem, Protesilaus says to Laodamia:—

> 'The invisible world with thee hath sympathized,
> Be thy affections raised and solemnized.'

If we cultivate our sympathies with the invisible world according to the new fashion, our affections are likely to sink even below their ordinary level, to become more frivolous than is their wont.

But in fact what I have called a new fashion is a very old one; there have been traders in spiritual enchantments in all ages. St. John intimates that they abounded in his time. We know that they did. All the writings of the Apostles are full of allusions to them. The Apostles appear to have thought that they had scarcely any more important vocation than to deliver the poor and the rich from the moral dangers to which they were exposed from such men as Simon Magus and Elymas, and from such women as the poor girl at Philippi, who brought her master much gain by soothsaying. But you will observe this difference between their treatment of these cases and that which is common among us. They do not deny that these people had powers, and were able to produce startling effects. They do not say, 'You are merely using natural, mechanical ' agents to create an impression that you have some spiri- ' tual faculty, that you have relations with the unseen ' world.' Probably they would have had some right to make these assertions. If they had known more of physical laws themselves, and had cared to apply their knowledge, they might have shown that the enchanters were 'one-eyed leaders of the blind;' that they had just enough acquaintance with Nature to deceive those who had none. This may have been so; but if the Apostles had been perfectly certain in every given instance that it was so, I doubt whether they would have made the same use of their information which we should make of it. For they would have felt that whatever form a lie happens to take, the lie itself is spiritual and not material, the product of a bad spirit, and to be denounced in that character. They would have felt also that it was *not* a lie in these men to speak of themselves as spiritual, and as subject to spiritual agencies, and as spiritual agents themselves upon other men. These appeared to them great truths, which it was very shocking that any should play with, as if they were not truths, but means of earning money or admiration.

It was not a matter of doubt, but of certainty, that men and women were thrown into convulsions and ecstasies. They boasted that it was the effect of spiritual or demoniacal power. The Apostles could not deny it, and had no desire to deny it. If men are spirits and have a dim notion that they are, and yet have a very faint apprehension of their spiritual dignity, they must be continually sinking into spiritual slavery; they must be the victims of spirits—clothed with bodies or unclothed, speaking to them through mortal organs or without them— which are subtler or stronger than themselves. If they can be raised out of that slavery, if they can acquire the liberty of moral, accountable beings, children of God, *that* is infinitely desirable. It might not be at all desirable, but a great loss to them, that they should be told, 'All your 'sense of being subject to a will stronger than your 'own, of being its tool and instrument, was a mere 'imagination. It meant nothing.' There are philosophical frauds, as there are pious frauds; this, it seems to me, is one. The conscience of a man who has felt the bondage must reject the message. The Apostles would not defy the witness of the conscience. But if they bade the demonised man rise up in Christ's name, and claim the rights of a man, the use of his will and reason,—the conscience did not reject them, but welcomed them.

They claimed the power to do this, not because they had been endowed with a spirit which distinguished them from other men, but precisely as God's witnesses that it had pleased Him to baptize all nations, to bestow His Spirit upon a family taken from all classes of men, specially from those who were not mighty, or rich, or noble, or learned. The casting out demons in the name of Jesus of Nazareth, the proclaiming Him to be the anointed of the Father, was the affirming that this Spirit had been given to *men*, that their chains might be broken asunder, and they might look up as redeemed children to the Father of Spirits. St. John is not here asserting this power for himself, but he is explaining in what sense and for what end it had been committed to him, by telling his flock that it is for *them to try the spirits whether they be of God*. Each one of them, he affirms, might do this for himself, nay, *must* do it for himself. The argument whether the spiritual influences that were acting upon them were pernicious or healthy, wicked or charitable, must be pursued in the secret chambers of their souls. But there, in those chambers, they would find, if they sought, the Spirit of all truth, who would enable them to discern between the spirits which were of His own nature, which were working together with Him, and those which only came to fill them with self-conceit, to draw them from their fellows and from God, ultimately to make them victims of every cheat. The Apostle, though unable to follow them into recesses into which only God might enter, could yet supply them with a test which his own experience had ascertained to be infallible.

'*Hereby know ye the Spirit of God. Every spirit that confesseth that Jesus Christ is come in the flesh, is of God. And every spirit that confesseth not that Jesus Christ is come in the flesh, is not of God. And this is that spirit of antichrist whereof ye have heard that it shall come, and even now already is it in the world.*'

Something of what is implied in the confession that Jesus Christ is come in the flesh—something of what is implied in saying that He is not come in the flesh—we have heard in that passage of the second chapter where he spoke to us before of the antichrists. Something more of what each implies we shall learn as we proceed in this chapter. But one doctrine was contained in it which greatly concerns spiritual teachers and prophets of all ages, of all countries, whether constituting an order or starting up to proclaim what the members of an order have left unproclaimed. To confess that Jesus the anointed is come in the flesh, is to confess that there is a medium of spiritual communications between the visible and the invisible world, between earth and heaven. It is to confess that there is one Mediator for all men. And for any man to say that the visible world is divided from the invisible, and that only by the arts of some priest, or seer, or 'medium,' the chasm can be bridged over, and an intercourse created between them; this is to deny that Jesus Christ is come in the flesh. The denial may be made by those who in words affirm their faith in Him most loudly. Every spiritual person who thinks highly of himself, and does not clothe himself with the humility of Him who became a servant, and does not desire to assert for every man the rights of fellowship with God and His Son and His angels, must seriously consider whether he is not one of these antichrists.

He continues, '*Ye are of God, little children, and have overcome them; for greater is He that is in you than he that is in the world. They are of the world, therefore speak they of the world, and the world heareth them.*' In what sense and on what grounds the men of the Ephesian church were exhorted not to love the world, or the things that are in the world; why it is affirmed that, if they do, the love of the Father is not in them, we have considered already. Here the world is again formally and directly opposed to God; the spirit of the world to the Spirit of God. Here again it is assumed that the little children of the flock have a right to claim the position of being *of God*, sons of God; or, to speak more correctly, that they have no right to take up any other position. The danger is, that they may be tempted to forsake that which has been given them, to forget their birthright. In resisting those who promised them such spiritual illuminations as would set them above the commandments, above their fellows, above the faith of a Christ who had taken flesh, in resisting these seducers and determining to maintain the state of little children, to abide in the Father and the Son,—they had overcome a world spirit, a spirit which acknowledged the world as its parent, and which the world was quite ready to own as its child. For though the lust of the *flesh* and the lust of the *eye* have so much to do with the nature of a world, yet the world has its own *spirit* too, or rather a legion of spirits, which fulfil its commands and take possession of its servants. All those tempers which lead men to worship what they see or to worship themselves, or to pursue some vision of selfish glory and happiness, are such spirits; mighty over our feeble wills, but not so mighty as the Spirit of God, who is drawing them back to their Father's house, when they are most inclined to wander in search of another home and another father.

To understand the next verse aright, we have need to remember what the Apostles' work on earth was, what they were living and dying to do; otherwise, we may easily read it in a sense which is not only not the true one, but exactly the reverse of the true one: '*We are of God; he that knoweth God, heareth us; he that is not of God, knoweth not us; by this we know the spirit of truth and the spirit of error.*' 'Is not that,' an opponent may exclaim, 'the 'very temper of a sectarian? *We are right, every one* '*else is wrong. God approves of us, God dislikes all else.* '*You are safe only among us; you must be the servant of* '*the prince of lies, if you do not join with us.*' Let it be admitted at once that the words are not only capable of being so interpreted, but that they have been interpreted so again and again; that we are all continually tempted so to interpret them. And now consider whether St. John could have intended us to do this; whether we shall be yielding to his authority and following his example, if we turn them to this use.

He was the preacher of a Gospel to all nations. That Gospel was the announcement that Jesus Christ had manifested the Life of God, and had opened the kingdom of God to men. The main opposition to this Gospel proceeded from the Jewish sects, each of which desired to attract proselytes

to itself, each of which denounced all out of its pale as false and evil. Another part of the opposition proceeded from the worshippers of visible and divided Gods who were bidden to turn from idols to the one living God. When the Church was formed, its great difficulty arose from the sects which sprang up within it, each fraternising in the name of some leader, each denouncing the leaders whom others followed. Those of whom St. John is speaking here as leaving the unpopular Church for the world which welcomed and embraced them, were the founders of sects, each to be distinguished by some opinion and by the name of him who had been its parent. Reflect on these facts, and I think you will come to the conclusion, that when St. John said so boldly, '*He that knoweth God knoweth us*,' he signified that those who were weary of all opinions and sects, and wanted a Living God, the Father of a whole family in heaven and earth, would find the doors of their Church open day and night to receive them, would find that they were claimed among them as brothers. And in like manner that when he added, '*He that is not of God knoweth not us*,' he must have meant to say, ' Those who are seeking ' for something else than a Living God, for something else ' than the Father of a family,—must and will turn from us. ' We shall have no attraction for them. For in this uni-
' versal name we are determined to fraternise.' And the final words, '*By this we know the spirit of truth and the spirit of error*,' will naturally and necessarily imply, ' We rest all upon this issue. We are not careful to prove ' that we are right and that you are wrong. We simply ' say, God is Truth, and those that forsake Him and His ' fountain of living water for any muddy cisterns and earthly

'springs, such as are to be found in schools, sects, systems, are
'in error. And all we have to do is to abide in Him, and
'leave the judgment of ourselves and of all men to Him.'

The context of St. John's life and writings would, I think, very sufficiently fix this sense of the passage and not the other to be *his* sense. But if any doubt remains in your minds, then turn to the immediate context of this very verse.

'*Beloved, let us love one another: for love is of God; and every one that loveth is born of God, and knoweth God.*' We have reached one of those passages to which I alluded in a former Lecture, those on which St. John's fame as the Apostle of Love is founded. And what are we to say of it? Are these words, '*Let us love one another,*' less strict and severe words than the words, '*Be ye holy,*' which are used in the Old Testament? Has it been more easy to follow this exhortation than that? No; this has been *the* precept in the whole canon of the Bible, which men have found in practice to be the hardest; the one which they have failed most signally in keeping. Oh! how many times we can most of us remember when we would gladly have made any compromise with our consciences, would gladly have made the most costly sacrifices to God, if He would only have excused us from this duty of loving, of which our nature seemed utterly incapable! St. John knew that men would feel this, that they must feel it. He knew the tricks to which they would resort to persuade themselves that they were obeying this commandment, even when they were transgressing it most flagrantly. He sets it down, therefore, not as a mild substitute for other and earlier rules, but as one which contained them all in itself, and to observe which demanded a power such as all the resources of our human nature and of the world do not supply. And do not suppose that he made the exhortation easier by saying, 'Let us love *one another.*' It is far easier to feel kindly, to act kindly towards those with whom we are seldom brought into contact, whose tempers and prejudices do not rub against ours, whose interests do not clash with ours, than to keep up an habitual, steady, self-sacrificing love towards those whose weaknesses and faults are always forcing themselves upon us, and are stirring up our own. A man may pass good muster as a philanthropist who makes but a poor master to his servants or father to his children. If the members of the Church at Ephesus had such love to one another as St. John demanded, there was little fear of their failing in love towards those that were without.

I might have used a stronger word, I might have said there was no fear at all, for this reason. St. John says, '*Love is of God.*' As if he had said, 'I know very well
' that there is no stock of love in you upon which you
' can draw that will not soon be exhausted by the
' demands that are made upon it. I know also that no
' opinions or doctrines upon one subject or another, will
' enable you to love one another. Love is of God. It is
' out of His nature you must derive your power of loving;
' every other will prove utterly inadequate. "*Every one*
' *that loveth is born of God.*" From Him comes the original
' capacity to love, by Him it is daily renewed. The loving
' man has drawn his first breath of life from Him; he
' receives a fresh breath from Him each morning, as the
' flowers and trees receive a fresh birth with the rising sun
' and a fresh baptism in the dew. And "*he who loves knows*
' *God.*" He has communion with the mind of God; he

'learns what He is by that which he receives from Him.' It is from an infinite, illimitable Being, then, that St. John bade his little children seek the love which they wanted in every day's intercourse with one another. Would that infinite, illimitable Being suffer them to restrain their sympathy with any circle narrower than His own? If He bestows His heat and His rain on the unthankful and the evil, would their bounties and affections be confined to the grateful and the good?

How often do we hear the first clause of the next verse quoted as if it stood alone; as if it were a rapturous exaggeration of one quality of the Divine Nature, as if it indicated a forgetfulness of other qualities which balance and counteract this! I read very recently in a religious periodical of large circulation and high authority, that the assertion, '*God is Love*,' has no doubt a great attraction for 'the natural man,' and that it ought not to be suppressed; but that, on the other hand, it ought to be carefully guarded by other statements which are less agreeable. Can the writer of this passage ever have read St. John's Epistle? Can he have recollected the tremendous sentence which precedes this,—the sentence of which it is the explanation, '*He that loveth not, knoweth not God*'? Is that a sound which is pleasant to the natural man, in him, or in me, or in any one? Does it not make the 'natural man' in us tremble and hide itself, as if it were excommunicated and cut off from the presence of God for ever? For St. John certainly means what he says. He is not playing with this awful and divine language. No; he is driving us to despair with it; he is telling us what is required of us,— certain that our consciences will echo his decree;—on purpose that he may force us to forsake all confidence in our feelings, natural and acquired, in our philosophy, in our humility, in our religion; on purpose that we may fly from ourselves to the Eternal God, who has what we have not, who is what we are not. '*God is Love*,' is not a proposition uttered in a sudden ecstasy; it is the final revelation to which all others have been tending. Without it all others are mere deceptions and contradictions. Without it there is no ground for individual faith or individual conduct to stand upon. Without it there is no human society. Without it there is nothing left for us but Devil Worship or Atheism.

Some people calling themselves Christians dare to speak of the Incarnation of Christ and the Death of Christ, as if they restrained or modified this primary test, by the application of which St. John discovered what is the Spirit of Truth and the Spirit of Error. Hear how the Apostle speaks of Christ's manifestation. The statement is familiar to us. It has gone through the whole Epistle. I have tried to examine each word in it accurately. But I wish you to think of it in this connexion. '*Herein was manifested the love of God to us, that God sent His only begotten Son into the world, that we might live through Him.*' What Christ did was not to create love in God, but to show it forth. If we believe in Him as St. John bids us believe in Him, we confess that God is Love; only when we do so, are we partakers of His life, or, as it is expressed here, '*do we live through Him.*'

Then comes the full assertion of that great ethical principle which I have been endeavouring to develop in all these Lectures: '*Herein is Love, not that we loved God, but* that He loved us, and sent His Son to be the propitiation for our sins.' The reversal of this principle, the notion that in some way or other our love to God is the ground of His love to us, and the kindred notion that in some way or other He is to be propitiated to us, seem to me fatal to all sound ethical teaching and ethical practice. They are driving numbers to a system of Ethics from which the idea of God is excluded altogether; to Ethics, therefore, which will be consistently and throughout what the Christian Ethics are inconsistently, of this world and for the world; based upon selfishness and terminating in selfishness.

St. John lays the axe to the root of selfishness: '*Beloved*,' he says, '*if God so loved us, we ought also to love one another*.' The emphasis, I think, should be laid on the word *ought*. He affirms, as he did before, that Love is the law of the universe; that in loving, we do not perform an act of supererogation, but merely submit to a duty. If God so loved us, *not* to love is to resist a power which is at every moment acting upon us, and impelling us to all sympathy and all sacrifice.

Thus we are led back to the point from which we started. It seemed wonderful to speak of our dwelling in God, more wonderful to speak of God dwelling in us. But we have been taught by degrees why such language is necessary, why we cannot shrink from it without shrinking from the obligations which our existence as members of a human society involves. To maintain that God is unseen and yet most real; that His Love is the ground of our love; that we only love when we submit to His operations; what is this but to affirm and adopt St. John's doctrine in the length and breadth of it? He announces it therefore as demonstrated in this sentence, '*No man hath seen God at any time. If we love one another, God dwelleth in us, and His love is perfected in us.*' And he repeats also the 24th verse of the last chapter with which I began this Lecture, '*By this we know that we dwell in Him and He in us, because He has given us of His Spirit.*'

Other spirits, we have said, were to be tried by their likeness or unlikeness to His Spirit. What His Spirit is; how we may understand whether we are yielding to it or to some other; we have now learnt. We have been carried far out of the region of rapping and table turning. Questions about spiritual communications and spiritual life are nothing less than questions what we ourselves will be, whether we would have Hatred or Love to rule over us now and ever.

LECTURE XV.

THE PERFECTED LOVE.

1 John IV. 14—21.

And we have seen and do testify that the Father sent the Son to be the Saviour of the world. Whosoever shall confess that Jesus is the Son of God, God dwelleth in him, and he in God. And we have known and believed the love that God hath to us. God is love; and he that dwelleth in love dwelleth in God, and God in him. Herein is our love made perfect, that we may have boldness in the day of judgment: because as he is, so are we in this world. There is no fear in love; but perfect love casteth out fear: because fear hath torment. He that feareth is not made perfect in love. We love him, because he first loved us. If a man say, I love God, and hateth his brother, he is a liar; for he that loveth not his brother whom he hath seen, how can he love God whom he hath not seen? And this commandment have we from him, That he who loveth God love his brother also.

THE question presented itself to us in the last Lecture, 'When St. John bade the disciples at Ephesus love *one* 'another, did he mean that the world beyond their circle 'was to be excluded from their love?' I was not in haste to answer this question. I contented myself with hinting that the exercise of love is most difficult towards those with whom we are most in contact. St. John, however, does not leave us long in suspense. '*We have seen,*' he says, '*and do testify, that the Father sent the Son* (to be) *a Saviour of the world.*' That is the truth which became evident to the little band of disciples while they were showing love one to another; that is the witness which they were bearing;

they *existed* only to bear it. The blessing which they were inheriting was a blessing for the world. He who was the ground of their fellowship, the author and finisher of their faith, was the Saviour of the *world*.

Let us consider this testimony of theirs more attentively. The name ' *Saviour* ' was not with them, if it is with us, a technical name, a name out of which the life had departed; a Saviour was one who saves,—saves from actual misery and bondage. What actual misery or bondage had they been saved from? Is it not a misery that men of the same flesh and blood should be living as if they had nothing in common, nothing to bind them to each other, as if each stood in the other's way? They had been saved from this misery; they had found a common interest, a common Lord. They *had* looked upon God as far off from them, in the hours when they felt most they could not live without Him; they had found Him sometimes fearfully near, when they wished they could drive Him to an infinite distance. They had been saved from the thought that God and they were separated; they had been saved from the *wish* that He should be separated from them. The name *God with us* had become the dearest of all names to them. And yet the reverence for God, as the perfect Goodness, as the great enemy of all that was *not* good in them and the universe, had become immeasurably deeper than it had ever been.

Why? Because *the Father had sent the Son;* because they had believed that He who was with them, their helper and deliverer, was the Son of God; the Son in whom that Being of absolute goodness delighted; because they had learnt to call Him, in Christ, their Father. This was salvation; what more did they want?

They *did* want something more; but it was implied in what they had already seen and felt. Their Lord was the Lord of the *world;* they had a right to tell the world so; they had no right to suppress the proclamation. For this end had the Father sent the Son, not simply to gather a little body out of the world which should have His love and not the world's love in it, which should obey Him and not the world; but by that means to save the world. Strange as the message sounded in other ears and in their own, He was the Saviour of that world which treated them as aliens and outcasts. Its curse was their curse. Its members were divided from each other. The Father had sent the Son to save them from that division. He was the head of every man; the centre of human beings. The majority regarded God as afar from them; even though their consciences told them that it was death to be away from Him; they dreaded lest He should approach them; lest *that* should be their death. The Father sent the Son to save the world from this death; in the Son He reconciled the world unto Himself.

Supposing St. John had not been at liberty to use this language; supposing he had been obliged to tell the Ephesians, 'The Father has sent the Son to be *your* Saviour, *not* to be the Saviour of the world,' think what the effect would have been on the testimony which they bore in the world! The very word *testimony* would have been inapplicable. They might have *argued* with men to convince them that Christians were right and they were wrong, that Christians were happy and they were miserable; but they could not have *testified*, 'We have found the King to whom all in heaven and earth owe homage; we can tell you what He is.'

They might have spoken of a scheme of salvation, and explained most learnedly how different parts of it fitted into each other. They could not have *testified* as St. John does in the next verse: '*Whosoever confesseth that Jesus is the Son of God, God dwelleth in him and he in God.*' That is the message of a man who believes, as St. Paul told the Athenians—men given to idolatry, frivolous men,—that '*God is not far from any one of us, for in Him we live, and move, and have our being.*' For he added, '*Certain of your own poets have said, We also are His offspring.*' If they believed Jesus to be the Son of God, the barrier which divided them from Him in whom they were living and being—the barrier of ignorance, discord, hatred, was broken down; they were brought into the proper state of men; '*God dwelt in them, and they in God.*' If they believed that Jesus was the Son of God, the dream of the poet was found to be a true dream. They *were* the offspring of God; God had created and chosen them in His only-begotten Son; they could call Him their Father.

Was there, then, no blessing, no privilege, in the condition of Christ's flock? Might they just as well have been still a portion of the denying world? St. John shall answer, not I: '*And we have known and believed the love that God hath to us.*' This was the blessing, this was the privilege. The infinite misery of the denying world was, that it did not know and believe the love that God had to it; that it believed Him to have no love to it; that it refused all communion with love. That neither the belief of the Church or the unbelief of the world, affected the nature and being of God in the least, he affirms in the next clause, where he repeats the sentence I spoke of in the last Lecture: '*God is love.*' This is not an accident of His character, but its essence; not an aspect which it wears at certain times or to some fortunate persons, but that which is the same yesterday, to-day, and for ever, that which has no respect of persons. But here is the difference: '*He that dwelleth in love, dwelleth in God, and God in him.*' By dwelling in love, that love which Christ had manifested, by entering with heart and soul into it, by permitting it to govern them, they dwelt in God and God in them; they became partakers of His nature instead of aliens from Him, at one with Him instead of at war with Him.

I have spoken of a strange contradiction which there is in men's minds when they think of God. They feel as if it would be a dreadful thing to lose Him, and yet as if it would be a more dreadful thing to be brought near Him, to be in His open presence. If you consider how you have spoken yourselves, how you have heard others speak of the day of Judgment, you will understand what I mean. We complain that the world is not at all what it ought to be; that there is tyranny and injustice in high places; that there is not merely misery here and there, but a predominance of misery; that sickness and death seem as if they were stronger than health and life; that truth and honesty are often despised by those who pass with the highest reputation, even with a reputation for religion; that even men, whom we are bound to think sincere and good in the main, have much alloy mixed with their gold. We cry in our hearts, if not with our lips, 'When will the Lord of the 'earth set these things right? When will He put down 'those who abuse His Name and His power to the sanction 'of foul deeds? When will He restore peace, and drive 'out war? When will He put an end to hypocrisy, and 'vindicate that which is simple and pure?' What are these cries but repetitious of the Psalmist's prayer, that God will rise and judge the earth? And yet if any one should say to us, ' *The* day of Judgment, or even *a* day of ' Judgment is at hand,' what shivering and shrinking there is at the sound! How the very report of a comet being seen in the heavens shakes the minds of poor ignorant people who have a notion that perhaps it may have some commission from God against the earth! What a secret cry there is in the heart, ' O Lord, not yet! We would ' not meet Thee now! Leave the world and us to our sins ' and falsehoods, just a little longer.'

You know that this is so. Ought we to wish that it was otherwise? Not if, by losing either of these inconsistent tempers of mind, we lost any part of the truth for which it is bearing witness. Not if, by parting with the desire that God should appear and rectify the disorders and caprices of the universe, we lost the feeling that it is His purpose to do this; that every one who has any office or ministry whatever among men must give account of it to the great Householder, that every widow may cry to Him, 'Avenge me of ' my adversary,' with the certainty that He is *not* an unjust Judge, and will hear His elect, though He bear along with them. Not if, by parting with the dread of His appearing, we lost the feeling that whatever is hateful or untrue must be exposed to His clear eye, must be confronted with His perfect Love and Truth. Both these convictions are necessary to us; the misfortune is, that each should weaken and counteract the other; so that, except at certain crises in our lives, the judgment-day should be an object neither of distinct hope nor of distinct terror, only of an emotion which is compounded of what is poorest and least honest, least capable of producing any moral effect, in both hope and terror.

St. John grapples with this subject in the 17th verse. '*Herein is our love made perfect, that we may have boldness in the day of Judgment, because as He is, so are we in this world.*' Our translators have deviated from the exact rendering of the first clause in this verse. They did so in hopes of making the sense more clear. I am not sure that they have not made it less clear. He had been telling us that if we dwell in love, we dwell in God and God in us. However difficult and wonderful this language sounds, we may see, after a moment's consideration, that he could not have given a 'perfect' account of love, if he had resorted to any other. Take a very simple analogy. I want to describe the act of seeing. I speak of it as an act of my eye. That is true so far as it goes; but it is imperfect. Seeing cannot be considered only in reference to the eye. To describe it perfectly, I must take in the object upon which it is exercised. If the eye does not rest in that, does not lose itself in that, I do not really see. The law of love must be the same. I may describe love in the lover; but that is an imperfect description. To the perfection of love it is necessary that it should be both in the lover and in the object beloved. St. John tells us that *herein*, i.e. in this union of ourselves with God, is our love, (more strictly the love that is *with us*,) perfected. This is the completest idea of love, the only complete idea we can have. And he shows, at the same time, that it is the only practical idea of love ; that no other will stand the great test of all. If I look forward to God's judgment, relying upon the love that I have to Him, I must be continually haunted with the thought that all the weakness and wretchedness of my love will be brought to light, all the failures of every day and hour towards Him and towards my brother. A death-bed makes a man conscious of these failures more than of any others, nay, resolves all others into these. And suppose I could increase that love ten thousandfold, still counting it *mine*, still saying, '*It dwells in me*,' the terror of that judgment would not be sensibly diminished. I still cannot wish to be brought face to face with a Love which must show me how utterly unworthy and wretched mine is, how utterly unlike His before whom I stand. But if I give up altogether speaking, or thinking, or dreaming of love as *mine*, if I sink myself, lose myself in a love which is altogether above me, which comprehends me and the universe, *if it is the very love* which will be revealed at the last day that I am dwelling in, and that is dwelling in me, may I not have boldness to meet that judgment, may I not long to meet it?

'*Because*,' St. John continues, '*as He is, so are we in this world.*' Our battle with evil is His battle; whatever is right and wholesome in us is simply derived from Him. Why, then, may we not hail the termination of the battle, the obtaining of the victory? What interest have we in justifying that which we have been taught to feel is our plague and curse? How can we shrink from the manifestation of that perfect goodness, about which we have complained so bitterly that it was hidden from us? I am paraphrasing the words very feebly; but even what I have said may enable you to see the ground of St. John's confidence that the Judgment day was a day which could not make him ashamed.

But is it possible to be wholly rid of that fear of this day, which is so natural to us? St. John answers, '*There is no fear in love; but perfect love casteth out fear; he that feareth is not made perfect in love.*' The first proposition is at variance with many which are familiar to us. Love is often represented as anxious, timid, jealous. And there is truth in the representation. The affection which is on one side, which is not certain of a return, is and must be of this character; precisely because it is not the perfect or perfected love which the Apostle is speaking of. In every case that perfected love which each lover realizes in the other *casts out fear*. The torment of doubt and suspicion is over; there is no balancing to ascertain who has most; there is no mine or thine. Supposing such love to exist between the Creator and the creature, the Father and His children,— there would be no fear of any fuller manifestation of His glory; only a continual hope of it. '*He that feareth is not made perfect in love.*' 'Perhaps not,' you may say; 'but at 'least he is humble; and surely God honours the humble.' There is a mistake, I think, here. A man who doubts whether he does not love God better than God loves him, is not humble. A man who fancies that he loves his fellow-creatures better than God loves them, is not humble. He is giving himself credit for the very highest qualities; he has not learnt that he has no good thing—certainly, therefore, no love, which is the best thing—in himself. Blessed are the poor in spirit; therefore he must be stripped of those notions of his own riches, before he can be blessed.

These words of St. John about the perfect or initiated

man, like some which I considered in a former Lecture, were designed, I believe, to undermine the self-conceit of those who boasted of their great wisdom and great love, and despised the little children of the flock, who felt that they were very poor in both. He would have the Ephesians understand that, if they thought they knew anything, they knew nothing yet as they ought to know; that, if they thought they had any love, they were not yet confessing the source of love, and drinking entirely from that.

For '*We love Him, because He first loved us.*' Let no one cheat you of the simple force of these words by persuading you to understand the Apostle as saying that we love God out of *gratitude* for the love He shows to us. Some ethical writers are wont to talk much of the motives, to which, they say, man's nature is subjected; this motive of gratitude, they affirm, is one of the chief. I do not wish to argue the point with them; but I say they have no right to impute these notions to the Apostle, to make him put *motives* in the place of *God*. And which is the most elevating doctrine, theirs or St. John's? *They* would make me the slave of a certain set of influences which I feel I ought to con'rol. *He* represents God as acting upon me that I may be free, and may not be the tool of this motive or that. Let us, therefore, receive these words in that sense which is most agreeable to the context; let us understand the Apostle to say, 'We love God only because that true 'original love which is in Him is moving us and inspiring 'us; we could not love secondarily and subordinately if we 'had not loved primarily and absolutely.'

Taking these thoughts along with us, we shall understand much better the next verse. '*If a man say, I love*

God, and hateth his brother, he is a liar; for he that loveth not his brother whom he hath seen, how can he love God whom he hath not seen? And this commandment have we from Him, That he who loveth God love his brother also.' The man says, 'I love God.' St. John meets him with the question, '*What* do you love? An unseen being, if it 'is the true God whom you love: but an unseen being 'who has declared that the beings you see, you converse 'with, are made in His image; a Father who has said, '"These are my offspring." And these images of His 'have nothing that attracts you! this offspring of His 'you positively hate! There is but one word for such 'profession, from whomsoever it comes,—It is a lie. If 'the love does not descend, the hatred must ascend. If 'you have an aversion for the human likeness, you must 'have an aversion for the divine prototype.' And then he recurs to his old language: 'Love to the brethren is not 'a fancy, a taste, a sentimental preference. It is obedience 'to a commandment. It is doing what God says you are 'to do. To divide the love of God from the love of your 'brother, is to divide the love of God from obedience to 'God. It is substituting something else for the love with 'which He first loved you; and that something else cannot 'be love at all.'

I have tried to show you in these Lectures that St. John explains himself to us more clearly than I or than any commentator can explain him; that if we are really wanting help, he will afford it us. The mistake which students of the Scripture generally commit is this — they fancy the words are very difficult, and they must get some one either to untie or cut the knots which are in *them*. They do not consider that the knots in books would signify very little, if our own lives were not full of knots; that these are what we need to have untied; that if the Bible fulfils its purpose it will enable us to do that work which without it we have been unable to do. One who has blundered very much himself, who has been tormented with a great many practical riddles which he could not solve, is not, I hope, arrogant if he says to his fellow-men, 'This book has cleared ' up perplexities in my experience. I think they are ' essentially the same as those which you are meeting with. ' Shall we try together whether we can make out the ' oracles which it utters?' I fancy that what the Apostle says—nay, that the whole Bible—must look dark to us till it has cleared away some darkness of ours. I have found in St. John a light upon many dark passages in my own history and in the history of the world. I learn from it why religion and morality have so often appeared to be at variance, what errors destroy right practice, how evil practices have given birth to errors and nursed them into maturity; what the first lie was which has expanded itself into a series of lies. And I believe this teaching has an especial worth for our time; that it meets us even more directly and sharply than it met our forefathers; that it may tell us plainly, if we will listen, the secret of our weakness as well as of our strength.

The Psalmist says, '*Do not I hate them which hate thee, O Lord?*' '*Yea, I hate them right sore: I do count them mine enemies.*' St. John says, '*He that saith, I love God, and hateth his brother, is a liar.*' Are these two passages inconsistent? Does St. John pronounce his inspired ancestor a liar? Must we say that there is to be no hatred any longer, seeing that God is love? I am afraid we are saying or fancying this, and that it is one cause why there is so little love amongst us, why our love is so effeminate a quality, with so little of zeal and fire in it; why, therefore, it is so little like the love which was in Jesus Christ, the love which brought Him through His baptism of fire, the love which it is promised that He shall shed abroad in our hearts, when it is said, '*He shall baptize with the Holy Spirit and with fire.*' If we do not hate that which is contrary to love—that which is contrary to the nature of God—we cannot truly and earnestly love. If we do not wish to see what is contrary to love extirpated and destroyed, we cannot truly and earnestly love. That daintiness of ours which cannot bear such expressions as those of the Psalmist, must hinder for ever any real victory of good in us over evil, of the divine life over the death that steals so steadily and rapidly over us. For what are the enemies which rise up against us continually? Are they not bitter, spiteful, murderous thoughts of each other? Do not these torment us? Do not they very often get the mastery over us, and lead us to cruel words and deeds? Is it disobeying the new commandment by which St. John tells us we are bound, to hate them right sore, to hate them with a perfect hatred? Are we not bound to cherish such feelings in ourselves, to be awakening them on all occasions, on purpose that we keep the commandment not in the letter but in the spirit?

I know that there is always a danger of the hatred which we ought to cherish in our heart of hearts against everything which is cowardly, base, insincere, unlovely, passing into that hatred of *men* which is a breach of the commandment; yes, the danger often seems to be greatest in the strongest, most earnest minds. They are most eager for actual reforms; they cannot bear merely to be fighting with principles; they must denounce them as they see them embodied in acts and persons. No doubt this was a temptation of reformers in other days. They launched forth their denunciations against men, some of whom we cannot help regarding with respect and affection. They could not stop to measure one part of their character against another; they saw them only as apologists for that which their conscience told them was accursed, as opposers of that which they knew it was worth while to die for.

God give us their zeal, for their *zeal* was all good and loving! God teach us not to judge their fierce words, though we may not imitate them, though we may sometimes lament them! For we should ask ourselves very seriously whether our calm, measured, demure phrases may not conceal more scorn that is meant to wound the heart of the man we are censuring—more of what is essentially diabolical—than those which we call them bigots and savages for uttering; just because we do not loathe the essential evil as they did, because we do not care as much for the essential good. This self-inquiry is, as I have hinted already, the true way to a distinction between a hatred of principles and a hatred of persons. To see the evil, first of all, in our own acts, in our own selves; to recognise it as marring our sincerity and worth – as degrading us from the level God intends for us—this is a security which we can obtain in no other way for our loving the man whose wrong doings we hate.

But then, how is such self-inquiry to be carried on? Is

it not likely to be treacherous? Is not the judge on the side of the criminal? Not if St. John speaks truly; not if we dwell in God and God dwells in us. Then He is the judge Himself. Then when our acts, and words, and thoughts come up before our consciences—and some of them have a very clear brand of malignity and hatred upon them,—it is He who is bringing them to light; it is He who is saying, 'Thou art not loving thy brother whom 'thou hast seen; how canst thou be loving Me whom 'thou hast not seen?' And then it is not a vague wish which rises in us to be different; it is not a vague wish that we might love our brother; it is His own voice which is saying, 'Do this, for I am doing it; Be this, for I am love.'

While, therefore, I do find in these pages of St. John a condemnation of all experiments of Christians in ages gone by, to persecute their brother in the name of God and for His glory; whilst I do find here a very clear, authentic declaration, that, if *we* attempt any repetition of such courses, we are rebelling against Him and are setting up a false god in His place,—I do also perceive that a very awful obligation is laid upon us by the claims and boasts which we put forward to be specially tolerant, and merciful, and charitable. I say that to make such pretensions and not to fulfil them, or only to fulfil them by a lazy indulgence which permits any kind of wrong in others, which stirs up no life or energy in us, is to place ourselves far below the cruelest fanatics who had in them some zeal for human beings as well as for God, however it might be perverted by their selfishness and pride. But I say also that God would not allow us even to dream of such an honour for ourselves as the use of these titles and of these boasts implies, if He did not wish us to have the dream turned into a reality. We may have more charity, a deeper charity than we have aspired to, when our aspirations have been the grandest. For we may abandon the thought of having a charity or love of our own, and so may be perfected in love. We may yield ourselves to that love which passes knowledge, that love which is a consuming fire to destroy the grovelling, petty desires, the party spirit, the self-seeking that have made us a world of sects instead of a church of brothers. And so while some are fancying that they shall banish persecution from the world by banishing all thoughts of God from it, we shall find that it is only by giving glory to Him in the highest we can have peace on earth or good will among men.

16. 11. 42.

LECTURE XVI.

FAITH AND LOVE—THEIR RELATION TO EACH OTHER AND TO THE WORLD.

1 John V. 1—5.

Whosoever believeth that Jesus is the Christ is born of God: and every one that loveth Him that begat loveth Him also that is begotten of Him. By this we know that we love the children of God, when we love God, and keep His commandments. For this is the love of God, that we keep His commandments: and His commandments are not grievous. For whatsoever is born of God overcometh the world: and this is the victory that overcometh the world, even our faith. Who is he that overcometh the world, but he that believeth that Jesus is the Son of God?

THE Apostle has been treating of *Love*. He passes in the first of the verses I have just read, to *Faith*. Formal writers on Theology or on Ethics would have stopped to announce the commencement of a new subject. They would probably have told us that they had been discussing one of the great Christian virtues or graces; now the time was come for explaining the nature and signs of another. If we find no such intimations in St. John, we must not hastily conclude that he is indifferent to method. Perhaps he is more careful of it than those writers to whom I have alluded. Perhaps he knows better than they what is the method of the human spirit, what is God's method of awakening and directing the different energies with which He has endowed it.

At all events, experience has proved that very serious

practical inconveniences, and very interminable controversies, are the results of those artificial divisions which have been thought a valuable improvement upon the teaching of Scripture. Simple men, who have had to work and live, possibly just about to die, have been driven nearly mad by discussions upon kinds, qualities, and conditions of faith, upon the relative value of acts of faith and acts of love, upon the possibility of faith existing without love or love without faith. And those who raise these hungry questions are never able to settle them. They are debated backwards and forwards with a subtlety and refinement that does not the least hinder fierce and violent passions from coming forth on each side. For the combatants know that their discourses are touching what is most vital in themselves and in their fellow-men. They know that the bystanders, who smile and ask them why they are making so much ado about nothing, are wrong, and may one day feel how much is at stake in what now seems a mere fight of words; they are half conscious that they have conveyed this false impression to men's minds by their disputations; they are vexed and fretted by the contradiction; it makes them still more eager to confute their adversaries; it turns their zeal into gall and bitterness. A dreadful story, which those who engage in religious debates understand only too well, and which makes them sometimes tremble as they read the sentence, ' *Woe to the world, because of offences! for it must needs be that offences come; but woe be to him by whom the offence cometh. For it were better for him that a millstone were tied about his neck, and that he were cast into the depths of the sea, than that he should offend one of these little ones.*'

Without judging those who enter into these disputes in one interest or another—for if we judge, we shall certainly be judged—and only desiring as much as possible to keep ourselves out of them, let us try if we cannot find how St. John escaped the peril into which they have fallen; why he can speak of Faith and Love without setting them up as rivals; how he ascertains the claim of Love to the precedence which his brother Apostle St. Paul had assigned it in his Epistle to the Corinthians, while he gives to Faith all the dignity and rights which that same brother Apostle had claimed for it in his Epistle to the Romans.

'*Every one who believeth that Jesus is the Christ, is born of God, and every one who loveth Him that begat loveth Him also that is begotten of Him.*'

We are familiar with this language. We have seen before how the idea of a Divine birth, of Sonship to God, penetrates the whole mind of St. John. We have found now the acknowledgment of Christ as the anointed one, as endowed with the true Spirit, as manifesting the true life of God,—is connected with this divine birth, how His Sonship is made the ground of our sonship. Is there anything fresh to be learnt from this passage, then? Is it not a mere repetition of what we have been told more than once already? No! its position in reference to the statements in the last chapter invests it with a new meaning and importance.

We have heard the broad announcement, 'God is Love.' A man might say, 'That is enough for me. I am content. 'There is nothing to fear. The words are without excep-'tion, without limitation. They are inspired words. They 'are Apostle's words.' Even so. But what are these?

'*And this commandment have we from Him, that he who loveth God love his brother also.*' You liked the first words. Do you like these as well? Have you kept this commandment? Are you able to keep it? Because, if we may trust the Apostle who delivered the one sentence, this is indissolubly bound up with it. He seems to intimate that those tidings will be of no profit to us if these are forgotten. Thus we are driven to inquire, whether there is no link between the God, the absolute Perfect Being, whose name is Love, and ourselves,—the feeble, the imperfect, yea, more than that, the unloving. Or if we begin at the other end, we are forced to inquire, how it is possible to keep that command, which, as I said before, is the most difficult of all to keep.

I believe that *Jesus* is the Christ. That is to say, I believe that there is a living bond between me, the poor, helpless human creature, and the absolute perfect Being. I believe that His Love has come near to me in a human person, whom I may claim as the brother of me and my race. I believe that Person is the Son of God; that in Him dwelt the fulness of the Godhead bodily. I believe, therefore, that I am related to that Love which created the world, and all that is in it. I may claim affiance in it. Again, I believe that Jesus is the *Christ*. I believe that He is anointed with the Spirit of God to the end that He may bestow that Spirit upon men. I believe that the Spirit in Him was a uniting Spirit, a self-sacrificing Spirit, a Spirit of active, suffering, sympathising Love. I believe that that Spirit is acting upon us, and can work in us the love which is most foreign to our selfishness.

Here is faith; faith in its simplest form; faith in

its greatest might. It is simple, for this faith refers everything to God. It is the renunciation of every claim in a man to do acts of his own, to exist by himself. It is mighty, for by this faith the will of the man becomes altogether subject to the will of God. His might becomes its might. And so, as St. Paul speaks in the Epistle to the Romans, '*boasting is excluded.*' The man can boast of nothing; least of all can he boast of his faith. That is not something which belongs to him, a gift which he can carry about with him, and say, 'Now I am a believer.' It is exactly the reverse of this. It saves him, by emptying him. It delivers him from himself; it attaches him to another. He is just by faith, because he believes in a just God. He is loving by faith, because he believes in a loving God. Truly, faith is the gift of God. He awakens it in us, as He awakens everything in us that is living, everything that is necessary to our life as men. He awakens it, as He awakens in us the powers of seeing, speaking, remembering, thinking. But as I have no right to say, I am different from my neighbours—better than my neighbours—because I have the use of sight, of smell, of hearing, of speech; as I *ought* to say, 'How sad 'it is for any one not to have these common human endow-'ments,—what an awful calamity blindness is, and dumb-'ness, and deafness,—how sadly I have misused my 'eyes, and ears, and tongue;' so it is with faith. That is more essentially, more characteristically human, than seeing, hearing, smelling, speaking. To be wholly without it, is to be a beast or a devil. To be endued with it in the highest measure, is only to be a true man. To abandon unbelief for faith, is only to return to a proper, calm, even state, to a right mind, after having wandered among the tombs, and been exiles from our kind. Faith saves us, as St. Paul says; saves us from an inhuman condition; saves us by joining us to *the* Man who cares for all men, and has refused to divide Himself from any.

But is St. Paul then inconsistent with himself in saying that Love or Charity is greater than faith? Hear how St. John interprets him. God is Love. Christ's own Faith was in the love of His Father. *He* lived by trust. His glory was never to abandon trust, never to set up Himself. Faith, because it is Faith, must have something to rest upon. And that something is Love. If Love was not the ground of all things, there could be no Faith; there must be everlasting distrust; that is what we should be bound to cultivate in ourselves; or rather it would grow without any cultivation. And all Faith which does not look up to Love as its end, which does not look down upon Love as its root, is a mere phantasy or contradiction. It is a faith which does not believe in anything, or, most monstrous of all, which believes in itself, worships itself. But it is equally certain that all Love which we talk of as ours, or make a pretext for vanity, is a contradiction and a lie. Such love is without any object; it attaches us to nothing; it makes us incapable of being attached to anything. To talk of God bestowing Love upon us as if it were something which we could hold or get credit for, is indeed to set Love and Faith in opposition; but only because it makes one as utter a nullity as the other. So long as we adhere to St. John's language,—so long as we speak of our dwelling in God and God dwelling in us,—the *faith* by which we confess God's Love can never clash with the Love by which He works in us.

And so we understand the last clause of this verse, and see how necessary it is to that which went before. It was easy for a reader of St. John's Epistle to misinterpret the words, '*He that loveth not his brother whom he hath seen, how can he love God whom he hath not seen?*' The sense which has often been given them is, that we start from visible objects of Love, and so ascend by degrees to the invisible, and that any one who attempts to reverse the process,— any one who begins from the invisible, and descends to the visible,—is a deceiver. I am sure that St. John did not mean this, and that we are contradicting his previous statements if we suppose that he meant it. No doubt, God educates us by visible and imperfect parents—*fathers after the flesh*— to seek for Himself the invisible and perfect Parent, 'the 'Father of our spirits.' Through brothers and sisters, through the love between the sexes, through the marriage bond, we are prepared to apprehend the relations in which we stand to the Kingdom of Heaven. But it happens very often indeed, that the child never learns to say the Lord's Prayer in spirit and in truth, till it has lost the father on earth to whom it clung. His death perhaps first brings out the full consciousness that there must be One who lives for ever and ever. Not seldom the absence of love in the home circle drives it to seek a more perfect and enduring home. Not seldom shame for our indifference and coldness to those who have watched over us in our infancy forces us to turn to Him who has taken the blessings from us, and whom we feel we have grieved by our scorn of them. And, even if this were otherwise, St. John is saying nothing about our particular families and the lessons we may have learnt or not learnt in them. He is putting the question to us broadly, whether want of love to *any* brother, any man whom we have seen, does not imply want of love to the God whom we have not seen? Now to declare that we have a universal Love for our kind, and a special Love for each member of it, *before* we have any thought about God, before we have made any efforts after His Love, is certainly at variance with all experience; to declare that we *ought* to start with such a love, and that we can only climb to the love of God through it, would be a strange assertion for any man, an absolutely incredible one for an Apostle whose business was to preach the Gospel of God's Love to a loveless world.

Lest, however, there should be any doubt about this matter, St. John here tells us plainly that the *love of Him that begat* is the root and not the consequence of *the love of him that is begotten of Him*. That is the natural order; that, we may say it confidently, is the universal order. For even in those cases to which I have alluded, of the love of children for their parents; of brothers for sisters; of husbands for wives, and wives for husbands; it is God who is secretly kindling that love. Though it is directed to a visible object, though without the sight of that object it might never exist, He has created the affinity between them; He attracts those towards each other whom He has intended for each other. He may be leading them through the earthly partial affection to one that is higher and more comprehending; but *that* affection also is of Him, called forth by His Spirit, and, as we hope, stamped with His own immortality. In the earliest, simplest affections of which a child is capable, we are to discern the signs of His purpose. He is intending the creatures whom He has made in His image to share His own nature, to show it forth in all their intercourse with each other and with the world in which He has placed them. The forms which present themselves to our eyes are not as dear to Him as the spirit which is within them. But they *are* dear to Him. The face of man we call, and rightly call, the human face divine. He who was the brightness of the Father's glory had the face and features of a man. Painters have not been wrong in thinking that, though it was and must have been a face of sorrow, the sorrow, being the effect of intense sympathy, revealed the glory as nothing else could have revealed it. Those who refused to see God in Jesus because He had taken upon Him the face of a servant, worshipped another God than the God who is Love. If we refuse to see the image of God in our fellow-men, because their faces are marred with sorrow —even marred with sin,—we do not confess His redemption, we do not believe that Christ is the Head of every man, we do not look forward to the day when He shall say to the meanest of them, ' *These my Brethren.*'

One of these passages, then, throws back light upon the other. It tells why the love of the unseen God must involve the love of the seen man; why every man is walking about in a vesture of weeds and mourning to prove us whether we will recognize his celestial birth or deny it. And so we are able to profit by the test in the next verse, which at first may strike us as impractical, as if the unknown were tried by the more unknown. ' *By this we know that we love the children of God when we love God and keep His commandments.*' I meet a man who offends me in a thousand ways. All his modes of thinking are different from mine; he evidently regards me with dislike; he gives proofs of it; he is aware, as I am, that there is antipathy on my side. Perhaps I have some valid reasons for objecting to him. He says something which wounds my conscience as well as my vanity: I do not know exactly which he has wounded most. I cannot distinguish one impression of annoyance from the other; they are curiously, inextricably mingled. I ask myself whether I am not indulging in wrong feelings towards him. I half justify myself by the evil that I have detected in him. It occurs to me, that if I were in a proper state of mind, that evil would grieve me for his sake. I try to think of the good which other people say is in him · which there positively must be in him though I have not perceived it. All is of no use. My bitterness increases. I would fain persuade myself that I love him *in a sense;* because I ought to do so. But in what sense? Some sense that is compatible with personal unkindness, ill-will, malignity. What, then, am I to do? Shall I allow the thought of GOD to mingle with these other thoughts of mine? Why is that so startling a contradiction?

The Apostle was not wrong. My conscience shows me that he is right. I must banish Him that begat from me if I am determined to be at enmity with those that are begotten of Him. He will not dwell with my malice. But He can separate that which is base in me, from that which is true. He can make me own His image in my foe as well as in myself. He can make me abhor what is contrary to that image in both. And since He commands me to love this man whom of myself I cannot love, whom it is my instinct not to love, I can ask Him to take me under His government and to make me do that will which 1 know to be the right one, which I feel to be the blessed one.

'*For this is the love of God, that we keep His commandments: and His commandments are not grievous.*' Very comfortable tidings, if we take them in. God's love is not that vague, distant, abstract Essence which we often fancy it to be; nor that terrible excellence which we must somehow imitate and cannot; His Love is that we keep His commandments. He desires us to be like Him. The energy of that Love which called the universe into existence is with us to make us obedient. And, after all, it is not a very grievous thing to be told that we must love. It is not a specially cruel and tyrannical obligation which we are laid under. We should not perhaps be restive under it, if we once knew what it meant. We should not complain that God would not suffer us to be without that which constitutes His own blessedness. We might not be fiercely indignant because that is taken from us which has set us at war with ourselves and with all creation.

But what is this martial note which follows? How does it accord with the soft gentle music of submission which has just been ringing in our ears? '*For whatsoever is born of God overcometh the world: and this is the victory that overcometh the world, even our faith.*' I told you it would be so. The Apostle, whom the painters represent as so tender, is a warrior to the last. He has not given over fighting himself. He will not let us plead any exemption on the score of youth or age. All through his Epistle we have heard that the world is our enemy; that we must overcome it, or that it will overcome us. Now we know better why it is our enemy, and what we have to overcome. God is Love. God commands us to love. The world will not own God's love. The world commands us to be selfish.

The world says that we may enlarge our circle indefinitely, but that Self is and must be the centre of it. And we all are inclined to believe the assertion. It sounds most plausible. Sometimes we think it nearly self-evident. We wonder that any one can dispute it. At all events *we* cannot. ' We have seen,' as we say, ' too many ghosts of ' perfectibility to believe in them. We have thought of ' a fellowship not based upon each man's desire to trip up ' his neighbour, and to gain wealth and power for himself. ' We have been disappointed. It is time to take men as ' we find them, and not to give ourselves credit for being ' better than our fathers were before us.' That is as good as saying, ' We and the world have tried a wrestle, and the ' world has thrown us. Henceforth there is nothing better ' for us than to sprawl in the dust and confess our con- ' queror.'

Now, this is just what St. John was determined not to do. The world in his day was the same as the world in ours. It jeered at all efforts to assert any other principle than the principle of selfishness. It said, ' People ' have sacrificed themselves for their family and country; ' but nothing has come of it. Every man, of course, ' seeks his own advantage. Every one, of course, cares ' for his neighbour only just so far as he serves his ' turn. Why cannot you be honest? Why will you ' profess that you have some wonderful secret which can ' raise you above ordinary human motives?' Such words were very hard to bear. For first, as we have seen, what St. John desired was to be an ordinary man; not to set himself above his fellows in any respect; to claim nothing which he could not claim for them. His fight, and the fight of all the Apostles, had been with the religious Jews who would have a heaven to themselves, who would not let the kingdom of heaven be opened to all men. And next such words were hard to bear; for no one knew so much of his own selfishness, and of the selfishness that is in the heart of man, as he did. No man of the world could pour out declamations and evidence on that matter which he could not endorse and expand a thousand-fold out of his own experience.

'*But this is the victory that overcometh the world, even our faith.*' That faith of which he has been discoursing in this passage, that faith in the eternal love of God, that faith in Jesus as the Christ, the anointed of God, who manifested the nature of God, who imparts the Spirit of God; that faith carried him through all these arguments; that faith told him that the existence of no man, that the existence of no society, can stand upon selfishness. It must stand upon the opposite of selfishness, upon that which selfishness is seeking to undermine and destroy. Its root must be in love. That is the one binding force. Omnipotence is only in that. So far as any family or any nation has ever been held together, it has been held by the might not of selfishness but of sacrifice. So far as any man's soul has not been torn by contradictory passions, it has been kept at one by the same might. The world's mockery lasts from generation to generation, but each generation changes its note. Each generation accepts some new precious legacy from the self-sacrificing man, whose faith it has cast out as evil. It lives on because God maintains it by that principle which it declares to be good for nothing, to be prized only by fools and fanatics.

But we cannot overcome the world by reckoning the discomfitures which it has undergone, or by foretelling those which it has to undergo. This is the only victory which overcometh it, even our faith. Faith, not in its weakness, but in God's strength; faith in that love which embraces the world, and which, at last, subdues the world to itself. St. John appears to be afraid lest even his grand language should lead to vanity. The Church might be proud of its promised victory over the world, proud of the faith that was to win it. He must remind his disciples in *whom* the faith was placed, *what* they believed: '*Who is he that overcometh, but he that believeth that Jesus is the Son of God?*' It is not a special charm called faith, an endowment conferred upon certain favourites of Heaven that could give them a victory over the world. The notion of such an endowment might make them into another world more selfish, less godly, than that which they denounced. Only by believing that Jesus who died for all men is the Son of God, and only by seeking fellowship with all men, could they receive the Holy Spirit, and be the conquerors of the world's Spirit. And what was true for them is true for us. We must be led captives in the world's splendid triumph; we must put on its badges, and be dressed in its meanest livery; we must be the victims of its selfishness, and make our fellow-men the victims of ours; unless we believe that He who offered Himself as a sacrifice, is the Son of God. Believing in Him, we can assert for the meanest child of earth the right of a child of God. Believing in Him, we can be members of that society which will be growing wider, and diviner, and more blessed, when the world and all its selfish works have been burnt up in the fires of the last day.

LECTURE XVII.

THE WITNESSES.

1 JOHN V. 6—12.

This is He that came by water and blood, even Jesus Christ; not by water only, but by water and blood. And it is the Spirit that beareth witness, because the Spirit is truth. For there are three that bear record [in heaven, the Father, the Word, and the Holy Ghost; and these three are one. And there are three that bear witness in earth], the spirit, and the water, and the blood: and these three agree in one. If we receive the witness of men, the witness of God is greater: for this is the witness of God which He hath testified of His Son. He that believeth on the Son of God hath the witness in himself: he that believeth not God hath made him a liar; because he believeth not the record that God gave of His Son. And this is the record, that God hath given to us eternal life, and this life is in His Son. He that hath the Son hath life; and he that hath not the Son of God hath not life.

ST. JOHN told his Ephesian flock that faith in Jesus as the Christ the Son of God would give them a victory over the world. What world did they suppose him to mean? They were dwelling in the midst of a rich commercial city. Many of them might be engaged in commerce themselves. A system of thoughts, notions, habits, were connected with their commercial dealings; that system of thoughts, notions, habits characterised the *commercial* world. They were living in a city which had been colonized by Greeks, the most accomplished, subtle, imaginative of all people. A whole system of thoughts connecting the outward visible world and its doings, with the worship of beautiful beings whose forms could be represented in marble, and worshipped in splendid temples, had established itself in Asia Minor, had partly superseded the older faiths of that region, partly adopted them into itself. This system of thoughts and feelings with all the ceremonial, and modes of life in which it had expressed itself, surrounded these Ephesians continually; they were born into it; this was a Pagan *religious* world. But there were trading with these Asiatic Greeks, settled in the heart of their city, a portion of the family of Abraham. They had brought with them their traditions, which were so unlike those of other people; they had their own synagogues, differing in all respects, outward and inward, from the Greek Temples; they believed there was one Temple, and only one, in which acceptable sacrifices could be offered to the true God. Those *Jews* formed a world within the other world, a world which touched that at a great many points, and yet was hostile to it. Many members of the Ephesian Church had actually belonged to that world; all were exposed to its influence and its persecutions. Once more; the rich commercial city of Ephesus had bowed down to a city that was not commercial at all, to a city on the banks of the Tiber, which starting from small beginnings had at last embraced the countries which the Greeks had acquired and civilized, the countries in which Jews had established themselves, Greece itself, Judæa itself, within its vast dominion. Rome had introduced laws, institutions, maxims of government, of which Greeks and Asiatics felt the power, though they were conscious of having some kinds of wisdom which their masters wanted. Rome had a religion nominally resembling that of the Greeks, really different from it, seeing that it was inseparably connected with the State and its order. *Rome* had thus built up a world empire, and also a world within each city which it reorganised. Governors, magistrates, municipal officers, gave a new tone to every society it vanquished. They did not destroy the old local habits, but they grafted upon them new habits such as belonged to a race which believed that its destiny was to subdue all nations to itself.

Now St. John's disciples of course understood him to say, 'You know that the various tempers, and tone of thinking 'in all these worlds are not what you have learnt; that 'they contradict those old commandments which you heard 'from the beginning, and that new commandment which 'Jesus proclaimed; that all equally set at nought that 'name by which you are called. And over each of them, 'over all of them you can have a victory, if you believe 'Jesus to be the Son of God. You can be free from 'the world if you are bound to Him.' This, I say, he *must* have meant whatever else he may have meant: in this sense his earliest readers will have understood him, if they merely regarded his words as admonitions and encouragements to themselves. But you will feel, I am sure, that this is not the only way in which *we* can read the words. That Ephesian commercial world has passed away; that Greek world with its idolatries has passed away; that Jewish world has passed away; that Roman world has passed away. Each has left wonderful traces of itself behind; but its forms, habits, thoughts, are obsolete. And the faith that Jesus is the Christ, is the Son of God, has established a dominion in all the countries in which these worlds had so mighty an influence;—in countries which they did not reach, which were not dreamed of when they were in their glory. This faith has, by some means or other, in some very remarkable sense, actually overcome these worlds. And then the question arises, By *what* means?—in *what* sense has it overcome the world? If we can get these questions answered, we may be able to answer others which are at least as important to us. What is it that is still to be overcome? Can it be overcome for us by any power which St. John makes known to us?

You will wonder, I dare say, at the words of St. John which follow these respecting the victory over the world, the words with which the passage I am to consider this morning begins,—'*This is He which came by water and blood, not by water only, but by water and blood. And it is the Spirit which beareth witness, because the Spirit is truth.*'
' What has this to do with the battle between the Gospel
' and the world? If he had told us of the purity of the
' moral code of Christianity, of the simplicity of its worship,
' of its superiority on these grounds to the other religions
' of the earth,—we might, you will be inclined to say, have
' understood him; that might have accounted for some of
' the strange events which have happened since his day.
' But what can we learn from these incomprehensible ex-
' pressions about water and blood?'

I confess that this language of the Apostle satisfies my intellect as well as my conscience much better than that language about Christianity, and its moral code, and its pure worship, which is so much more popular, and, in the judgment of some, so much more philosophical. Supposing a better code of morals and a purer worship has established itself in the world, I want to know *how*. That is the fact to be explained; I must not take the fact as if it were the explanation. It cannot be assumed that men are naturally inclined to a worship and a code of morals which restrain and counteract their natural inclinations; to say so, sounds like a great paradox. And if you introduce a divine power, and say, 'God has done that for men which they could not have done for themselves,' I may be well inclined to accept the statement; I may admit that you have found the only possible solution of the puzzle. But since God has clearly not uttered a simple decree that men shall have a different worship and obey a purer code now than in the days of old; since no such decree *could* have effected that purpose, so long as we are constituted as God has constituted us; since there has been clearly a process at work, a process which has acted upon the minds and consciences of men;—I am driven again to ask, What has that process been? What testimonies have been borne to the minds and consciences of men which they have confessed by receiving the message of the Gospel?

In replying to this question, St. John does not, you perceive, introduce the word Christianity at all. No such word is found in the New Testament. Surely we may be most thankful for the omission. For what a vague phrase it is! How continually it stands for a hundred different meanings, or does duty for a meaning that is absent altogether! It is not Christianity of which the beloved Apostle and all the Apostles speak to us; it is Christ. It is not a collection of notions, habits, practices; it is a Person. '*Jesus is the Christ*'—that is the proclamation which was made by fishermen and tentmakers in the ears of a denying or a laughing world. We have seen that it meant something very serious to those who made it. The Christ was not an idle title, a name that was surrounded with no associations, that was capable of no definition. Ages of Jewish lawgivers and prophets had been spelling out its signification; ages of Gentile idolaters and philosophers had cast in the contribution of their necessities and their doubts, which it must satisfy, if it were what these lawgivers and prophets had said that it was. According to its simplest etymology, it must denote that whoever bore it was a King, and was endowed with a Spirit. The Apostles said that one had appeared who was *the* King of Men, who had received the Spirit *of God*. And that one, they said, was called a carpenter, and had been put to death as a malefactor.

If He had the dignity which was asserted for Him, how was it to be denoted? What were the signs of it? ' *This is He*,' answers the Apostle, '*who came by water and blood, not by water only, but by water and blood.*' The Gospel interprets the language; history interprets it. *He came by water.* When He descended into the Jordan, it is said the Heavens opened and a voice declared, ' *This is my beloved Son, in whom I am well pleased.*' And the Spirit descended upon Him in a bodily shape. The narratives of the Evangelists start from this narrative. There are short records in St. Matthew and St. Luke, which I am convinced are genuine, concerning His birth and circumcision, and His coming into the Temple at twelve years old. But the Baptism opens the history of His ministry. The Baptism is the key to every record of it. Because He is declared to be the Son of God, and endowed with the Spirit of God,

He is led up by the Spirit to be tempted of the Devil, each temptation turning upon His right to call Himself the Son of God. Because He is declared to be Son of God, He goes forth in power of the Spirit preaching to the poor, healing the sick, casting out devils, calling Apostles, enduing them with power, giving them wisdom. All these were manifestations of His inward Spiritual power, of His Kingly power. That power is exercised in the name of His Father, and to glorify His Father. The more attentively you read any one of the first three Gospels, the more you compare them together, the more you will find that they derive their coherency from their relation to the Baptism, that *by far the greater part* of their story appears to be an explanation of the Christ's '*coming by water.*'

But not all. If you read to the end of these narratives, still more if you add to them that of St. John himself, you will see why he affirms with such emphasis: '*Not by water only, but by water and blood.*' We dare not say that the Baptism is the subject of the Gospels, when we read the account of the Passion. The death of Jesus, the shedding of His blood, that is, that must be, the great sign of what He was, the key to all the work that went before it. He tells His disciples so again and again; it was the part of His teaching which most utterly puzzled and confounded them. His rejection by the chief priests and scribes, the delivering of Him to the Gentiles, are the subjects on which He spoke to them, especially when St. Peter had confessed Him to be the Son of the living God, and when His glory had been seen on the Mount of Transfiguration. It followed speedily upon His entry into Jerusalem as the Son and Heir of David. The last passover fixed the conviction in the hearts of the disciples, that His death was to translate the old covenant into the new.

The conviction worked slowly in the minds of the early Christians; there were innumerable revolts from it and reactions against it. I have spoken to you of some who utterly refused to connect the Christ with death; who said that the death on the cross must have been only an apparent one, or else that Jesus must have ceased to be the Christ before it took place. The Gospel of St. John struck at the root of this opinion. Dwelling more than all previous Evangelists on the original glory of Christ, on His life before the worlds, on His eternal union with the Father, He yet dwells more than all others on His giving up of Himself, on His shedding His blood, as the very sign of His filial character, as the test of His divinity. He merely alludes to the Baptism, does not formally describe it. But he introduces the discourse (which contains the essence of all His discourses) wherein Jesus declares Himself to be the true Shepherd, and to be loved by his Father, because He gave His life for the sheep. The wonderful words belong to His Gospel: '*My flesh is meat indeed, my blood is drink indeed.*'

But I said that history, the history of the modern world, explained these words as well as the Gospels. You ask for the signs which distinguish those who acknowledge Jesus as the Christ from those who reject Him. You ask this question of some Jew or Mahometan, who can, of course, only point you to some external mark, who has a very imperfect notion of what the disciples of Jesus believe, who would not admit that they had any moral superiority. He would say, 'They baptize their converts, and generally

T

'their children, with water; they hold a feast which celebrates the death of their Founder, for they say that the shedding of his blood was, in some sense or other, a sacrifice.' This would be the observation of an impartial, intelligent traveller of another faith, who had not, perhaps, made himself minutely acquainted with the peculiarities of Christians, but who had ascertained in a rough way wherein their customs differed from his own, wherein they were like each other in different countries, as well as through a course of ages. And this, if we had no other evidence, would surely add a general confirmation to the words of St. John. It would indicate that a faith which had established itself amongst a number of different races, which had overcome the opposition of a considerable portion of the world, was faith in a Person who had come by water and by blood.

Still you are not satisfied. If any of those good results which we suppose to have followed from the spread of the Gospel have followed from it, you must demand further, 'What relation was there between them and these signs?' It would strike every one that water is a sign of cleansing. No one can read the Bible—I might say, perhaps, the book of any writer, professional or unprofessional, on the human frame—without feeling that the blood had some connexion with the life. To say that water is not the only sign of the coming of the Christ, that blood is also a sign of it—an equally important sign— might therefore appear to be equivalent with saying, 'The Christ is not only a purifier, He is a life-giver; He does not only remove defilements from men, He imparts to them a quickening principle.'

We are advancing rapidly, perhaps too rapidly; for now the doubt presents itself; every page of Christian

history raises it. 'Yes! but what a wide gulf there is
' between the sign and the thing signified! You have the
' water sign on your foreheads, but where is the purity that
' answers to it? You have the blood sign on your door-
' posts, but where is the divine, holy, self-sacrificing life
' which it would appear to express?' Certainly the doubt
ought not to be evaded, or trifled with; but with solemn
earnestness to be searched out. Will the last clause of the
verse help us at all in the investigation? '*And it is the
Spirit which beareth witness, because the Spirit is truth.*'

We have seen that the very idea of the Christ, as St
John sets it forth to us, is of one who receives the Holy
Spirit that He may impart it. When he speaks of Jesus
as the Christ, he means this. If we accept his statements
at all,—if we would understand them, even though we do not
accept them,—we must allow him to tell us his *whole*
meaning; one part of it must be imperfect without the
other. He denies that the signs of water or of blood
have any power apart from 'the Spirit' which was in
Him of whose person, of whose work, they are the signs.
But he says also that they are true signs, signs of an
actual purity which belongs to our race in Him who has
come by water; signs of a holy, self-sacrificing, divine life,
which belongs to it in Him who has come not by water
only, but by water and blood. Therefore he does not say
that the Spirit makes any man that which he is not truly
and actually in virtue of his being a man, but that He *bears
witness;* that He awakens the spirit of man to know his
true state, to understand and to claim the purity and the
risen life which are his in the Son of Man. the head of the
body whereof he is a member.

The Spirit, St. John intimates, is as truly given as the water and blood are given. One is as much involved in the coming of the Christ as the other. And this Spirit beareth witness *because He is truth;* beareth witness against the falsehood which is in us, the falsehood which disposes us to dwell in our own selfish impurity and death, when Christ has come to make us partakers of His own holy nature, of His own free and perfect life.

This subject is so important and so interesting that we long for more light upon it. St. John is ready to give it; but between the sixth verse and the eighth, wherein he explains more fully what he has just been saying, a verse has been interposed which appears entirely irrelevant: '*There are three that bear record in heaven, the Father, the Word, and the Holy Ghost; and these three are one.*' Nearly all scholars, I believe, in our day, are agreed that this verse is spurious. If it was genuine, we should be bound to consider seriously what it meant, however much its introduction in this place might puzzle us, however strange its phraseology might appear to us. Those who dwell with awe upon the name into which they have been baptized; those who believe that all the books of the Bible, and St. John's writings more than all the rest, reveal it to us; those who connect it with Christian ethics, as I have done; might wonder that an Apostle should make a formal announcement of this Name in a parenthesis, and in connexion with such a phrase as *bearing record,* one admirably suited to describe the intercourse of God with us, but quite unsuitable, one would have thought, as an expression of His absolute and eternal being. Still, if it was really one of St. John's utterances, we should listen to it in reverence,

and only attribute these difficulties to our own blindness. As we have the best possible reasons for supposing it is not his, but merely the gloss of some commentator, which crept into the text, and was accepted by advocates eager to confute adversaries, less careful about the truth they were themselves fighting for,—we may thankfully dismiss it and proceed with the topic which has occupied us already:
'*For there are three that bear witness on the earth, the Spirit, the water, and the blood ; and these three agree in one.*'

In speaking of the state of mankind since Jesus was born into it, two facts require to be explained: 1. How any change has been wrought in the moral condition of the world. 2. Why that change is not greater; why, at times, we are disposed to deny it altogether, and to think that we are worse than the generations of old?

Supposing there were a Spirit continually witnessing with the spirits of men concerning a purification from evil, concerning a spring of good which all are meant to enjoy; does it not seem to you that we have an explanation of both these facts? A man heeding this witness, suffering himself to be governed by that Spirit who is bearing it to his heart and conscience, acquires an internal righteousness, an energy to do what he ought to do, to be what he ought to be, which a man without the same revelation, without the same assurance of a divine presence and co-operation, cannot have had. And yet, though this righteousness and Life are internal, the same revelation compels the man to declare that they are not his; to attribute all that is good in him to another, with a confidence which no man in the old world can have felt. The Spirit, the water, the blood, agree in this testimony; all alike signify to the man that the more inward his purity and regeneration are, the more entirely they must be referred to Christ, not to himself.

But supposing this inward testimony is borne to the conscience and heart of a man — for to that it must be addressed—and rejected; may there not be, must there not be, an internal impurity, an internal death, such as no man in the old world could have realized? Or what is more frightful still, a self-righteousness, a self-glorification, to which he must have been a stranger? To whom such states of mind are to be attributed, is happily beyond our knowledge. The Judge of all the earth, of quick and dead, only is able to discriminate. But does not each one know enough of what has passed in *himself*, of *his* struggles with a good Spirit, to be able to say, ' Such a state, so far darker
' than that of any Jew or Heathen, may be the portion of
' one who has been brought into the Christian covenant,
' just because he has been brought into it, just because the
' Spirit, the water, and the blood agree in their witness to
' the blessings whereof we have been made inheritors?'

One point more has to be recollected, that the great enigma which was started may be solved, so far as it is needful for our comfort and peace that it should be solved. Reflect that the Spirit, the Water, and the Blood all agree in the testimony that Good is mightier than Evil, that Christ has come to destroy the works of the Devil, and has not failed in the purpose of His coming. Thus we may explain the fact which would be otherwise unaccountable, that, though the numbers of those who reject the witness seem to our human eyesight immensely greater than that of those who accept it, yet that the former have failed, and the latter have succeeded. The meek have inherited the earth. They have had a power over it, a power to transform it in spite of the continued resistance of a majority possessed of all appliances and means to keep it in its degradation and darkness. So you may understand the progress of civility, the breaking the fetters of the serf, the existence of politics, of freedom, of humanity, in spite of that increased malice and devilry which the Gospel has called forth. So you may dare to anticipate all that holy men and prophets have said should be, and may be certain that the Spirit, the Water, and Blood are agreed in witnessing that it shall be.

'*If we receive the witness of men, the witness of God is greater: for this is the witness of God which He hath testified of His Son.*' You will remember that this subject of Testimony was brought before us in the very opening of St. John's Epistle. He had seen and handled that which was about the Word of Life; He had been sent to *bear witness* of that Eternal Life which was with the Father, and had been manifested to men. In speaking of this passage, I remarked that the Ephesians must have been often exercised with the question whether they should not know less of Christ after the Apostles had left the world than they did then, and whether their sons and grandsons would not lose something of what they retained. I showed you how directly St. John's words met this doubt, how they vindicated for him and the eleven their true position as eye-witnesses of that which could be seen of the Christ; how they declared that the Person who was manifested to them might be as fully known in the nineteenth century as in the first. Those who know what endless anxieties have arisen in all ages since, out of the inquiry how much testimony we have respecting the Christ, what testimony is of worth respecting any events that have been recorded of the past, what testimony it is possible for us to receive respecting anything which is supernatural, may be thankful that St. John did not hastily dismiss this topic, that he returns to it again, that he expresses his full judgment upon it. What that judgment is you might guess from the previous sentence; but it is well worthy of a careful examination. Starting from the belief that God is, and that it is God's purpose to reveal Himself, he boldly declares that we are not dependent for our faith upon the testimony of Apostles, upon the traditions of past ages, upon the authority and interpretation of doctors and Churches. Whatever value you may attach to these testimonies, whatever may be their respective degrees of credibility, there is a Great Judge, a standing Court of Appeal to which these decisions may and must be referred; one who is separating the chaff from the wheat in them every moment; one who alone is able to give them any weight over the Conscience and Reason and Will of man. The witness of men may be great, the witness of God is greater. This, I believe, is sound philosophy, in which we must all at last acquiesce. I conceive the Scotch philosopher, Hume, was right, that no mere human testimony, or combination of human testimonies, could be of weight enough to procure credence for anything that transcends the limits of human experience. He had of course to explain, as well as he could, how it is that men in all countries of the world have been dreaming of God, have been feeling that they could not exist without God. He had to account as well as he could for the manifold experiences of what is supernatural, of what is higher than themselves, which men, not in one country but in all countries, have spoken of. There are but two ways; one was Hume's way, that of supposing that all the deepest and most earnest thoughts of the most earnest men in the world pointed to nothing. The other is to suppose that they pointed to some Person, whom they could not reach; that all their confused guesses were calls to Him to make Himself known; that He Himself had awakened those calls; that He *was* testifying to men of Himself; that He was purposing to testify to them fully of Himself. Between Atheism, in its most direct and absolute form, and the conviction that God is manifesting Himself, and that His testimony to us is above all human testimony— is the ground and strength of all human testimony—I believe we shall soon find that there is no alternative. Those who have put forth the doctrine of Positivism in our day are driving us to this discovery. We owe them infinite thanks for it. They are bringing the battle to a point. It will be fought out, not as it has been in former ages of the world, with confused noise, and garments rolled in blood, but with burning and fuel of fire. Everything will be involved in it. Wit, letters, science, humanity will for a time be glorified, as if they were substitutes for God. Then they will go down into the unfathomable pit of Atheism. Or they will be seen to have derived their greatness and glory from the God who so loved the world as to give His Son for it; they will rise to a new life; humanity will have that excellence in the Son of Man which men have fancied they could win for it by casting off His yoke. The earth will come forth a bride adorned for her husband, shining with the radiance of her Creator and her King.

'*He that believeth on the Son of God hath the witness in himself: he that believeth not God hath made Him a liar; because he believeth not the record that God gave of His Son. And this is the record, that God hath given to us eternal life, and this life is in His Son.*'

As there has been much talk among us about external testimonies and the weight that is to be assigned to them, so there has been much talk about an inward witness, which some might claim and others not. Here St. John speaks of this inward witness very emphatically, '*He that believeth on the Son of God hath the witness in himself.*' In fact, he could not understand any witness to a man which was not a witness to a man *in himself*. A mere vision presented to the eyes, if it was the clearest possible, was nothing, unless it signified something to him who used the eyes; unless it entered into his heart and conscience. But St. John never for an instant sanctions the vanity and self-glorification of those who say that Christ is for them and not for the world. If they believe in the Son of God, they believe in a Christ for mankind. The inward witness is of such a one. And if they believe not in a Christ for mankind, a Christ who has reconciled God and Man, St. John is very broad and simple in his assertions respecting them: '*They make God a liar.*' They deny the revelation He has made of Himself in the Baptism and the Death of Jesus; they deny the witness which the Spirit and the water and the blood are together bearing respecting Him.

Good men—some of them men whom I honour and revere—want to get rid of all outward testimonies of God's love,—of the water and the blood,—and to dwell exclusively on what they call the internal testimony of the Spirit. I do not undervalue their doctrine as a counterweight to much that is coarse, sensual, external, in the language of Churchmen; I think God has appointed it, as a protest against our idolatries. But I do not admit for an instant that they are wiser than St. John, or that they know as well as he did what the witness of the Spirit is. I find them continually setting aside His witness by confounding Him with the thoughts which He inspires in them; with the spirits to which His witness is borne. I think they must do this, and must become very exclusive, and also very often the victims of casual impressions, of nervous ecstasies or depressions, if they are not willing to receive God's testimony to others as well as themselves. This is the blessing of the '*Water and the Blood.*' They speak of a gift, a gift of eternal life to Mankind; a gift not bestowed upon those who are conscious of it, but upon all, in that Son who died for all and lives for all.

The words which follow contain the only possible limitation of this gift, and they are in very truth not a limitation but an expansion of it, '*He that hath the Son hath life: and he that hath not the Son of God hath not life.*' We have no life, we can have no life in ourselves. The Spirit does not witness to us of a miserable, partial, selfish, new life, which is given to us because we are Christians or believers, or have certain rare emotions. He testifies to us of a Universal and Everlasting Life which dwells in the Son of God; which we may enjoy, if we do not desire to be separated from the great family in heaven and earth that is named in Him.

LECTURE XVIII.

THE NATURE OF PRAYER—VENIAL AND MORTAL SINS.

1 JOHN V. 13—17.

These things have I written unto you that believe on the name of the Son of God; that ye may know that ye have eternal life, and that ye may believe on the name of the Son of God. And this is the confidence that we have in Him, that, if we ask any thing according to His will, He heareth us: and if we know that He hear us, whatsoever we ask, we know that we have the petitions that we desired of Him. If any man see his brother sin a sin which is not unto death, he shall ask, and he shall give him life for them that sin not unto death. There is a sin unto death: I do not say that he shall pray for it. All unrighteousness is sin: and there is a sin not unto death.

WE are approaching the conclusion of the Epistle; the words, '*These things have I written*,' indicate that St. John is about to give an explanation of its general purpose, if not a summary of its contents. Thus much is obvious on the first reading of them. His object was not to make proselytes of those who lay outside the Christian Church. He addressed himself to '*those who believed on the name of the Son of God.*' They were baptized into that Name; they publicly confessed that Name; it was the Name which drew on them the charge of blasphemy from Jewish rulers and scribes; it was the Name, when associated with the person of Jesus the Crucified, which excited the contempt or hostility of the worshippers of the Greek divinities. All acts of united worship among the disciples, all their sufferings, recalled this Name.

But if they had no need to be convinced of its worth or its power, what good was an Apostolical Epistle to do them? St. John makes answer: '*That ye may know that ye have eternal life, and that ye may believe on the name of the Son of God.*' You will wonder at the last clause. It sounds as if he proposed to convert them to a faith which they were possessed of already. Before you determine that it is actually so empty of meaning, consider the first clause. That, at all events, is not a commonplace. 'Ye have eternal life.' Not 'ye *may* have it; sometime hence ' this unspeakable blessing may be bestowed on you, or ' on such of you as deserve it.' But, 'it is yours now. The ' gift has been assured to you.' I think many Christians of his day and of ours would rather be startled by the strangeness than by the simplicity of this assertion; would deem it very unlike the notions which they had associated with their traditional faith.

Yet it cannot be said that St. John is introducing a new doctrine at the close of his letter. In the first verses of it he adopted the very language which we meet with here. The Eternal Life is said to have been manifested that they might partake of it, and that so their joy might be full. There has been no inconsistency in any of the sentences which followed that early sentence. All have represented Eternal Life as shown forth in Jesus Christ, as given to men in Jesus Christ. All have been signifying that to believe in Christ is to believe in one who has the Eternal Life of God, that Life which is intended for man who is made in the image of God, that life the loss of which is

Eternal Death. The verse with which I concluded the last Lecture had the same burden: '*He that hath the Son of God hath life. He that hath not the Son of God, hath not life.*'

You can understand, then, why the Apostle wrote to those who believed in the Name of the Son of God, '*that they might believe in the Name of the Son of God.*' He does not wish to rob them of any faith they had. He does not seek to persuade them that it was good for nothing. It meant far more, not less, than they supposed. He would show them how much it meant, what rights they had which they were not claiming. And this not merely to increase their comfort, not even to enlarge the scope of their knowledge; but to save the belief they had from degenerating into the pride which is the enemy of all belief. If their faith was in a Christ in whom there was *not* Eternal Life for all men, who only might bestow something called Eternal Life on certain persons, hereafter; they might soon learn to compliment themselves on their superiority to the Jews and Heathens who had not this faith. They might find a certain comfort in looking forward to *their* exclusion from the blessings which were in reserve for the chosen flock. And yet, all the while, their notion of these blessings would become more and more vague; the Eternal Life would be a mere expression for a certain amount of conceivable or inconceivable happiness. Strange, no doubt, that we should find a compensation for the distance, indistinctness, unreality of our hopes for ourselves, in thinking that other men are cut off from them altogether! Strange;—and yet no reader of history, no reader of his own heart, will deny that our dark unregenerate nature does find a miserable consolation in this thought; or that it mixes in fearful confusion with thoughts which have their root in the *regenerate* will, with the zeal and affection which God Himself has inspired!

St. John permits no vagueness and no exclusiveness. He tells them of a life, an actual divine life, which has been manifested in the Son of Man to men. This is, this must be, the blessing which God desires for His creatures, which God only can bestow upon them. This must be that which they want *here*. The full fruition of this Life, separated from all the vanity, selfishness, death which mingles with it now, must be what the saints enter into when they cast off their mortal rags. St. John then wrote that all who believed in the Son of God then, or should believe on Him hereafter, might believe in Him in this moral, human, divine sense; not in a sense which might become immoral, inhuman, ungodly.

'*And this is the confidence that we have in Him, that, if we ask any thing according to His will, He heareth us: and if we know that He hear us, whatsoever we ask, we know that we have the petitions that we desired of Him.*' He has told us that we *have* eternal life. 'What then have we to ask 'for? Is there anything better than eternal life?' Such a question as this would be a most reasonable one if Eternal Life were what so many of us take it to be, a state of repose after toil, a state of security not of dependence. But who that uses language faithfully, associates Life with inanition, and not rather with the highest activity of all powers and energies? Or who that has learnt from bitter experience that to be independent of God is to be in death, can dream of a state which shall have any worth or any security apart from Him? No; '*Ask and ye shall receive*, is a higher promise than 'Ye shall receive without asking.' And it is the climax of all St. John has been telling us about the gift of Life to say, that '*if we ask any thing according to God's will, He heareth us.*'

But some one may say, 'We gain nothing by such 'asking as that. No doubt, if we pray according to God's 'will, we are right. But why might not we let that Will 'take its course without our prayers?' The thought is so natural that, after we have replied to it in ourselves a thousand times, we find it starting up again as strong as ever. In fact, no replies of ours to it are of much avail. God answers to it out of the whirlwind. Sufferings of body and soul drive us to pray, whether we expect much good from the effort or not. We pray, because we feel that things are not as they ought to be; we pray, because we secretly confess or faintly hope that there may be some Power in the Universe which would set them right. We have very dim and confused notions what that Power can be, or why things should have gone into disorder in spite of it, or whether it is itself the author of our misery. Nevertheless, we pray; the sense of evil goading us on. If we stop at this point of knowledge, dark superstitions, such as I spoke of in former Lectures, gather round us, and take possession of us. A number of different Minds and Wills seem to be ruling the universe and tearing it in pieces; which are in favour of us, which are adverse to us, we cannot tell; by degrees the sense of guilt within us makes us deem all as our enemies; the only question is, how we can disarm them or escape from them. Then comes the Revelation of Jesus Christ. The Son of God enters into our world. He finds, as we do, that it is full of darkness, strife, enmity. But He says,—He proves,—that this darkness, strife, enmity, are not according to the Will of His Father. Instead of succumbing to them Himself, instead of calling upon men to submit to them as decrees of an immutable destiny, He is fighting with them every hour. His death, which looks as if it were their final triumph, is the proclamation of their defeat. A WILL, then, is declared to be at the foundation of all things, at the foundation of the whole visible and invisible, material and spiritual Creation, which is a Will to Good and only to Good; which is a Will that all should be saved and should come to the knowledge of the Truth.

But this is not all. That endless question, Why did not Omnipotence prevent the existence of evil, is settled for the Conscience, the Heart, the Reason of men. Whatever restless thing in us craves for another settlement, *they* declare, 'No omnipotent decree *can* take the evil from a voluntary creature; *can* make him blessed. The Will of man was made in the image of God; it must be in harmony with that Will or be miserable. No power but Love can establish that harmony. The Revelation of Jesus Christ declares that Love is *the* power of God; that Love is at work to restore this harmony; it is all we want to be told; what remains is, to ask with boldness and confidence that all wills which are struggling with this Will may be reduced into obedience; that whatever disturbances in the natural world, the world of involuntary creatures, have been the results of our rebellion, may first be turned into instruments for quelling it, and then may be removed for ever.

U

Is it nothing, then, to be told, '*that if we ask any thing according to God's will, He heareth us; and that if He heareth us, we know that we have the petitions which we desired of Him?*' Nothing!—is it not everything? If we believed that, would not every thought of our hearts be a prayer, our work a prayer? Should not we be certain, that whatever tyranny, anarchy, falsehood, there is in the universe, or in ourselves, must be contrary to the Will of God; that when we ask for the removal of that, He heareth us; that however long the struggle may seem to us, we actually have what we desired of Him? The enemy is doomed; from the judgment-seat of Christ its death has been pronounced; only God would have us working with Him for its extinction; only He would have us understand, and act upon the understanding, that all which is against Him is against us; that all which aims to set up another Ruler instead of Him, is aiming to make us wretched slaves. Prayer, then, is not the howl of a set of Baal worshippers, crying and cutting themselves with stones, to a Power which they want to compel into consent with their own wild, selfish, cruel inclinations. It is the response of creatures—conscious of these wild, selfish, cruel inclinations, conscious of having yielded to them, conscious of having thus set themselves at war with the perfect and living Will—to the fixed resolutions of that Will, to its hatred of whatever is perverse and base, to its gracious, gentle, and therefore all prevailing inspirations.

Many are inclined to pass over this sentence (which is the fulfilment and practical application of all we have heard from St. John concerning the Love of God and its manifestation of Jesus the Anointed Son, and the gift of His

Anointing Spirit to bind His family into one) as if it signified almost nothing. They treat the next two verses differently. Upon these they dwell; upon these they found conclusions. I will dwell upon them too; they are worthy of all the thought we can give them.

'*If any man see his brother sin a sin that is not unto death, he shall ask, and he shall give him life for them that sin not unto death. There is a sin unto death: I do not say that he shall pray for it.* [The more exact rendering of the last clause would be, *Not concerning that am I saying that he should ask.*] *All unrighteousness is sin: and there is a sin not unto death.*'

These sentences have led to a distinction which has more affected the science and the practice of Christian Morals than any other that I know of. You cannot open a book of Devotion written by a Roman Catholic, or any of their numerous books on Casuistry, for the rich or the poor, without meeting with the phrases, *Mortal* and *Venial* sin, and without some announcement of what sins are mortal and what venial. I have no language to express the amount of positive transgression, of self-deception, of tyranny, which, I think, has been caused by the doctrines and decrees that have been promulgated in different ages, and are promulgated now, on this subject. My impulse might be simply to denounce them. But I have learnt from my own experience, and from the experience of far wiser men, that this is never a safe or right way of treating prevalent opinions and habits of thought, if they seem to us ever so mischievous.

In the last volume of the Sermons preached at Brighton by the late Mr. Robertson, there is one remarkable even among its noble and beautiful companions, 'On *Absolution.*' It does, I am sure, express the innermost mind and heart of the writer. Profoundly impressed, far more profoundly than those who are loudest in their declamations against Romanists, with the moral evil which has flowed from the maxims and practices respecting Confession and Absolution, that are sanctioned among them, he yet maintains that the fullest justice must be done to the principle which is at the root of these maxims and practices; otherwise there can be no deliverance from the superstitions of votaries or the assumption of priests. This remark, which comes to us from the grave, or rather, from one of that redeemed company who are witnesses and helpers of our struggles upon earth, is just as true in the case before us as in the one to which it was originally applied.

The distinction of mortal and venial sins will be, as it has been, the cause of indulgence to sin, of utter confusion as to the nature of sin and of deliverance from sin, of a money value being set upon sins, if we do not show what there is in this distinction which commends itself to the conscience, which is demanded by the conscience. St. John's words, I believe, contain what we need. If we consider them carefully, we shall see how strikingly *his* teaching respecting the sin unto death illustrates and vindicates that teaching respecting the answer to prayer, which has come under our notice already.

'*If we ask anything according to His will, He heareth us.*' 'How!' one of his readers might exclaim, 'Did I
' not ask fervently, by day and by night, for the forgiveness
' of that friend or brother whom I saw going fearfully
' astray? And was it not all useless? Did he not, so far

'as I can judge, die in his sins? Were not some of his
'last acts some of his worst? Is it not, then, the Will of
'God to forgive sins? How can I judge of His will from
'the cross of Christ, if this is not His Will?' People
must have said this then; for they are saying it now. It
is one of the profoundest causes of distress to earnest,
true-hearted women, mothers and sisters; to them,
because their affection, their compassion, yes, and
their faith, is generally stronger than ours, and because it
nearly always takes an individual direction. Therein lies the
power and the weakness of women. Their devotion ought
to be balanced,—alas! how rarely it is!—by a deeper feeling
on our parts of the plagues and sins which are consuming
nations, Churches, mankind; of the war which God is
carrying on with these; of the sacrifices of individual life
which He makes that the greater ends of His government
may be accomplished. Out of these two elements together
might a real Christian communion be formed, because the
love of the brother would be sanctioned by a perfect trust
in the Will of the Father.

That you may see better how such a doubt as that
I have supposed might be met, consider how an ordinary
father would answer the complaint of a daughter who had
been pleading for the restoration of a reprobate brother to
the house from which his offences had banished him. He
would say, 'My dear child! you are quite right to ask me
'to forgive this boy of mine. You know how I care for
'him; you know how entirely it is my wish to have him
'amongst us. I have forgiven him one offence after
'another; you felt, and I felt, that by showing him for-
'giveness I was taking the best course to bend him

' and to attach him to us. That is true up to a certain
' point. But there are offences about which it is not true.
' There are offences implying an alienation of heart from
' me and from you all, which the manifestation of forgive-
' ness will not remove. I believe he has committed *such*
' offences. I believe it would not do him good, or you, his
' brothers and sisters—I believe it would not be right in me
' —to send him word that he might come to us, after he has
' fallen into this state. We must leave him alone; we
' must appear to forget him; wait and see whether my
' treatment or yours will be the most satisfactory in the
' end.' I can suppose the daughter adding, in great
sadness, ' But, father, how can *I* know whether his offences
' are of the first kind or the last?' ' My dear child,' he
would answer, ' you cannot know, and I do not require
' you to know. Leave the judgment of that to me. Ask
' as you like for your brother; I shall not blame your
' ignorance; only if, in the greater wisdom for which I
' am sure you give me credit, I decide that he has done the
' acts to which your kind of discipline would be unsuitable,
' do not fancy that my mind is different from what in all
' other cases, in all your past experience, you have found
' it to be.'

I believe this human analogy is a strictly accurate one.
It would not be accurate—it would not apply at all—if
St. John had spoken of sins unto death, as those which
make it impossible for a man to repent and turn to God,
of sins not unto death as those for which a man may be forgiven. But he says nothing of the kind. He limits himself
to the case of one who is asking for another; asking when
that person has given no apparent signs of wishing to be

a better man. What the petitioner desires is the restoration of such a one to the communion of the Christian family, to a participation in the Life of Christ. In many cases, he is told, the wish—the God-inspired wish—will have an accomplishment. The sinner will be brought into the fold. But there are cases in which the separation is more complete, when there has been an habitual resolute separation from all that is good and true; when good is abhorred, and evil becomes good. 'I do not,' he says, ' speak of such cases. I do not hold out promises con-' cerning them which may be disappointed. *All unright-* ' *eousness is sin;* every departure from the commandment ' is a separation from Christ.' ' *He that sinneth,*' as he said before, ' *has not seen Him, neither known Him.*' But ' *there is a sin not unto death ;*' one which interrupts communion, but does not destroy it. Every one's conscience, I think, recognises *this* difference. Each one of us knows how little indulgences of bitterness, of insincerity, of distrust, harden into states of mind. Each one may have felt the death creeping on him, may recollect how its progress has been arrested. He cannot, therefore, wonder if he is told that the same process goes on in other men; that the all-seeing eye detects when the disease which was functional has become organic and mortal; that He acts upon that knowledge.

You perceive not only that St. John does not say what acts are mortal, what are venial or pardonable, but that it is essential to his object that he should not say it. What he is teaching is entire dependence on the Will of God, entire confidence in that Will; a readiness, therefore, to trust Him even in cases where He seems to refuse what He has promised to grant. He is teaching also that death is the refusal of that Eternal Life which is given us in Christ. It must, therefore, go on in the *soul* of a man. Who can say that an external act which is no flagrant enormity, which does not look like an enormity at all, which is even admired by men, may not be hastening this death? For what can hasten it so much as hypocrisy; what sin can be so mortal as that? Yet if it were set down in a thousand books as mortal, what would the hypocrite be the better for the information; how would any one be the better able to convict him of it?

The reason why persons have attempted what St. John would not attempt, what it would have been inconsistent with every one of his maxims to attempt, is this: The Church claims to have communion with the life of God. This is the meaning of its Sacraments, especially of the Sacrament of the Lord's Supper. If it does not signify that such a communion has been established between God and us in His Son, it signifies nothing. We do not claim too much for it, when we say that this fellowship is involved in it and expressed by it; on the contrary, by making that assertion we secure it from degenerating into a charm or ceremony; we do not allow ourselves or any to find a virtue in the mere service apart from Him of whom it testifies. But if it has this character, to cut men off from this Sacrament is as much as denying that they are partakers of the life of Christ. What an awful proclamation! Yet if no person is banished from the communion of the Church, men may be recognised as belonging to it who would be excluded from any society in the world, whom decent unbelievers would utterly refuse to mix with. It is because the sacrifice of Christ is complete, and because the communion of the Church declares it to be for all, that this disgrace should not be suffered. Men who have committed flagrant transgressions have said publicly,—'We renounce the life of Christ; we 'do not choose to be His servants:' the Church with fear and trembling must ratify their decree against themselves.

This is what St. Paul told the Corinthians they must do —what he blamed them for not having done without his authority—in the case of a man who had committed incest with his father's wife. Such a man, he said, *must be delivered to Satan.* In other words, he must be told, ' You 'have chosen the devil for your master: you must go and 'serve him. You must receive his wages; you must learn 'that these wages are death.' He does not shrink from that very expression. He says, *he must be given up for the* DESTRUCTION *of the flesh.* That is as much as saying, the man had committed a mortal sin. Here, then, seems to be a precedent for pronouncing what are mortal sins. A man reading this passage may ask triumphantly, How can there be any discipline in a Church such as St. Paul demands, such as the consciences of us all declare there ought to be, if we are not able to affirm, that certain transgressions are grounds for excommunication; that certain transgressions may be pardoned by the Church because they are pardoned by God?

I state the case as strongly as I can, in favour of making this arrangement of offences. And now let us see what St. Paul's precedent, which I admit to be decisive, actually says.—1. Hear the end of the passage. The man is delivered to Satan for the destruction of the flesh, *that his spirit may be saved in the day of the Lord.* The man has committed a mortal sin. By treating it with righteous severity, it may ultimately be found not mortal. God may remove it, though we cannot. 2. Hear the sequel of the story. In the Second Epistle to the Corinthians St. Paul recurs to this very case. He declares his belief that the notorious offender is penitent; he desires the Church to forgive him; he forgives him; he and they are to assure him of Christ's forgiveness. 3. Consider what St. Paul omits to do, as well as what he does. The Church of Corinth was the one which stood most in need of directions respecting the nature of moral offences, as well as respecting the treatment of offenders. To no Church does St. Paul speak so much on these subjects; for none does he enter into so many minute questions of life and conduct. And yet nowhere, in either of his Epistles, does he make a classification of sins; not when he had this one crime of incest forced upon his notice does he put it into a catalogue, and say, You are to reckon it with this and this and this mortal crime; you can distinguish it from that and that and that venial crime.

The precedent of St. Paul, considered in all possible aspects, proves that he did not conceive *he* had any authority as an Apostle, as one who had had a revelation of Jesus Christ, to lay down rules and maxims about the sins which should be pardoned and should not. And he makes us feel why he would not, why he dared not, exercise such authority. He wanted the Church in every exercise of its discipline to feel that it was in the presence of the Judge of the whole earth; that it must not venture to cut off any one of His children from Him by any act or decree of its own; that it must simply inquire, feeling the awfulness of the duty, 'Has the man sentenced him-'self? has he done any act which constitutes a formal re-'nunciation of his affiance in, of his allegiance to Christ; 'has he refused to communicate with us and with Him?' And even if it is determined, after solemnest deliberation, that he *has* done such an act, even then his exclusion is not to be regarded as cutting him off finally, but as a means of saving him finally: even then it is possible that the Church on earth ought at some time or other to readmit him among its members.

So then St. John's caution in defining is not greater than is St. Paul's in practice. The one says—'This 'is a sin unto death, I am not speaking of that when I 'tell you that your prayers for your brother will be an-'swered'—and then is silent. The other coming into direct contact with one of these deadly cases, being obliged to legislate about it, not avoiding in the least degree that responsibility, not allowing the Corinthians to escape from their share of the responsibility; yet imposes upon himself and them the obligation of committing everything to God, of not anticipating His judgment. And here then, in the principle and in the conduct of both these Apostles, exhibited in such different circumstances, I find our protection from the definitions and divisions of Church doctors. St. Paul and St. John show us why those who have claimed a wisdom higher than theirs, have also claimed a wisdom different from God's, and therefore most destructive to His creatures.

If those who have affirmed certain sins to be mortal, and certain sins to be venial, had adhered to their own statements, their doctrine might have been a presumptuous or a cruel one; but it would have been far less injurious to morality than it has been. In effect, mortal sins have been declared to be as much within the scope of the Church's forgiveness as venial. Out of its infinite treasure-house of pardons there may come relief for every conceivable, almost for every inconceivable, transgression. And then the question has been, On what terms will the Church bestow these infinite pardons? Shall they be dealt out freely, or shall there be certain acts done to procure them? If certain acts, of what kind shall they be? 'Certainly,' the Church has said, 'The man must give proofs of his wish to 'be pardoned.' The proofs may be submitting to severe penances; they may be deeds of charity to the poor; they may be presents to the Church itself. Consider what comes of this! Penances which might be good to make a soft flexible temper capable of endurance; deeds of charity which might be good as witnesses of a common brotherhood; gifts to the Church which might mean a devotion to the general weal or a confession of God's care for all; become vile selfish contrivances for averting a threatened sentence, for purchasing a possible good. Deeds, which should flow out of God's love, are means for buying off His wrath. And as good loses its nature and principle, so does evil. Evil becomes not a detestable, accursed state, the state of separation from God the perfect Good, but something which brings a punishment that may be severe, that may be everlasting, that may be avoided by certain compensations. Conceive the inward perplexity, the trickery, the money-worship, which such notions must introduce into the hearts of a people, of the rich and of the poor. Conceive the still worse effect which they must have on the minds of the priests, who have power to play fast and loose with mortal and venial sins, with terrors and with pardons, with dispensations and excommunications!

About all these things we in Protestant countries hear warnings enough, warnings often so fierce and ill-timed that we cease to believe there is any ground or necessity for them. Would to God there were not! But the facts are clear and patent; it is a childish affectation of liberality to deny them. It is, indeed, a solemn duty to acknowledge that beneath them there lies, in every Roman Catholic country, a better faith, a deeper Gospel, which they have overlaid and half smothered, but which they have not destroyed. It is a duty to see that we assert that better faith, that deeper Gospel, for them and ourselves. It may be hidden from us as well as from them; the same tempers of mind, differently exhibited, may undermine it for both. If we do not adopt St. John's interpretation of the faith of Christ the Son of God; if we do not think that God has manifested the true eternal life in Him, has given it to mankind in Him;—we may be confusing eternal death, the separation from the divine Life of which His sacrifice and death have made us heirs, with certain outward punishments to be inflicted here or hereafter; we may begin to ask whether *we* cannot make compensation by outward acts or inward, by some great deeds or by professions of faith, for our sins, and so escape their punishment. And so our English morality may become as insincere, treacherous, venal, as any Papal morality ever was. On the other hand, if we declare that the sacrifice of Christ was made for the whole world, that the eternal righteous love and truth of God are revealed in Christ to every sinful man; that he may cast off his death, his unrighteousness, hatred, untruth, and enter into possession of them; we shall be bearing a testimony which the same creeds and sacraments bear to Romanists and to Englishmen, a testimony to which there will be a response in the inmost conscience and heart of the Catholic as well as of the Protestant.

3 Nov '42
5 Dec '42

LECTURE XIX.

CHRISTIAN CERTAINTY.

1 JOHN V. 18—21.

We know that whosoever is born of God sinneth not; but he that is begotten of God keepeth himself, and that wicked one toucheth him not. And we know that we are of God, and the whole world lieth in wickedness. And we know that the Son of God is come, and hath given us an understanding, that we may know Him that is true, and we are in Him that is true, even in His Son Jesus Christ. This is the true God, and eternal life. Little children, keep yourselves from idols. Amen.

CAN we be certain of any principles in Ethics? St. John declares that we can. He says that he has not been making probable guesses about the grounds of human actions, the relations of man to God, the nature of God Himself. These are things that he *knows*. Nay, he is not content with claiming this knowledge himself. He uses the plural pronoun; he declares that his disciples, his little children, '*know*' that which he knows.

I. What do they know? He had just said, '*All unrighteousness is sin: there is a sin not unto death.*' He says now, '*We* KNOW *that he that is born of God sinneth not.*' You may remember that we met with this language before. I inquired how it was consistent with the words, '*If we say that we have no sin, we deceive ourselves, and the truth is not in us.*' Evidently we could not bring these statements into accordance by modifying either. We could not, for instance, pretend that he meant merely that those who were born of God did not sin a great deal, very terribly. Or again, that he did not address himself to Christian men, to 'true believers,' when he spoke of confessing sins. These would have been dishonest subterfuges, which would have robbed us not of one of the Apostle's assertions, but of both, and would have left an impression on the mind of every reader that he was himself an untrustworthy man, who played loosely with words. I said, we must determine to construe each sentence accurately, to give it its full force; then we might consider how they should be reconciled. So we discovered that the apparent contradictions in St. John arose from a *real* contradiction in us; that sin itself is a contradiction, and that we cannot express ourselves rightly and satisfactorily about it, so as to describe undoubted facts, without using phrases, which, when they are looked at on the surface, clash with each other. The way to ascertain the meaning of each, and the veracity of each, was to bring them home to our consciences. 'Man, 'dost not thou know certainly that there is something 'wrong in thee, something that is struggling against the 'truth in thee? Darest thou deny it? Hast not thou found 'that when the truth is strongest within thee, when it is 'clearest to thee, thou art least disposed to question the 'existence of this enemy; thou art most aware of his pre- 'sence? Is it not, then, thy indifference to truth, thy wish to 'ignore it, which leads thee to say, " I have no sin in me?" 'Is there not a self-deception, a lie, in that denial?' I do not think any man will bear this probing without being either brought to the confession which St. John demands of him, or stammering and shuffling in a way that is equally decisive about the fact, though far less creditable to him.

But in the process of this inquiry, what has come to light? There is a *truth in him,* in the man who confesses his sin. There is a truth against which the sin is fighting; there is a truth with which the man has a right to associate himself, to say, ' It is for me ; I am for it.' There is a truth which authorizes him to disclaim his sin, to say, ' I ' will none of it; closely as it approaches me, I entirely ' repudiate its pretension to be a part of me, or to govern ' me.' The confession of the sin that is in us is nothing less than this disclaimer, this renunciation, of the sin. But to *whom* do we confess the sin? *who,* besides ourselves, do we conceive is interested in that renunciation? We confess the sin to GOD ; we believe He is interested in our renunciation of it. Why? Because we confess that the '*truth in us*' is His truth ; that it is there because we are related to Him ; there, because we are not our own, but His. The *sin* is the denial of this relationship ; the setting up to be independent of Him. The *truth* which the sin rebels against is, first, the truth that is in God Himself; secondly, the truth that we are born of Him, that we are His children.

Here, then, is the vindication of the proposition, taken in its broadest, strongest form : '*He that is born of God doth not commit sin.*' Fix upon a set of persons, proclaim, ' These are God's children ;' and you must dilute the doctrine, you must reduce it almost to nothing, in order to make it coincide with the facts of these persons' lives. But take the Apostle to say to each man, ' that in you which ' is born of God doth not commit sin, and if you habitually, ' at every moment, claimed your rights as a child of His, ' *you* would not commit sin ; ' and I believe the conscience which confesses sin would cry, '*I know it;* it is so. I know 'it by every righteous act I have done, I know it by 'every wrong act I have done. I did righteous acts 'because I yielded myself to God, because I owned Him 'as my Father; I did wrong acts because I would have a 'way and will of my own; because I would not own the 'truth; because I would not say, "He is with me; He is 'the root of what is right in me."'

There is no part of St. John's Epistle which more than this convinces me that Christian ethics are, in the highest sense, *scientific* ethics; nay, that we cannot have a science of ethics, in the full sense of the words, till we accept the principles which the Apostle sets forth to us. For that there are confusions in the world, innumerable confusions, all acknowledge; we may not call these confusions 'sins;' perhaps we avoid the word. But, at all events, they produce some of the effects which men attribute to sin. And evidently there can be no *science* of *confusions*. They set at nought science; by their very name they refuse to be brought into any order. Accordingly, writers on ethics are driven to speak of the happiness that men *might* attain, the virtues that men *might* exhibit. They affirm, and rightly affirm, that these are intended for man; that these are according to his constitution. They say, 'If men only knew what their constitution is, even what 'their physical constitution is, how many evils might they 'avoid! If they were only better educated, what blessings 'would follow!' All which may be exceedingly true, but practical people do not heed it. They reply, 'We cannot 'pursue ideals. Somehow or other, we suppose things 'will last for our time. We were not born to set them

'right. The world is very corrupt, no doubt. But are we
'not a parcel of it?' Thus the science of life and the business are set in continual opposition, and every day makes
the distance between them greater and the conflict fiercer.

But is it so if I can say to every man, 'Friend, thou art
'not part and parcel of the world; thou art not pledged and
'sold to its corruptions; thou hast another parentage; thou
'art a man; thou art a child of God; and as such thou
'art holy and righteous; as such the corruptions and
'anomalies of the world are odious to thee, are thy enemies;
'thou hatest them; thou art at war with them. Yes!
'understand thy constitution! Know what thou art by the
'law of thy creation, of thy redemption. Take up thy
'freedom'? Are the science of life and the business of life
in hostility then? No; for the science of life is expressed
in the words, ' *He that is born of God doth not commit
sin;*' that is the law of our existence. ' *And he that is
begotten of God*' (the tense of the participle is different, but
there is no change in the word, as our translation might
lead you to suppose) ' *keepeth himself, and that wicked one
toucheth him not.*' This is the practice of life. By reminding ourselves of our true birth, by betaking ourselves
to our real parent, we may separate ourselves from the sin
that is in us, we may resist the evil spirit who would persuade us that we belong to him, not to the God of truth.

The Apostle then, I think, has vindicated his first
assertion. He not only *knows* himself,—he can appeal to
his readers in one age or another, whether they do not
know,—that he that is born of God sinneth not. If their
answer at first is in the negative, he is sure that one day
they will reply with a confidence as great as his own, 'It

is so.' Kepler, the astronomer, said he could wait for men to discover the true law of the heavenly bodies. ' If ' God has waited six thousand years, I can wait two ' hundred,' said the noble physical discoverer. The Apostle could speak as calmly and bravely, more cheerfully. ' God in His Son has declared Himself to us as our ' Father. We may tell men that they are His children. ' In His own due time He will confirm our words to the ' Universe, if now there are but a few little children here ' and there who give heed to them.'

II. And thus his next assurance explains itself to us, which sounds, perhaps, to many, both audacious and uncharitable. ' *We* KNOW *that we are of God, and that the whole world lieth in wickedness.*' ' *We know that we are of God*' is an equivalent statement to this, ' We know by ' repeated experiments that there is in ourselves no good ' thing; that we cannot of ourselves do the things which ' we ought to do. We know also, by repeated experiments, ' that when our Lord taught us to say, "Our Father," ' He did not mock us, nor encourage us to mock God. ' This prayer we have ascertained to be a true prayer; if ' that is false, everything in the universe is false; it is the ' foundation of our thoughts, acts, hopes; they have no ' other.'

But, '*We know that the whole world lieth in wickedness,*' or ' *in the wicked one!*' What can one make of such an assertion as that? I do not want to make anything of it but what I find. How could St. John account for the fraud, cruelty, superstition, tyranny, which he saw in the Pagan world and the Jewish world? Were they of God? Did they come from the will of God? Were they not to be explained by the fact that Jews as much as Pagans did not believe that God was a Father; did not believe that He was Love; did not believe that He had reconciled the world to Himself in His Son; did not believe that they were the children of God? Were they not, then, believing a lie; confessing the Spirit of Lies? Were they not making him their father; receiving his inspirations?

You say that St. John and the Ephesians might *think* so, but could they *know* it? In replying to a similar objection, I alluded just now to the speech of a famous German, who prepared the way, by his discoveries, for our Newton. There was an Italian predecessor of Newton, as brave, as true-hearted;—I mean Galileo. I am sure you have often heard those words of his, which he is said to have shouted through the door of the chamber in which he had been confined by the Inquisition, for saying that the Earth moves round the Sun; '*However, it does move.*' The Cardinals said it did not; the learned men of his time said it did not; the popular opinion of the time said it did not. And this impudent Galileo cries out, ' It goes on in spite of you; and you, cardinals, doc-
' tors, people, are moving with it. And you cannot set aside
' God's doctrine by yours.' He cast his bread upon the waters. He knew quite well that it would be found after many days. St. John's arrogance is of the same kind.
' Doctors of the Sanhedrim,' he says, ' High Priests of
' Rome, Senators, Emperors, Philosophers, People, you
' believe God not to be a Father, but to be a tyrant, or a
' mere vague Essence; not to have claimed men as His
' children, but to be at a hopeless distance from them,
' and not to care for them at all. I, a fisherman, and

'this silly flock of Ephesians, say, "However, He *is* a
'Father; however, we *are* His children." And we know
'it. We know that you are asserting a lie, and that we
'are asserting a truth. We can venture all on that convic-
'tion. Other days will judge between us. It will be seen
'whether the mighty majority or the contemptible minority
'has spoken the thing as it is.'

Perhaps you may say to me, 'Oh, then, now at all
events you change your note. *You* appeal to majorities
'against a minority.' I do no such thing. Galileo's truth
does not rest upon the verdict of a majority; a few have
been forced to confess it by irresistible evidence; it has
commended itself to mankind by its practical results, by
the powers which it has enabled men to wield, by the
confusions which it has scattered. St. John's truth does not
rest upon the verdict of a majority. There never has been
a time when it has had a majority in its favour. There
never has been a time when the very same classes which
contradicted Galileo's doctrine have not contradicted it and
tried to hunt it down. The Inquisition has been far more
active in proclaiming 'God is not a Father, God is a
Tyrant,' than in saying, 'The Earth does not move round
the Sun.' Cardinals have been more busy in hiding from
men the truth that they are reconciled to God in His Son,
than in hiding from them any proposition of astronomy.
And we who are removed from the influence of the Inquisition and Cardinals, are not more ready than those who
are under their influence, to think of God as a reconciled
Father; we are just as ready as they are to regard Him as
a tyrant and an enemy. And, in general, philosophers
amongst us, as in the ages immediately after Christ, pour

contempt on the notion that it is possible to know anything of God, to know that He is a Father, to know that He loves the world. London working men must learn to adopt the daring tone of the Galilæan fisherman. They must begin to affirm boldly, 'God has taken us to be His 'children, seeing that we have that nature in which 'Jesus Christ died. It is so; though all the philosophers, ' all the theological doctors, all the priests, all the rich, ' the easy and comfortable people in Christendom suspend ' their mutual hatreds to affirm, " *You*, at all events, are ' fools ; *you* can know nothing." '

But is not this confidence—this claim to certainty—that which has been the great warrant and cause of persecution in other times? might it not become so in ours, if the opportunity were afforded us? No doubt, you and I should be in the same danger of becoming persecutors, as any men in former days, provided we had the same external power as they had ; for the internal temptations are not less in us than in them; we are not less internally dogmatic and proud, and anxious to crush every one's thought but our own; therefore let us pray that we may never have the means of indulging these vile inclinations. But it is not true that calm trust has made any man a persecutor. He who trusts, like Kepler, can wait. As the prophet said, ages before Kepler was born, '*He that believeth doth not make haste.*' Those who say, 'God is the Father of men in Christ,' must be sure that He will prove Himself to be their Father. Till we have lost our senses, we cannot suppose that we shall make our fellow-men more ready to embrace that truth by proving that we are not their brothers. No! depend upon it your temptation and mine to put down one who differs with us, has a different origin from this. When we have some opinion which we are *not* sure of, which we *cannot* rest in, yet which is dear to us because it is ours; then the impulse to crush those who will not accept it, who cannot see the force of our arguments, is very strong indeed. Habits of courtesy, deference to the rules of society, may restrain it to a certain extent, but not completely; those who cannot get the most effectual weapons try others; bitter epithets, secret slanders, are substituted for the gag of the ruling dogmatist and the dagger of the fanatic. An individual Christian is often very furious and intolerant at a certain stage of his life. For the conviction that he exists to proclaim a truth which concerns all men, and which it is miserable for men to reject, mingles strangely and incoherently with the thought that this truth is *his* opinion which *he* is to defend against all assailants, which *he* is to establish. Hence a fierce effervescence, like that produced by the meeting of an alkali and an acid ; hence, oftentimes, indifference, when that effervescence has subsided, like the neutral salt in the other case. And if the result be otherwise, it is always, I believe, because God substitutes the certainty which comes from dependence on Him for the positiveness which is the result of confidence in ourselves or in any human authority. With respect to Christian rulers, when they have persecuted, it has always been from a distrust in the certainty of God's own truth, leading very naturally and directly to the notion that it is their duty to enforce positive decrees of their own in exchange for it.

III. Once more St. John says, '*And we know that the Son of God is come, and hath given us an understanding, that we*

may know *Him that is true, and we are in Him that is true, even in His Son Jesus Christ.*' The two former propositions had vindicated such a knowledge for handicraftsmen and women as the wisest of the earth had not dared to boast of. What was the source of it? How could they explain their advantage over prophets and kings, Jewish as much as Heathen? They could only say, '<u>The Son of God has come.</u> He from whom prophets and kings derived their
' illumination; who they said must be; who they be-
' lieved would manifest Himself not as their king, but as
' the King of men; not as their light, but as the Light of
' the world; He has not disappointed their expectation, has
' not cheated the race which, in every country and period,
' had been feeling after such a ruler, such a teacher. He has
' come; *we* KNOW *that He has;* for whereas we were seek-
' ing God where He was not to be found, calling upon Him
' where He was not near—asking earth, and sky, and sea to
' tell us whether He was not with them, and receiving the
' same dreary answer from all;—now *He has given us an*
' *understanding, that we may know Him that is true;* <u>the</u>
' <u>eyes of our spirits have been opened to discern the Father</u>
' <u>of our spirits</u>; <u>to confess with awe and trembling</u>, not a
' being whom we have created, but <u>Him who is, and was,</u>
' <u>and is to come</u>; not one who depends upon our thoughts,
' feelings, imaginations, but <u>Him in whom we are living and</u>
' <u>moving and having our being</u>. Not as if the Absolute
' Truth and Goodness were brought down to our level; not
' as if He were less awful, less perfect now than in the days
' when Solomon declared that the heaven of heavens could
not contain Him, how much less the house which he had
built; but <u>that He has met with us in that Son</u>, in whom

'alone He declared Himself to the generations of old;
'but that He has come in whom we were originally created
'to be sons of God; but that we are in Him, even in Jesus
'Christ, and can therefore call His Father our Father, can
'therefore say that the truth in which He dwelt before the
'worlds is a truth for us and in us.'

IV. '*This is the true God and eternal life. Little children, keep yourselves from idols.*' So St. John concludes his Epistle. He was a Jew, you see, to the last. His work was to bear witness against idols; his work was to testify of the living and true God. He existed only to do this; he existed only to save his own generation, to save the generations to come, from worshipping a lie, from seeking a happiness that would prove to be a lie. '*This* Jesus Christ,' he says, 'in whom we are created, of whom we are members, 'this Lord of our spirits, this Light of our understandings;
'this is He in whom alone we can find the true God. This is
'He whom men have been seeking in heaven and earth, and
'in the waters under the earth. This is He in whom alone
'they can find that eternal life, for which they are thirsting,
'and which they are trying to find in the visible earth,
'or in some fantastic heaven, or in some depths which none
'have been able to sound. Little children, believe that you
'have not to ascend into heaven, or to go into the furthest
'corners of the earth, or to go down into the abyss of hell,
'that you may find God. He is near you; He is with you.
'Trust Him; abide in Him; be perpetually renewing your
'life at His fountain; then you will not bow down to the
'creatures of His hand; then you will not confound the
'bright images cast forth by the minds which He has made
'in His image—which He has endued with a portion of His

'own creative power,—with your Creator and Father. You
'will adore Him, in His Son, and He will enable you, by
'His Spirit, to offer up yourselves, and all your powers, and
'the earth which He has placed under you, as sacrifices to
'Him.'

I had meant to conclude my Lectures with these words; there are none in which I would rather gather up all that I have said to you, or wished for you. But I cannot resolve to pass over the two short letters which St. John addressed to an elect lady and to Gaius. In these letters I discover the simplest, broadest statement which I have seen anywhere, that the foundation of all Christian life, of all practical morality, is TRUTH. Alas! how few of us believe that! how few that believe it dare to act upon the belief! Therefore, I should be shrinking from a duty, I should be leaving this treatise most imperfect, if I failed to claim the Apostle, who has been suspected of sacrificing everything to Love, as a witness for a principle apart from which love is a worthless and contemptible affectation.

LECTURE XX.

TRUTH IN THE WOMAN AND THE MAN.

THE SECOND AND THIRD EPISTLES OF ST. JOHN.

The elder unto the elect lady and her children, whom I love in the truth; and not I only, but also all they that have known the truth; for the truth's sake, which dwelleth in us, and shall be with us for ever. Grace be with you, mercy, and peace, from God the Father, and from the Lord Jesus Christ, the Son of the Father, in truth and love. I rejoiced greatly that I found of thy children walking in truth, as we have received a commandment from the Father. And now I beseech thee, lady, not as though I wrote a new commandment unto thee, but that which we had from the beginning, that we love one another. And this is love, that we walk after His commandments. This is the commandment, That, as ye have heard from the beginning ye should walk in it. For many deceivers are entered into the world, who confess not that Jesus Christ is come in the flesh. This is a deceiver and an antichrist Look to yourselves, that we lose not those things which we have wrought, but that we receive a full reward. Whosoever transgresseth, and abideth not in the doctrine of Christ, hath not God. He that abideth in the doctrine of Christ, he hath both the Father and the Son. If there come any unto you, and bring not this doctrine, receive him not into your house, neither bid him God speed: for he that biddeth him God speed is partaker of his evil deeds. Having many things to write unto you, I would not write with paper and ink: but I trust to come unto you, and speak face to face, that our joy may be full. The children of thy elect sister greet thee. Amen.

The elder unto the well-beloved Gaius, whom I love in the truth. Beloved, I wish above all things that thou mayest prosper and be in health, even as thy soul prospereth. For I rejoiced greatly, when the brethren came and testified of the truth that is in thee, even as thou walkest in the truth. I have no greater joy than to hear that my children walk in truth. Beloved, thou doest faithfully whatsoever thou doest to the brethren, and to strangers; which have borne witness of thy charity before the church: whom if thou bring forward on their journey after a godly sort, thou shalt do well: because that for his name's sake they went forth, taking nothing of the Gentiles. We therefore ought to receive such, that we might be fellow-helpers to the truth. I wrote unto the church: but Diotrephes, who loveth to have the preeminence among them, receiveth us not. Wherefore, if I come, I will remember his deeds which he doeth, prating against us with malicious words: and not content therewith, neither doth he himself receive the brethren, and forbiddeth them that would, and casteth them out of the church. Beloved, follow not that which is evil, but that which is good. He that doeth good is of God: but he that doeth evil hath not seen God. Demetrius hath good report of all men, and of the truth itself: yea, and we also bear record; and ye know that our record is true. I had many things to write, but I will not with ink and pen write unto thee: but I trust I shall shortly see thee, and we shall speak face to face. Peace be to thee. Our friends salute thee. Greet the friends by name.

St. John's First Epistle, like most of the Epistles in the New Testament, is addressed to a Society. He may have instructed that Society in the principles of Christian Morals. But has he given any hints about the kind of character which he desires most, which he admires most, in an individual? Has he set before us any example—besides the great Universal Example—of that which he would wish us to be?

At first sight it seems strange that such letters as these to the Elect Lady and to Gaius should have been preserved, and that they should form part of the Canon of the New Testament. If you knew how many Gospels, professing to contain narratives of our Lord's acts upon earth,—how many Epistles professing to come from Apostles and apostolical men,—had been cast aside, you might wonder even more that these had stood the wear and tear of eighteen centuries, and had kept their place among the sacred books. For they have nothing which could recommend them to the taste of the ages which received them; much which

was uncongenial to it. There was a craving in the earlier ages, as there has been since, for stories of startling events; of miracles such as Apostles might have been expected to perform. Ecclesiastical writers, a century or two after the age of St. John, talked of his having been cast into a cauldron of boiling oil, and of his coming out unhurt. How gladly would they have found some hint or allusion to confirm that tale in a letter which was attributed to him! But these letters contain no such hint; they are of the simplest, most commonplace kind. Again, the notion became prevalent very soon in the Church,—it gained strength every century, outward circumstances conspiring with inward feelings to deepen it,—that the morality of the Gospel was of a new and peculiar kind; that the strong *male* qualities which were admired in the old world were discarded by it; that its graces were wholly passive and feminine; that the woman was not only raised by it to a higher level, but that it was her glory to be alone; that the less she had to do with wedlock and the bearing of children, the more blessed and holy her life was. How eagerly would any confirmation of these sentiments from the last of the Apostles, from him who was emphatically the Apostle of the coming dispensation, have been welcomed! What a delight to find him who had been brought up a Jew, who, as such, had been taught to think nobly of wedlock, and even to regard barrenness as a curse of womankind, saying, 'Now all this is changed; the Incar-
' nation has introduced an entirely different ideal of life
' into the world; not only is it not now possible for women
' to do the noblest services to the commonwealth and to
mankind, though they are not mothers of children, but

' to be so is to reduce themselves to a lower level, to make
' themselves less dear and precious in God's sight.' Some
occasion for proclaiming these great Christian maxims, if
he held them to be such, the Apostle would surely seize.
And what an occasion is here! A letter to an Elect Lady!
To one who has chosen the good part, or whom God has
chosen to be His handmaid! Now, if ever, we shall find
what we are looking for. Ah, no! This Elect Lady has
children. She is addressed as a mother. The aged Jewish
Apostle does not drop a hint that he thinks less nobly of
that calling than Abraham, or Moses, or David, or Hannah,
or any of those on whose words or on whose deeds he had
loved to dwell in his youth.

These are reasons which may make us sure that the old
Church would not have forged such an Epistle as this
second (I will speak of the third presently), and would not
have been specially inclined to admit its claim to apostolical weight and authority. They are, therefore, reasons
which may make us confident that we are not wrong in
accepting it as a genuine witness of the mind of St. John,
conveyed in his own childlike manner. So considered,
I believe we shall find that, short as it is, few documents
have been bequeathed to us of greater interest and significance.

I have referred to one characteristic of this letter already.
It is the one which presents itself to us the moment we begin
to read. *The elder*—(the Apostle does not care to describe
himself by any greater title than that; he is adopting the
tone of an elder brother, rather than of a father)—is writing
to a *lady* of whom we know nothing except from his account
of her,—to one on whom he bestows the title of *elect*. What

that title means we shall soon learn from himself. In the meantime the lady is not alone. She is surrounded by her family; he addresses her children as if they were inseparable from her. He says of them all, '*Whom I love in the truth, and not I only, but all they that have known the truth; for the truth's sake which dwelleth in us, and shall be with us for ever.*'

Here is a word repeated three times in one sentence. Is it an idle repetition? Why does the Apostle begin with speaking to this lady and her children of the *truth?* why does every passage that follows relate to living in the *truth*, or walking in the *truth?* Evidently this is the key-word in the mind of the writer. Whatever else he says has reference to this. He says that he *loves* them. But it is impossible to pretend that the emphasis is on the verb *loves*. He loves them in the truth. Others love them as he does. But it is '*they that have known the truth.*' There may have been many winning and graceful qualities in this lady, and in one or in all of her children. Doubtless there were. But the Apostle, and those who love them most, love them for '*the truth's sake which dwelleth in them, and shall be in them always.*'

I must fix your attention upon this last clause. As you are now familiar with St. John's language, its form will not surprise you. This phrase, 'dwelling' or 'abiding,' is that which has met us so often, which we have ascertained to be the characteristic phrase of his former Epistle. But we want it that we may not go astray respecting that expression which is occupying us here. We are frequently told—and told by persons to whose authority on many subjects I defer—that truth belongs to Propositions.

Mr. Mill sets forth this maxim with his usual admirable precision at the commencement of his 'Logic;' in doing so, he is perfectly in accordance with a great number (a large majority) of Church doctors. They have maintained that agreement with certain propositions constitutes truth, that disagreement with them constitutes falsehood. And seeing that people in general cannot be expected to arrive at safe and certain conclusions about propositions concerning the deepest and most difficult subjects, they have said, and laymen have acquiesced, that there must be some infallible dictator to determine which propositions on such subjects are true and which are false.

What I wish you to observe is, that St. John cannot agree with Mr. Mill and with these Church doctors in this judgment of theirs; he cannot look at truth from their point of view. To speak of the '*truth which dwelleth in us*,' meaning thereby the assent to or agreement with certain propositions, which dwelleth in us, would have been nonsense. To speak of loving this lady and her children in the agreement with or assent to certain propositions, would have been also nonsense. If we are not prepared to accuse him of such absurdity,—if we will permit him to explain what he means, without binding him by notions of which his writings give us no hint,—we may perhaps find that he is not so far from common sense and common life as he is from the wisdom of the schools; that he is not the less able to help *us* because he may have put himself under their ban.

The last words, almost, of the general Epistle were, '*He hath given us an understanding, that we may know Him that is true, and we are in Him that is true, even in His Son*

Jesus Christ.' Long before we arrived at this sentence, we found him speaking of *our dwelling in God, and God dwelling in us;* we found that we could not dilute the expression, or empty it of any of its awfulness, without contradicting every previous statement of the Apostle, without setting at nought altogether his idea of the Christian revelation. If we apply these observations now, we cannot adopt any other inference than this, that the Truth which dwelleth in us, and will dwell in us for ever, is He Who is, and was, and is to come, that true God whose life eternal Jesus came to manifest, that we might be partakers of it and might show it forth in our acts. Truth, according to St. John, is not dead, but living; not a notion, or set of notions which we comprehend, but a Being who comprehends us; not a theory concerning God, but God Himself. And therefore he can love *in* this truth; he cannot love out of this truth. For there is no love but of God, and God is love; therefore all who know this truth, who are in communion with it, love one another for its sake, by its power.

And therefore he can go on: '*Grace be with you, mercy and peace, from God the Father, and from the Lord Jesus Christ, the Son of the Father, in truth and love.*' Grace, in Scripture, comprehends all the senses that it bears, separately and apart, in our common dialects. When you say of a royal person, 'How *gracious* he is;' when you say of a beautiful woman, 'What *grace* there is in her;' when you speak of a man not having the *grace* to return a benefit that has been done to him; you indicate some aspect of *that* grace which the Source of all good bestows upon men; which becomes in them a comeliness answering to His from whom it is derived; which awakens the reaction that we call gratitude or thanksgiving. And this Grace being manifested towards creatures who have need of daily forgiveness, is inseparable from Mercy; which, like it, proceeds from the nature of the being who shows it, and becomes an element in the nature of the being to whom it is showed: the merciful obtaining mercy. And this Grace or Mercy flowing forth towards creatures who have been alienated from their Creator, who have been at war with Him,—and being at war with Him, have been, necessarily, at war with each other and themselves—becomes Peace or Atonement. But that the Grace, because it is royal, free, and undeserved, may not be supposed to be capricious; that the Mercy may not be taken as dependent on the mercy which it calls forth; that the Peace may not be judged by the results which it produces here, where oftentimes the proclamation of it is the signal of fresh fighting; they are declared to come from God the Father and from Jesus Christ the Son of the Father, in *truth and love;* these being the essential Godhead; these dwelling absolutely in the Father; shining forth to all in the life of the Son; while the Spirit in whom they are eternally united, imparts them to the family in heaven and earth.

For Heaven and Earth are truly united when an apostle has bestowed this heavenly benediction on pilgrims upon earth. See how easily he passes from one to the other: '*I rejoiced greatly that I found of thy children walking in the truth, as we have received a commandment from the Father.*' Who these children were we can form no conjecture; nor do we want to form any. They were probably very simple people, nowise noticeable in the crowd around them, except by doing their common business more faithfully, by being freer than others from pretension, by judging their fellow-creatures less, by not being at the mercy of boasters and charlatans. They were true in word and deed, true in life; such men as one meets with from time to time in all classes; such as one is sure St. John would have rejoiced to meet with; for no cause but this, that they are true. They do not talk of their sincerity; no people so little; they are afraid of their own insincerity; they feel continually tempted to it; they do not think any people in the world as much in danger of becoming hypocrites as they are. But they walk in the truth; they live not in themselves, but in Him who is true. They depend upon Him to keep them true, and to tell them of their falsehoods. They are sure that His truth is compassing the whole universe. They desire that every man should know it, and that it should make him free. This was the truth of the children of the elect lady; and this was her own. She was a true woman, as they were true men or women; not affecting anything high for herself; not wishing to be anything else than God had made her to be; fighting against the vanity and conceit which might make her wish to shine in the world or in the church, as a model of beauty, or wit, or saintship. Such a woman, whatever be her outward condition, must have the grace of a lady, because she has the grace of God.

This lady and her children are walking in the truth, ' *as we have received a commandment from the Father.*'

In lecturing on the former Epistle, I have had frequent occasion to speak of the connexion between love and keeping the commandments. It is a subject to which St. John often recurs. It belonged to that office which I conceive was peculiarly his, of uniting the old world to the new, the Law to the Gospel. A Jew who *walked in the ordinances of the Lord* habitually recollected that the Lord had taken his nation to be a people of inheritance to Himself, that he was devoted and consecrated to the service of an unseen King. One who *walked in the truth*, after Christ had appeared, was not different from his ancestor; he, too, was under a commandment; he, too, was simply obeying a will. Only it was a will which had revealed itself. He was brought into direct contact with the Mind which the law expressed, with the Spirit of Him who gave it. It was a grander and more responsible, more divine, position; but it might be described in nearly the same language; it equally involved obedience; the obedience of a child; a *Father* had given the commandment.

But He who was now revealed as a Father, had always been a Father; therefore the Apostle says, '*And now I beseech thee, lady, not as though I wrote a new commandment unto thee, but that which we had from the beginning, that we love one another.*' No one was more likely than a woman to think that the precept of loving was something altogether different in kind from the precepts of the old law; no one was more likely to say, ' Love has nothing ' to do with precepts; it springs up unbidden in the heart.' And no one was more likely than a woman to suffer from these very natural opinions; to turn love into a mere taste and sentiment; to suppose it had its origin in herself, and that its continuance might be trusted to her strong feelings; to separate it from obedience; to make it unpractical; so to divorce it from self-denial and endurance. Nothing would be so fatal to all that is noblest in the female character, to the sacrificing and persevering affection for which women have been so eminent, as this temper of mind. Nothing, therefore, appears more entirely appropriate than the Apostle's double admonition, which is enforced in the following verse: '*This is love, that we walk after His commandments; this is the commandment, That, as ye have heard from the beginning, ye should walk in it.*' The repetition of this sentence in so very short a letter would appear unaccountable, if St. John had not been made aware—or if that Spirit who guided his thoughts had not been aware—that the woman would be taught by high authorities to set the virtues of the new world in contrast with those of the old; to exalt feminine peculiarities above those of men; and so would learn not to walk in the truth, but to think she was most godly when she was most despising the order of God's universe.

It is not, however, to this class of teachers that St. John directly alludes in the next verse: '*For many deceivers are entered into the world, who confess not that Jesus Christ is come in the flesh. This is a deceiver and an antichrist.* You have heard already who these deceivers were, and why such a hard name as that of antichrists is bestowed upon them. They had left the church because they could not tolerate the notion that the Son of God had taken an actual body, and had died in it on the cross. They were far too spiritual, they said, for any such earthly doctrine. Their Christ had entered into the world to save the spirits of certain elect people who had been enslaved by the vile flesh which they said was the cause of all evil. A plausible, tempting theory,—one which appealed to many noble instincts in the persons who listened to it, and supported itself by some of their saddest experiences, while it flattered their conceit and their exclusiveness. It addressed itself with peculiar power—so we gather from many passages in other Epistles, so we might guess if we had not these passages — to the minds of women who were vain of their intellectual or spiritual gifts, and who had perhaps known too much of the corruptions and perils of their time.

These were often the prophetesses, as well as the receivers, of the maxims which treated the flesh as essentially evil, and denied Christ's association with it. St. John was more deeply convinced, even than his brother apostles, that this denial involved the denial of the *whole* Gospel. It said that they were not witnesses of a reconciliation of God with men; it said that Christ had not shown forth the eternal life of God, in the acts, words, death of a man; it substituted another Christ of a different nature and character from Jesus; it set up a proud Spirit coming in his own name, for a Son who submitted in all things to a Father's will, and glorified Him. St. John cannot express those convictions more strongly than he expressed them in his general letter; but he applies them with earnestness to the case of the particular lady to whom he is writing here. He warns her of the danger which her dread of evil, her spiritual desires, her humility, may expose her, if she does not adhere to the plain commandment which she had from the beginning: '*Look to yourselves, that we lose not those things that we have wrought, but that we receive a full reward.*' He uses—dexterously, we might say, if dexterity meant as it ought to mean, that which belongs to the right, and not as it does often mean, that which is clever and opposed to straightforwardness — he uses the very phrases which the deceivers were probably in the habit of using. They would urge their disciples not to miss the full reward; not to be content with the low condition of the novice; to aim at initiation into the highest mysteries, at the perfection which was reserved for the elect. And they would talk—we know in the next century they did talk—of arriving at a knowledge of GOD by some wonderful process, by some special road; obedience to the outward law being an unnecessary means to the end, the transgression of it being sometimes a sign that they had reached a further stage in spiritual elevation. To such pretensions, I doubt not, St. John alludes: '*Whosoever* TRANSGRESSETH, *and abideth not in the doctrine of* CHRIST, *hath not* GOD. *He that abideth in the doctrines of Christ, he hath both the Father and the Son.*'

The tenth and eleventh verses have been rather favourites, with some religious men, Romanists as well as Protestants. For the sake of them, the disagreeable passages in the rest of the Epistle have been forgiven; it has been thought to possess a certain inspired and canonical worth. I do not esteem them above the rest of the letter, but I esteem them as a part of it, and I am anxious to know what use we ought to make of them. '*If there come any unto you, and bring not this doctrine, receive him not into your house, neither bid him God speed: for he that biddeth him God speed is partaker of his evil deeds.*' St. John himself—one of a small despised minority, belonging to a body who were called heretics by the great body of the Jews, who were denounced as rebels against the gods, probably as absolutely atheists, by the heathens,—St. John, writing to a lady whom he loves in the truth, who he believes is walking in the truth, warns her not to receive into her house, or bid God speed to teachers who were proclaiming a certain doctrine which he believed to be mischievous. Such a sentence delivered by a person for whom we have a profound reverence, obliges us to ask, What the doctrine so condemned is? The answer is explicit. It is, *that Jesus Christ has not come in the flesh.* On this answer, I believe, the whole of modern history is a commentary. To the belief that Jesus Christ the Son of God *has* come in the flesh, I can trace an idea of *God* diffused through society which is at variance altogether with the dark superstitions to which the world had been prone; an idea of *Man* and his true greatness entirely different from those debasing notions which the religions of the earth had sanctioned; an idea of the worth and sacredness of *all* men whatsoever and of all common *occupations* which these religions had utterly discouraged. I can trace through the history of Christendom a continual *conflict* with this idea of God, of Man, of common men, of common occupations; a continual effort to restore, under the name of Christianity, under the sanction of the Christian priesthood, those dark thoughts and superstitions (and to make them darker) which the belief that Jesus Christ has come in the flesh has shaken, and is destined, as I trust, at last wholly to undermine. Had those men, then, whom St. John denounces as deceivers and antichrists,—those men who went forth boasting that they had a purer and fuller revelation than the common one,—succeeded in their purpose, had they drawn the Church generally after them,—every blessing which we owe to the Gospel would, I judge, have been lost; every curse which we owe to the superstitions that existed before the Gospel, and that have corrupted it, would, I judge, have been multiplied a thousand fold. Here is justification enough for the Apostle, if he wanted justification. Not to have warned the Elect Lady of giving entertainment to such men, of bidding them God speed, would have been not merely to leave *her* at their mercy, but to withhold from the ages to come a lesson that was at least as necessary for *them*.

Once more, then, I demand, 'How may I take advantage ' of this lesson?' It is easy to fix upon certain persons and say, 'These are heretics, these are infidels ; St. John meant ' that you were not to receive them into your house, or bid ' them God speed.' Most assuredly, in as far as they are teaching and preaching that Jesus Christ is not come in the flesh, I will not bid them God speed; I will, God being my helper, warn them with all the power I have, that they are doing an injury to their fellow-men, that they are robbing them of the truth which is the one great barrier against a cruel conception of God, against a degrading conception of humanity, against worship of riches, against the degradation of labour. But I am also bound to remember that there is no courage whatever, no imitation of St. John's example, in denouncing men who are denounced already; those who belong to a minority, I being in a majority. I must be prepared, God being my helper, also to lift up my voice against any denials of Jesus Christ being come in the flesh, which have had and still have the sanction of numbers, the weight of authority, on their side ; against any practical denial of the *principle*, while the mere form of words which asserts it is lazily admitted, perhaps passionately defended. I cannot in the least pretend to be obeying the apostolical authority unless

I am prepared to take this course, though it may be a far less easy and convenient one than the other. PREPARED, I say, each of us should be to take it, if God shows us by evident signs that some outrage has been committed upon this great divine and human doctrine, which is doing extensive mischief under high authority; and that He means us to bear witness on behalf of it. So Luther felt when Tetzel sold indulgences in his own neighbourhood under the direction of Leo X. That was a denial of Christ which was more certain to undermine the faith of the Gospel than any nominally infidel teaching;—of which there was abundance in the sixteenth century, the abuses of the Church having produced a very general unbelief. But in the meantime the right course for those who feel deeply that Christ is the Centre of the universe, the source and spring of life to all men; that He took flesh for the sake of all men; is to be purging their own minds of whatever is inconsistent with this doctrine, and to be asserting it as often as they have the opportunity, by their acts even more than by their words. I conceive that I should not be asserting it, either by act or by word, if, in seeming compliance with St. John's words, I refused to receive into my house a person whom others called, or who called himself, a heretic or an infidel. I should, by so doing, be confirming him in his notion that Christ is *not* the common brother of men; I should be doing just what the Pharisees would have had St. Paul and St. John do,—that which in Christ's name they refused to do,—separate themselves from the Gentiles.

The last sentences of this letter to the Elect Lady remind us that it is what it professes to be, a letter to a friend; that the friendship was the more natural and human because it was grounded on the truth, and that other ladies also elect were, like this one, not nuns but mothers. '*Having many things to write unto you, I would not write with paper and ink: but I trust to come unto you, and speak face to face, that our joy may be full. The children of thy elect sister greet thee. Amen.*'

At first you may be chiefly struck with the resemblance between the second and third Epistle. They have a common characteristic. Gaius *is found in the* TRUTH, like the elect lady; Gaius, like her, *walks in the* TRUTH. Truth of life, grounded upon trust in the living and true God, is that which St. John desires and prizes in man as much as in woman; all qualities are trifles in comparison with that; it is the substance, apart from which all qualities are mere shadows. The elder writes to him with all affection; he is his well beloved; he wishes him health and advancement; outward and inward; the sound mind, in the sound body. Yet his great joy is that the brethren testify of his truth. No joy is like that to the old man. His children might be reputed as brilliantly pious or charitable; but are they *true?* That is what he cares to hear; those tidings satisfy him.

But notwithstanding this fundamental likeness, I think you will feel at once that the letter to the man is materially different from the letter to the woman. Their truth has the same root; it is the same essentially; but it is differently exercised. The elect lady is in the midst of her family, liable to the visits of strangers, some of whom she will entertain cordially, some of whom may have mischievous designs. But the acts of Gaius are *before the Church*. His tastes and occupations are public. Instead of being warned against the seductions of false teachers, he is commended for the charity with which he has brought forward on their journey men who were devoting themselves to Christ's cause among the Gentiles, and who for that reason were suspected by certain men coveting preeminence in the Church. Herein are the duties of the man; herein are his dangers. Simple duties;—those of using the opportunities that had been given him, to be a fellow helper with the truth, to aid honest, disinterested, misrepresented labourers. Nothing grand, nothing above the standard of humanity; but just the acts that spread a blessing around; just the acts that discover the truth within. Simple dangers;—the wish for authority; the jealousy of others; the impatience of guidance. Nothing terrible, nothing which Christians in general regard as sins; only an entire departure from the life of Christ; only the causes which have torn the Church in pieces. Diotrephes, of whom we have a sketch in the 10th verse, was probably a Jewish Christian, determined to assert the superiority of the circumcised race in the Church; not able to exclude Gentiles altogether; but throwing impediments in the way of those who would open the door to them; consciously or unconsciously glorifying himself in the name of his nation and of God; a pattern of tens of thousands who were to arise afterwards, and who would attain the dominion they claimed, when there was no longer a venerable apostle to put down their prating, to expose the essential meanness of their pride.

St. John's hints for avoiding the influence and tyranny of such men, for not being tempted by the example of their ambition, are very childlike. Wise doctors would smile at them. I question whether you will find any as effectual. '*Beloved, follow not that which is evil, but that which is good. He that doeth good is of God: but he that doeth evil hath not seen God.*' Diotrephes was no doubt a wonderful talker; a man who overawed all with whom he came in contact, by his confidence in himself, and by his denunciations of those whom he wished to crush. It was a great temptation to encounter such a man with his own weapons; to give fierce word for fierce word; contempt for contempt. But those who sincerely loved what was good; who cleaved to that; recognised it in whomsoever they found it; confessed it to be God's; hated whatever was not good; whatever was base, malicious, intriguing;—these men would really overcome the blusterer; for they would never aspire to be like him. Such a quiet, steady love of good the Apostle appears to bring before us in the person of Demetrius; one who had good report of all men, and of the truth itself; one of whom the Apostle himself could speak confidently. Who he was, we may know in that day when the truth itself shall bear witness of him, and of all who have loved it in all ages; and when every form of pretension and falsehood shall flee away. Why may we not believe that in that day also the Apostle, and those in far off countries and ages who have learnt the truth which he spoke with his lips or wrote with pen and ink, may speak with each other '*face to face, may greet each other by name?*'

I have one word to say before I conclude this Lecture. We are sometimes told by Christian apologists, that women have acquired an honour since the preaching of the Gospel which was almost denied them in the old world; and that because the feminine type of character is commended to us by the example of Him who was emphatically the Sufferer. I believe both assertions have a foundation of truth in them; but that they are not true: and therefore would not have been adopted or commended by the Apostle. It is not true that women were not honoured in the old world. I have alluded to the Jewish feeling about mothers. In that character the highest and divinest promises rested upon them. But they do not only appear as mothers. Deborah is a judge and a prophetess of the people. Miriam leads the songs which celebrate the deliverance of the nation from Pharaoh. Greek history, again, pays high honour to women. The Trojan war, the subject of its earliest legends, of its noblest song, is undertaken in vindication of female honour and the sacredness of the marriage bond. In the Homeric poems, the freewoman is treated with reverence; even the captive taken in war is not without honour. The Roman State, which almost rests on the authority of fathers, was anything but neglectful of the mother and the wife. The traditional origin of the Republic is the retribution for the wrong done to Lucretia. One of the earliest stories, that of Coriolanus, illustrates the honour which even the proudest, most wilful son paid to her who had borne and nursed him. Some of the noblest recollections of the perishing commonwealth are connected with the name of Cornelia the mother of the Gracchi, and Portia the wife of Brutus. It is dishonest to overlook these facts; and being dishonest, it is unchristian. We do not honour Christ by disparaging that which took place before He dwelt on earth. If we believe St. John, He was before all worlds. He was in the world and was the Light of men. The Greek reverence for women, the Roman reverence for women, was as much the effect of His teaching and culture as that which the purest knight exhibited in the middle ages, or that which appears in the best men of our day. He came upon earth in the midst of a foul and adulterous age. Jews, Greeks, Romans, under the Cæsars, had almost equally forgotten the sacredness of marriage, the holiness of women. And that Society was <u>therefore</u> doomed. The Christian Church came into it and did not renovate it; but was partly corrupted by it, partly was the cause of its destruction. The worst Christians became like the world into which they had fallen. The better stood aloof from it; they thought they were not to touch it, taste it, handle it. They could, therefore, do it no good, and they bequeathed to after times the notion that the Christian age was not to recover and restore that which had been right and true in the former ages, but to set up an opposite standard of its own. God, however, was working out His own ends, and the ignorance of His servants could not defeat them. He raised up the Gothic or Teutonic race; gave them in their barbarism and paganism a reverence for women and for human relationships which those whom they conquered had lost; made them at the same time fierce protestants on behalf of the manly virtues, against the effeminacy of priests and monks. So He prepared the way for a homelier morality, as well as a deeper faith; a morality and a faith which should have Truth for their ground.

But is not this Teutonic reverence for manliness inconsistent with the example of Jesus Christ? I say, No; emphatically, No. Jesus Christ is the Sacrifice; you cannot describe Him by any other name which is so characteristic and so glorious. But He is the King sacrificing Himself for His subjects. Read the Gospels, and see whether they do not regard Him first of all as a King; whether they do not present Him to us speaking with authority, commanding the winds and waves to be still, casting out the unclean spirits, ruling the multitudes, causing His accusers to tremble and fall down. Hear Him as He stands before Pontius Pilate in His hour of submission and surrender, just before He is crucified, uttering these royal words— '*For this cause was I born, and for this cause came I into the world, that I might bear witness of the Truth.*' Jesus Christ, the Head of humanity, exhibits the perfect type of that nature which belongs to the man and the woman. Neither the woman is without the man, nor the man without the woman, in Him. But He does not sink the attributes of the man in those of the woman. He clothes the woman with the glory of the man. Truth is essentially the manly virtue. But He proclaims it as the test of His Truth that He does not come in His own Name; that He glorifies His Father; that He does His Will; that to fulfil that Will He becomes a servant. Here is Truth wedded to Obedience, the characteristic of the Woman. She can live in the Truth, she can die for the Truth, without departing from her feminine simplicity and dependence. About opinions and propositions she may not know much; if she sets great store by them, the probability is that she will surrender herself to some priest of her own choosing and become anything but truthful in St. John's sense; helping also to destroy whatever there is of truthfulness in her director. But living Truth, the truth in a person, she can confess; that she can represent in her own character and acts.

What I have been just saying has a very intimate connexion with a subject which you will find largely discussed in Ethical books, sometimes at the very threshold of them. The eminent writer, of whom I spoke in my first Lecture, begins by affirming that every study and pursuit aims at some End; that there is an End which men as men are pursuing. This end he designates by a word which I think he would gladly have exchanged for another, if he could have found it. I told you how anxious he was to avoid any allusion to his country's faith, what pains he takes to construct his Ethical system without it. But the language of a country *must* express the habitual convictions of that country; its faith will insinuate itself whether you wish it or not. The Greeks were emphatically worshippers of Dæmons; that is to say, of powers intermediate between the supreme unknown Being, whom they sometimes called Fate, and human creatures; powers partaking of human feelings, passions, caprices. Their notion then of the best possible condition of existence for a man was of one in which the Dæmons were on the whole propitious to him; the word *Eudaimonia* indicated what they most desired. The philosopher must take this expression—awkward a one as it is for his purpose—and must try to discover some definition of it which shall, as little as possible, recal its etymology, which shall have as little as possible to do with Dæmons and their influences.

You may think this was the misfortune of his Paganism. Partly but not altogether. Pope is placed in a dilemma as serious by the English language, in which he wrote, and of which he was a great master. He speaks of '*Hap-*'*piness* as our being's end and aim.' Now what is the derivation of 'happiness?' Evidently it is connected with that which *happens;* its root is Hap or Luck. Can you suppose that Pope, or any sound-headed thinker, regarded the end of man's being as good Luck? Of course not; he is as anxious to forget the meaning of his English word as Aristotle is to forget the meaning of the equivalent Greek word. All that either means to say is, 'There is what the 'Algebraist would call an *x,* an unknown quantity, which 'all men are in search of. They call it *Eudaimonia,* or 'Happiness or Luck. *We* are to find a value for this *x.* '*We* are to fix a meaning to this loose phrase, which shall 'take out of it, as far as may be, all associations with mere 'accident or chance; which shall change it into something 'real, permanent, substantial.'

That admirable man whom I have quoted in a former Lecture, refers in a striking Sermon, on 'The Christian Aim and Motive,' (Robertson's Sermons, 3d Series, p. 238,) to Pope's line, and expresses himself about it in this strong language. 'Brethren, Happiness is *not* our being's end and 'aim. The Christian's aim is Perfection, not Happiness, 'and every one of the Sons of God must have something 'of that spirit which marked their Master; that holy 'sadness, that peculiar unrest, that high and lofty melan- 'choly, which belongs to a spirit which strives after heights 'to which it can never attain.' Mr. Robertson is not contradicting Pope so much as he would at first appear to do. He is rather finding a value for the unknown quantity. He pronounces its value to be *Perfection.* I am sure that what he means is as right as the language which he adopts is bold and striking. Man cannot be satisfied with anything short of what is Perfect. He must have perpetual 'unrest' till he finds what is Perfect.

When so profoundly reverent a man as Mr. Robertson attributes this unrest to Jesus Christ, we are obliged, just because the word gives us a start, just because it shocks us, to ask what he can intend by it. The answer, I believe, leads to a very important and radical principle. The Son of God did not rest in Himself, but in His Father; apart from Him it was impossible for Him to rest. And this is also true, as the preacher says, of all the sons of God. They can have no rest in themselves; they must have a 'peculiar unrest,' a discontent with everything that is their own. But Jesus Christ says, 'Come unto me all that are 'weary and heavy-laden; for I am meek and lowly of heart; 'and ye shall find rest to your souls.' It was His own rest to which He invited them; the rest and satisfaction in a will which was perfectly true and good. Because He rested in that will, because He delighted in it, He had a perpetual sorrow in seeing it resisted, a 'baptism'—such were His own words—' to be baptized with, and how was He 'straitened till it was accomplished?' But this sorrow was not only compatible with the rest of which He had spoken; one was inseparable from the other. He who dwells in the truth, must suffer till truth triumphs once and for ever.

In one sense I can admit that man is always striving after the unattainable. Truth will always seem deeper, broader, higher, the nearer we approach it; the more we converse with the eternal, the less shall we dream of comprehending it. . But does not our unrest come from the desire to hold that in the hollow of our hands which holds us; in which we are living? Christ came to deliver us from this unrest. He plunged into the deep waters. They sustained Him; He tells us that they will sustain us. The unfathomable truth of which He bore witness is our home and dwelling-place. To be in fellowship with that, is to be perfect, as our Father in heaven is perfect. To be struggling with whatever opposes that, in ourselves and in our brethren, is to be entering into Christ's work on earth. And this truth, though it is ever discovering more of its wonders and its glory, is the same that·was in the beginning, the same that men in every age have sought and struggled for. Some of them called it the favour or good pleasure of capricious *Dæmons*. What they wanted, what their inmost hearts told them must be, was a righteousness and love, without variableness or the shadow of a turning. They called it, and call it still, Happiness. What they want is that which is beyond all chance or hap, a Being in whom their being can find its end and aim. They have climbed up to heaven, and gone down to the deep in search of it. Lo! it is near to them; their hearts may turn to it and repose in it. They hoped to find it in some condition of their own minds. They do find it when, worn out with their own efforts, they say, ' Thou who art the truth, Thou in whom is the eternal life, ' hold us up, for we are Thine.'

ON POSITIVISM AND ITS TEACHER.

I HAVE alluded in the 17th Lecture to the theory of *Positivism*, and have spoken of the battle between it and the doctrine of St. John, as, perhaps, the last which will be fought in the world; as one which will be no battle merely of words or merely of swords, but in which all human interests will be involved. *Auguste Comte* had the wisdom to perceive, and the honesty to proclaim, that we are in an age of Science; that the words Knowledge and Science are synonymous; that whatever by its nature *cannot* be known, must, in such an age, be assumed not to be. This being the major of his syllogism, what was the minor? *That* was furnished not by him, but by a multitude of orthodox Christian theologians and philosophers. *They* have said, 'GOD 'cannot be known. *That* He is, we have probable reasons for 'thinking; throw in the danger of doubt, *if* our guesses should 'prove true; and that is sufficient warrant for believing His 'existence, or acting as if we believed it. *What* He is we can 'only describe by negativing certain conditions of our own 'nature. The Bible, what we call the Revelation of God, tells 'us certain things which we have to believe about God, because we are ignorant, and must be ignorant, of that which He really 'is.' *Comte* held that such a belief as this cannot stand in an age of *Science*. I am convinced that he was right. But I am convinced also that it could as little stand in an age of *faith*

If St. John belongs to an age of Faith, he teaches that which seems to me the only possible doctrine for an age of Science; that GOD *can* be known; that the knowledge of Him is the root of all other knowledge; that we are only capable of knowing our fellow-creatures, and of knowing the world of nature, because we are more directly related to Him than to them; because His knowledge of them is imparted in a measure to the creatures whom He has made in His image. If this be so, Science demands God, as its foundation; the effect of denying God will be to rob us of all the fruits of Science; ultimately of all belief in the possibility of Science.

But in the meantime the life of Auguste Comte seems to me to give us a beautiful and consolatory intimation how God guides an earnest man out of his theories, and if not into an acknowledgment of Himself, at least so many steps in the way to the acknowledgment of Him, as can leave us no doubt of what the seeker will behold when he is no longer bewildered by the mists of this world. The following sketch of his career appeared recently in 'The Leader:'—

<small>The main facts of his history are soon told. Born, in 1797, of Catholic and Royalist parents, he was educated at one of the Bonaparte lyceums, where he early distinguished himself by his love of speculation, and his profound dissatisfaction with the existing philosophic schools and actual social condition of his country. On leaving college he became acquainted with the celebrated Saint-Simon, and being attracted by his personal character, and charmed by the originality of his views, he joined the band of brilliant disciples which the genius and ambition of that distinguished social reformer gathered around him. Being the youngest amongst them, he was known as the Benjamin of the Saint-Simonian school;—a soubriquet which his enemies maliciously said his subsequent career fully justified, his philosophical system being, according to them, a genuine Benjamin's mess. As a favourite pupil of Saint-Simon, Comte not only assisted him in the preparation of his text-books, but undertook, in 1820, at the suggestion of the master, an independent work designed as an exposition of the scientific basis of the system. This work, entitled 'Système de Politique Positive,' while approved of in the main by Saint-Simon, was</small>

described by him as defective in its exposition of the religious and sentimental aspect of his views. On the death of its founder in 1825, Comte deserted the Saint-Simonian school, to found one of his own; and during the next twenty years devoted himself to the elaboration of an original system of scientific thought, since known as the 'Positive Philosophy.' The great text-book of his system, entitled 'Cours de Philosophie Positive,' extending to six thick volumes, gradually appeared at intervals between the years 1830 and 1842. During this time he led a quiet, scientific life, as Professor of Mathematics in the École Polytechnique; and almost immediately after the conclusion of his great work published two popular treatises connected with the subject of his chair, one on Analytical Geometry, the other on Astronomy, both of which were very successful. In 1844 he issued an outline and defence of his system in a single volume, entitled 'Discours sur l'Ensemble du Positivisme.' Soon after the publication of this work, an emotional crisis happened in his history, through which he became conscious that his own system was defective—as his early exposition of Saint-Simonism had been—on the religious side. The occasion of this was an ardent but virtuous attachment to a lady named Clotilde, whose death, a year after he had first met her, left him miserable in himself, and dissatisfied with his philosophy. Comte's life divides itself into three eras; in the first, he is a disciple expounding the views of others; in the second a master, a philosophic legislator, unfolding a system of his own; in the third an apostle, proclaiming a new religion. In the first period he naturally accomplished but little, and his efforts in the last were, as we have said, to a great extent abortive; but in the middle era, that of his philosophic activity, he accomplished a scientific reform such as few men can ever individually achieve. Whatever may be thought of the positive philosophy either as to the perfection of the parts or as to its completeness as a whole—and it is undoubtedly open to criticism in both respects—it cannot be denied that to Comte belongs the honour of being the first who grasped the true principle for the co-ordination of the sciences; that in an age of vast speculative and scientific activity he first rose from the empirical classification of facts to a genuine science of principles. Even his enemies allow that he possessed great general force of intellect, rare speculative power, and that he reaches the happiest generalizations in every branch of science he undertakes to expound.

From this profoundly interesting narrative we learn that human love awakened Comte to a conviction of the inadequacy of his philosophical scheme. He must have a religion to graft upon it. There is no help for it; he must deny facts—facts which he has realized—if he pretends that his notion of Science is sufficient to explain *them*. His followers perceive clearly—and complain bitterly—that by taking this course he is giving up the principles for which they had hailed him as the last great discoverer, as the man 'who had grasped the true principle for the co-ordination of the Sciences.' If there is something that lies beyond this Science—an indefinite, immeasurable Love, which is not and cannot be included in it,—a Love which must have a Worship in some way attached to it,—we are *not* in the age of Science, we must still beg some contributions from the bygone age of Faith. Nor is it only Comte's consistency which is imperilled by this his later experience. His new worship *must* have all the superstition—I would say boldly more than all the superstition—which has been found in the worship of any age or any country. It is grounded simply upon a feeling,—a deep human feeling, but still upon a feeling. It must be liable to all the varieties and excesses of that feeling. Christianity, Mahommedanism, Hinduism, Buddhism, have always, in their most corrupt forms, recognised a Science as somehow connected with them; *this* religion is avowedly an excrescence upon, and a violation of, the ascertained principles of Science. Of what changes and developments, of what outrages upon Reason and Morality, must it not be susceptible?

And yet it is as much the offspring of experiment,—true, honest, practical experiment,—as any which ever led to a change in the opinions of any physical student! I leave the disciples of Comte to ponder on these apparent contradictions. The more their study is accompanied by a reverent and affectionate admiration of their master, and by a determination to part with none of the *convictions* into which he had been the means of leading them, the better. The more they determine not to part with any of the genuine and recognised characteristics of the scientific temper, patience, quietness, courage, awe,—the less I fear for the result. And if there comes in, apparently to disturb this temper, some pure but overpowering human attachment or passion, I trust they will give it entertainment as Comte did, and not resolve to be inhuman, lest they should be unscientific. Then, I think, they will find at last that a GOD, of whom it can be said, 'He is Truth, He is Love,' is the ground on which an age of Science rests, as much as an age of Faith; that Science without Him becomes a System which must exclude all new facts, which deals at last only with dead things; that Faith which is not based on Him becomes a belief in that which is not; in that which the believer *chooses* to hold; therefore an imposture.

THE END.

RICHARD CLAY AND SONS, LIMITED,
LONDON AND BUNGAY.

CONTENTS

THE BIBLE—

    History of the Bible

    Biblical History

    The Old Testament

    The New Testament

HISTORY OF THE CHRISTIAN CHURCH

THE CHURCH OF ENGLAND

DEVOTIONAL BOOKS

THE FATHERS

HYMNOLOGY

SERMONS, LECTURES, ADDRESSES, AND THEOLOGICAL ESSAYS

www.ingramcontent.com/pod-product-compliance
Lightning Source LLC
Chambersburg PA
CBHW031423230426
43668CB00007B/411